MAIN STREET TO MIRACLE MILE

American Roadside Architecture

Chester H. Liebs

Bulfinch Press
Little, Brown and Company
Boston Toronto London

To L.H.L., K.N.H., P.L., and T.H.S.

Second printing, 1989

Acknowledgments of permission to reproduce copyrighted illustrations appear on pages 251–252.

Library of Congress Cataloging-in-Publication Data
Liebs, Chester H,
    Main Street to Miracle Mile.
    Bibliography: p.
    Includes index.
    1. Commercial buildings—United States.
2. Architecture—Environmental aspects—United States.
I. Title.
NA6212.L54   1985   725'.2   85-12940
ISBN 0-8212-1586-8

This paperback edition does not include the color plates.
MPC
Designed by Patricia Girvin Dunbar

Bulfinch Press is an imprint and trademark of Little, Brown and Company (Inc.)
Published simultaneously in Canada by Little, Brown & Company (Canada) Limited

Printed in the United States of America

Contents

Preface

AS LEWIS MUMFORD pointed out in *The Brown Decades* (1931), "The commonest axiom of history is that every generation revolts against its fathers and makes friends with its grandfathers." Now that the twentieth century (the very name once personified all that was modern) is an octogenarian, perhaps it is time to set aside the controversy that adheres to one particular creation begun by our grandfathers—the American motorway and its brash pictorial and lingual commercialism—in order to gain some insight into one of the more neglected areas of American architecture and culture.

Though not necessarily regulated by so precise a generational pendulum, the cycle that Mumford described is a familiar one. With *The Brown Decades*, Mumford himself became one of the first to whittle away at the antipathy toward all things Victorian which characterized his own age—a prejudice that persisted another fifty years until finally dissipated by the recent craze for all manner of Victoriana. Mumford's fathers, before him, had rekindled a popular interest in the material culture of colonial times. And we, his sons and grandsons, have begun to explore Mumford's own era through the visions of city and suburb of twentieth-century reformers, architects, and planners. Now is also an appropriate time to explore a long-spurned reality nurtured by the motorcar and the highway and the consumer society that followed the industrial revolution—the new genre of commercial establishments that have clung to the perimeters of our cities, have sapped their centers, and have bisected our suburbs in long corridors of structures, signs, and symbols forming a cultural landscape that is quintessentially American.

Heretofore this subject has usually been treated either very broadly or in small segments. Probably the best-known work is Robert Venturi, Denise Scott Brown, and Steven Izenour's *Learning from Las Vegas* (1972), in which the authors employ the architecture of the American roadside as a metaphor for the process of design and underscore their particular interest in a greater role for popular symbolism in contemporary architecture. Never intended as a history of roadside building, this brilliant, provocative, and ground-breaking book presents a compelling argument for the design philosophy of its authors. More recently a growing number of scholars have studied specific aspects of commerce along the American highway, among them Warren Belasco with his fascinating work on the early evolution of tourist camps, motels, and auto touring. Over the past few years, a spate of attractive books of photographs—most often of outlandish wayside buildings—has also helped to spark increased public interest in and knowledge of roadside architecture (a complete list of the many people who influenced my work can be found in the note on sources that precedes the Selected Bibliography).

Since roadside commercial buildings are most often first viewed from that most ubiquitous of twentieth-century vantage points, behind the windshield of a moving car, I begin *Main Street to Miracle Mile* by setting the reader in motion along a generic highway stretching from the key commercial intersection of a typical city, past the outer reaches of the urban fringe, to the open countryside. To this familiar spatial sequence, I then add the dimension of history by examining phases in the evolution of wayside commerce—from the turn-of-the-century Main Street to the interchange cluster of the 1980s—as they appear along a hypothetical asphalt-and-concrete time line. A chronological framework emerges for placing in context one of the most common yet confusing of twentieth-century visual experiences—driving down the roadside commercial strip.

In a similar way, I have sorted out the insistent cacophony of competing images with which roadside buildings are cloaked, by breaking the visual components of this fundamentally commercial communication into a series of "pictures" used over time to lure the speeding motorist off the highway. Like any medium that successfully motivates people to part with their money, the roadside business—in its package of building, sign, and image—signals its message directly and with economy in a visual/verbal language that is not only easily understood by the customer but also, through simile and metaphor, plays on subtle and perhaps unconscious visual associations. These associations are subject to change with time—with the shifts in values and priorities of the society as a whole.

Behind the exterior sales costumes, roadside businesses also provide some kind of service or product for their customers—be it gas, food, lodging, and amusements or groceries and automobiles. In order to serve its specific function, each roadside building type evolves from an architectural program that changes over time in response to economic conditions and new technology. Thus the gasoline station acquires and then loses its car repair bays, while the supermarket steadily grows in size as more and more products are displayed along its interior highways. Therefore, *Main Street to Miracle Mile* concludes by following a series of roadside building types—auto showrooms, gas stations, supermarkets, miniature golf courses, drive-in theaters, motels, and roadside restaurants—as they have evolved over the past nine decades.

As with any first survey of a vast subject, and perhaps any first book, errors of judgment, fact, omission, and interpretation are almost surely to be discovered. I ask for each reader's understanding of any such deficiencies and hope that the merits of this effort will overshadow the shortcomings. I also hope that this work will stimulate further scholarship and improve our understanding of how the automobile, coupled with an emerging commercial revolution, helped shape the physical environment of twentieth-century America.

Chester H. Liebs
Burlington, Vermont

Acknowledgments

MANY PEOPLE and organizations kindly helped in the preparation of this book. I am extremely grateful to Miriam Trementozzi for coordinating the initial archival and photographic research and organizing the preliminary bibliography. I am also indebted to Peter Hawley, Diane Cohen, Deborah Gilbreath Andrews, and Marcia Cini for their invaluable research assistance; Bruce and Geneva Peach, Amanda Burke, Laura Taylor, Carolyn Perry, and Clare Sheppard for much-needed clerical and administrative support; Dore Gardner and also Fine Grain for their superb photographic printing; Nina Asher, Laurel Ginter, Richard Longstreth, and Neil and Mainey Stout for their critical reading of the manuscript; and Michele Plourde, who stalwartly expedited the revisions and served as my guide into the computer age.

The book would also not have been possible without the kindness and generosity of Walter Beinecke and the Osceola Foundation, and my good friend Robert Sincerbeaux and the Eva Gebhard-Gourgaud Foundation and Cecil Howard Charitable Trust, who collectively have helped underwrite so many of my activities over the past decade. Much appreciation is due the University of Vermont, which provided both a grant to help in the initial research and a sabbatical leave that gave me the opportunity to develop the manuscript and field-check information along thousands of miles of highway across the continent. Special thanks to the Society for Commercial Archeology and also the University of Vermont History Department and its Chairman, William Metcalfe, for constant encouragement and support.

I would also like to extend my sincere appreciation to the numerous archivists, collectors, curators, and others who resourcefully located photographs and answered queries. Those especially helpful include John Baeder, Richard Drew, Frederick G. Frost, Jr., Connell Gallagher, David Horvath, Paula McDougall, Brita Mack, Cynthia Read Miller, Philip Mooney, Joan Morris, Ellie Reichlin, Nadia Smith, and Lenore Swoiskin.

There is also a long list of scholars, designers, business owners, public officials, and friends who gave their valuable time for the benefit of *Main Street to Miracle Mile* in ways including everything from fund-raising and stimulating conversation to the loaning of valuable materials—even taking photos in remote locations for me in the course of their travels. Many thanks to Stanford Acher, John Axtell, Doris Backer, Linda Bassett, Joseph Bedway, Mary Ann Beinecke, Edith Lutyens Bel Geddes, Margaret Beyer, Roger Brevoort, Kathleen Brooker, Donald Cael, Lynn Callowhill, Garnet Chapin, William Chapin, Ellen Chapman, Alexandra Cole, John Cooke, Jody Ladd Craig, Sharon Cumiskey, Karen Czaikowski, Mary Davis, Eric DeLony, Susan DeWitt, Edward and Sharon Dintaman, Carol Dubie, Geraldine Duclow, Mark Edwards, Maria Epsimos, Charles Fish, Francis Francois, Peter Fuller, David Gebhard, Robert Giebner, Frederick Goldberg, Maureen Gustafson, Avery Hall, H. Thomas Hartman, Alan Hathaway, Hope Headley, Alan Hess, G. Michael Hostage, Mary Humstone, Michael Jackson, Byron Johnson, Lydia Jones, Marjory Kinney, Gregg Kloenne, Robin Krawitz, Arthur Krim, Philip Langdon, Steve Levin, Mrs. Chester Lewis, Stuart Lottman, Barbara Lowry, Charles Lyman, Jonathan Malone, Lloyd Marsh, Philip Marshall, Mary Means, Stanley Meston, John Miller, Richard Mouck, Joe Oldham, Everett Ortner, Roger Osbaldeston, Norman Ott, Ann Pritzlaff, Suzanne Roberson, J. C. Rogari, Lars Rolfsen, Mertie Romaine, Lynn Rozental, C. R. Schnardthorst, Stu Schneider, Gloria Scott, Keith Sculle, Dan Scully, David Shelton, Ronald Shelton, Donald Short, Ed Silva, John Stef, Julie Stokes, Charles Sullivan, A. B. Tideball, Ginny Troutt, Gale Turley, and Douglas and Eve Yorke. (I hope I will be forgiven by anyone accidently not included in this long list.)

Finally, my deepest appreciation to Robin Bledsoe for setting high standards for both writing and photography; to my editor, Terry Hackford, for her unfailing encouragement, optimism, and wise counsel; and most especially to Kathlyn Hatch for providing more moral support than I ever deserved, helping solve knotty snags in logic, and giving countless invaluable suggestions for improving the content and wording of the manuscript.

S P A C E

From Main Street to Miracle Mile

THE MOVIE THROUGH THE WINDSHIELD

During the nineteenth century, a gradual, yet profound, revolution in travel was taking place, forever altering human understanding of time, distance, and perception of the landscape. In 1812, it took an average of six days to travel by stage across the rugged mountain barriers from Philadelphia to Pittsburgh. Forty years later, the same trip could be made by train in sixteen hours,[1] and by the end of the century the entire run took a single morning. The lurching and jouncing of the stagecoach and the frequent stops to change horses, eat, or spend the night, had become a memory of travel past. Now it was possible to go to the depot, buy a ticket, step into a train coach, sit down by a window, and relax—gazing at an endless procession of cities, towns, villages, farms, and wilderness streaking by.

Trains may have been fast, but they were not without their limitations. Passengers could alight only at certain designated stops along a route rigidly determined by the location of the track. On foot or horseback, travelers could go almost anywhere, albeit slowly, while the train temporarily incarcerated its passengers.[2] Freedom to roam the landscape had been traded for speed.

train → car.
tend → hotel

Then the twentieth century made its debut, along with a new form of land transportation—the automobile. Small, gasoline powered, private passenger coaches sans rails, automobiles could roll along the same routes as horses and wagons, only faster and for greater distances. The owner of a car could choose exactly when and where to go and what to see, confined only by the location and condition of the roads.

Within a few years, cars began streaming from the nation's auto factories, and the demand for places to drive them soared. Before long hundreds of new highways laced the continent, and countless older roads were widened and paved. Mass-produced, inexpensive autos such as the

> It is in the nature of the automobile that the city spreads out thus and far away.
>
> —Frank Lloyd Wright
> "America Tomorrow"

Santa Fe Railroad advertisement; Life, 14 March 1907. Watching scenery from a railroad passenger coach had been (and still is) basically a passive experience. The landscape streams by as if it were painted on an endless canvas being drawn past the window on giant rollers like the moving background of a stage play. Only the engine crew could see the rails converging toward the horizon and everything else that lay ahead. (Santa Fe Industries.)

Model T Ford flooded the marketplace, cars became widely affordable, and suddenly, large segments of the population had an alternative to rail travel. By the early 1920s, for the first time in history, it was possible to cleave through miles of scenery in a single day, with the power to start, stop, or change the sequence of onrushing images by merely stepping on a pedal and turning a wheel.

This freedom to start, stop, or change direction at will made the automobile more than a means of moving from one place to another. Each tiny, motorized, rubber-tired vehicle with its padded seats offered an alternative not only to the railroad, but also to the newfound magic of the cinema palace and silver screen. Simply by whirling the crank and opening the throttle, the windshield of any car could be transformed into a proscenium arch framing one of the most fascinating movies of all—the landscape played at high speed.

At first windshield moviegoers saw a roadside environment tailored to earlier modes of transport. In cities motorists dodged pedestrians, bicyclists, trolleys, and horses and wagons as they threaded their cars around unforgiving curbs and right-angle corners designed for slow-paced vehicles. In the country, mileage markers, tollhouses, stagecoach inns, and other horse-age artifacts popped in and out of view. In either place, the thump of tires on steel rails at grade crossings was a constant reminder of the latticework of railroads superimposed on the landscape.

Soon highway building became the great editor of windshield perception. Trees were cut. Buildings obliterated. Front yards taken. Hills lev-

Rare candid view (most likely in western Maryland along the old National Road) of a convoy of motor tourists; photograph 1912. In contrast to railroad passengers, motorists were active participants rather than passive observers and had an engineer's-eye view as the automobile penetrated the landscape in a continuous race toward the vanishing point at the end of the highway. They could speed through the landscape head-on and had the power to change the sequence of onrushing events by merely pushing a pedal or turning a wheel. (Author's collection.)

U.S. Route 1, Hyattsville, Maryland; photograph 1983. Once auto travelers saw a corridor of commercial buildings (far left) when they passed through Hyattsville, Maryland, on the way from Baltimore to Washington. In 1929 the downtown was bypassed with a viaduct (right). Now motorists, unless they elect to take the older route, see the back of downtown flickering through slots in a concrete guardrail. This is but one of thousands of examples of how highway construction has edited windshield perception. (Author.)

eled. Valleys filled. Curves flattened. Meanderings straightened. Right-of-ways widened. Bypasses built, and traffic rerouted. Features that once appeared to leap into view as a car rounded a curve could now be seen far ahead. Instead of grand facades, backs of buildings greeted motorists as they followed the new bypass route through town.

But probably the most dramatic change in the windshield movie was the wholesale injection of "commercials" into the roadside panorama. The need to sell goods aggressively had been a predictable by-product of the industrial revolution. Advertising signs already inundated the nation's thriving Main Street business districts by the mid-1850s, and toward the end of the century, advertisers had begun to erect large billboards beside railroad tracks and streetcar lines to catch the attention of passengers streaking by. However, it was not until automobiles became relatively commonplace that widespread commercialization of the landscape began in earnest.

About the time of World War I, sharp-eyed entrepreneurs began, almost spontaneously, to see ways to profit from the motorist's freedom to halt the windshield movie and step out into the picture. Shops could be set up almost anywhere the law allowed, and a wide variety of products and services could be counted on to sell briskly in the roadside marketplace. A certain number of cars passing by would always be in need of gas. Travelers eventually grew hungry, tired, and restless for diversions. Soon gas stations, produce booths, hot dog stands, and tourist camps sprouted up along the nation's roadsides to capitalize on these needs. As competition increased, merchants looked for new ways to snag the new market awheel. Each sign and building had to visually shout: "Slow down, pull in, and buy." Still more businesses moved to the highway—supermarkets, motor courts, restaurants, miniature golf courses, drive-in theaters. By the early 1950s, almost anything could be bought along the roadside.

Over the next thirty years, the windshield movie was even more drastically edited, more vigorously commercialized. Highway construction ripped through city and countryside at an even greater rate. Four lanes. Six lanes. Eight lanes. Bigger bypasses. New alignments. Interstates. And with each change in routing, speed, and access, business was not far behind. Giant corporations edged their way into the roadside marketplace, and shopping malls, fast-food restaurants, convenience stores, and highway hotels became familiar roadside fixtures.

Now, as the twentieth century creaks toward its final decade, the excitement of driving anywhere, anytime, has dimmed, and the automobile has assumed its place as an accepted component in the daily routine of commuting, shopping, and recreating. Gazing at moving images through the windshield of a car, along with moviegoing and watching television, has become one of the primary visual experiences of twentieth-century life. Yet, while the plot of the latest film or TV drama is often dissected down to the minutest detail, the visual events seen while driving have become so familiar that they barely register at any level above the subconscious. The script of a trip along a busy trunk road from the city center to the open countryside might read as follows:

Inch out of parking place. Drive down Main Street past glass-box office towers interleaved with old buildings fixed up like new. Farther out traffic eases. Wheels jerk occasionally on old streetcar tracks peeking out through the pavement. Pass through row after row of little, one-story shop fronts with a myriad of signs: supermarket, taxes prepared, learn to drive, launderette, dentist. Suddenly eyes dart forward, foot slams on break to avoid hitting a car that has just cut in ahead.

Butcher shop, law office, auto parts. About every half mile, this passing parade is halted by a red light dangling above a busy intersection presided over perhaps by a bank, movie theater, church, or gas station.

Eventually shop fronts disappear while more gas stations, hamburger stands, and tiny shopping centers slip in and out of view. Most of these structures are now set back from the sidewalk and have clusters of parked cars out front.

A fork in the road appears. Follow traffic onto four-lane highway. Larger signs begin rushing by the edges of the windshield—jet cleaners, executive car wash, discount mart, carpet city. Yellow arches perched high on a pole appear in the distance and rapidly draw closer. A big green reflective sign announces Interstate 17. Swerve left to avoid semi merging off cloverleaf, then under the underpass. Cars and trucks everywhere. More signs. The road widens into six lanes of starting, stopping, turning cars and trucks all jockeying to beat the light at the shopping mall. Then the staccato of signs increases in intensity as the traffic picks up speed again. Holiday Inn, Ramada Inn, Texaco, Burger King, Wendy's, Arby's, Mobil. A quick glance in the mirror reveals the angry-looking grill of a tractor trailer pressing close behind. . . .

K Mart, Midas, 7-Eleven, Star Cafe, Nite-O-Rest Motel, Putt Putt Miniature Golf, Twilight Drive-in Theater. Gradually the bombardment of commercials diminishes, traffic picks up speed, and the road narrows to two lanes. A sense of relief takes over similar to that felt by a skipper who, having negotiated the busy harbor, is now free to sail the open sea. Trees, farms, cows, barns, fences zip by, interspersed with an occasional roadhouse or village of tiny tourist cabins. As the next city approaches, the cycle is reversed. Signs increase, traffic builds, malls appear, followed by interchanges, rows of little shops, and finally, another town center.

A drive such as this unfolds in a scramble of streets, cars, signs, and buildings. As the eye darts <u>from traffic to catch a quick glimpse of the</u> <u>visual episodes speeding by,</u> the initial effect <u>is that of a screenplay with-</u> *parking everywhere.* <u>out an intelligible plot.</u>

Yet there is order in this <u>rush of images</u>—a pattern that is often re-peated from city to city across the United States. By deciphering this pattern, it is possible to trace the evolution of the commercial landscape. Thousands of clues lie hidden along the flowing ribbons of roads like bench marks along a seemingly endless time line. When discovered, sorted out, and decoded, these traces reveal a fascinating story, first writ-ten by the earliest settlers, then amended, added to, and rewritten over time, with the latest episode heavily reworked by the automobile. It is <u>the</u> <u>saga of the spread of commerce from traditional business centers along</u> <u>Main Street to today's Miracle Miles of signs, buildings, and parking.</u>

MAIN STREET: CAR MEETS COMMERCE

The first stop along the roadside commercial time line is the corridor of business activity in the heart of most towns and cities—a corridor known literally or generically as Main Street. By the mid-eighteenth century, the majority of colonial port cities contained some form of primordial Main Street that served as a corridor for trade. Describing his travels in 1748 along the east coast of North America, Swedish botanist Peter Kalm ob-served that Philadelphia's Market Street (still to this day a bustling com-mercial artery in what is now the nation's fourth largest city) was already "the principal thoroughfare where the market is kept." While exploring the Hudson River port of Albany, farther north, Kalm noted "a street [today's Broadway] which . . . is five times broader than the others and serves as the market place."[3]

As settlers journeyed inland along roads and waterways in the early nineteenth century, they founded hundreds of new communities, each with its own Main Street. In road towns, such as Brownsville, Ohio, that sprang up along the National Road (begun in the Jeffersonian era and now U.S. 40), the turnpike itself became a Main Street lined with churches, stores, stagecoach inns, stables, and rooming houses for drov-ers. Main Streets also appeared in river cities such as Cincinnati and Louisville on the Ohio, or St. Louis, Memphis, and Natchez on the Mis-sissippi, as well as in towns that sprang up along man-made waterways—Utica, Syracuse, and Rochester on New York's Erie Canal, for example.

The coming of the railroad created the greatest stimulus for Main Street commerce. Through the downtown depot and railway freight house, goods arrived and local products were shipped out, newcomers alighted, visitors tarried, and residents set forth to explore a larger world. Fortunes were made, communities prospered, and by the late nineteenth century these developments could all be read on the frontage of a commu-nity's principal street.

In villages across New England, modern three- and four-story brick commercial blocks began to crowd out older structures along village greens,[4] while scores of new shop fronts ringed courthouse squares across

the Midwest. Main Street even boomed in remote Western track towns, from Green River, Wyoming, to Livingston, Montana,[5] where rows of false-front buildings near the railroad advertised to people riding by, and reassured those already there, that the town was prosperous and would continue to grow.

But nowhere was this surge of expansion more evident than in the cities, where population skyrocketed in the fifty-year span between 1860 and 1910. Retail trade along commercial thoroughfares such as New York's Broadway increased dramatically, in large part because of new networks of urban railroads—the rapid transit systems—that injected thousands into the heart of town each day to shop and work. As the cost of land along the nation's urban Main Streets escalated, buildings grew taller and more closely packed.

Although they differed widely in size, scale, and density, by the turn of the twentieth century most Main Streets shared a number of characteristics. Whether in Lewiston, Maine, or New Orleans, they had become the hardest working thoroughfares in town. Main Streets were usually the first to be lit with gas and later with electricity, the first to sport a streetcar line or elevated railroad or subway, and the first to be paved. They also served as the civic and religious hubs for the communities around them. Main Street was the home not only of stores and offices, but also of imposing churches, theaters, banks, hotels, courthouses, city halls, war memorials, libraries, and other banners of community well-being. The corridor formed by these varied structures, jammed tight along both sides of the sidewalk, became the ideal setting for speeches, parades, and celebrations.

Most importantly, all Main Streets—from bustling city shopping districts to a tiny strip of shop fronts strung along a railroad track—were magnets for trade. Over their shop counters, the wares of factories and highly productive mechanized farms were distributed. Time and development had transformed the embryonic thoroughfares noticed by Peter Kalm into the principal places of exchange for the industrial revolution.

Dense rows of commercial buildings anywhere from one to more than ten stories forming a wall of facades along the sidewalks interspersed with an occasional church or other noncommercial edifice, well-lit and surfaced streets that thronged with activity—such was the general appearance of Main Street when the first automobiles chugged into town at the dawn of the twentieth century.

At first the new vehicles functioned essentially as carriages with motors and simply joined the traffic stream of horses and wagons, bicycles and trolleys. At the onset, merchants looked upon the new vehicles as a novelty, then as another product to sell and service and an added way for customers to come downtown to shop. Soon livery owners began repairing cars in addition to boarding horses; bicycle and carriage shops became makeshift auto showrooms; and stores began selling gas along the sidewalk. Motorists simply parked their cars at the same curb where they would have tethered their horses and wagons and ate at the Main Street restaurants, shopped for groceries at the Main Street markets, bought clothing at the Main Street haberdasheries, and if they were from out of town, stayed at the Main Street hotels.

By the 1920s, motor vehicles were not only more numerous, but faster and larger, and it became increasingly evident that Main Street was the invention of a bygone era and had not been designed for the automobile. Cars required maneuvering room far in excess of the horse-powered vehicles they were rapidly replacing. With more automobiles on the streets, the demand for gas outlets, salesrooms, and repair shops soared, while motorists wishing to shop grew impatient with crowded streets and lack of parking.

Especially in larger cities, where these problems were most acute, municipal governments took stopgap measures to accommodate the auto. They pushed back curbs, widened streets, and installed an array of directional signs, lights, and traffic controls to help the more nimble and potentially lethal motor traffic intermingle safely with horses, wagons, darting pedestrians, and lumbering, unmaneuverable streetcars. Private business also contributed its own share of modifications by demolishing an occasional structure to make room for a parking lot or drive-in filling station.

But buying and clearing valuable urban land was often prohibitively expensive, so Main Street became increasingly congested. A growing number of center-city merchants actually began to regret the day the auto came to town. As one Georgia cigar-and-soda-fountain-store owner, Thomas H. Pitts, lamented in 1926:

When I first came to Atlanta . . . horse cars ran out Edgewood Avenue. [Now] most of the shops that were there in the early part of the century have van-

Broadway near Bleecker Street; from King's Views New York, 1906. During the opening years of the new century, the horseless carriage made its debut in the Main Street traffic stream. (Author's collection.)

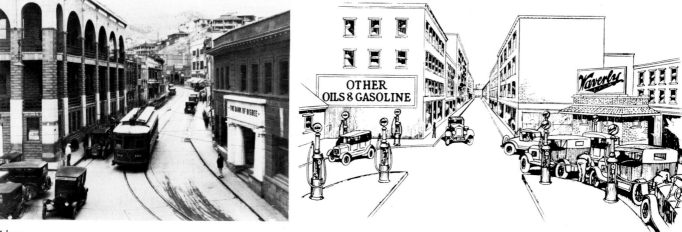

Above:
Main Street, Bisbee, Arizona; photograph c. 1920. By the 1920s, motor traffic began to crowd out the streetcars along Main Street. (Arizona Historical Society.)

Above, right:
Illustration from Waverly Oils advertisement. By the mid-1920s, efforts to provide auto-convenient services were causing the gradual breakup of the dense corridor of buildings along Main Street. (National Petroleum News, 8 October 1924.)

ished. . . . I think the real thing that did it was automobiles, and more automobiles. Traffic got so congested that the only hope was to keep it going. Hundreds used to stop; now thousands pass. Five Points has become a thoroughfare, instead of a center. New traffic rules have made it impossible to park an automobile within two or three blocks of Five Points, and the traffic signals keep everything moving. . . . The place where soda fountain trade is, is where automobiles go, and one must have wide spaces for curb service. A central location is no longer a good one for my sort of business.[6]

THE TAXPAYER STRIP: MAIN STREET BY EXTENSION

Mr. Pitts reacted to changes along Main Street by choosing to close his store for good. There was, however, a less drastic alternative open to big-city merchants faced with a similar dilemma. They could set up shop in a rented store space in one of the dozens of single-story commercial buildings sprouting up by this time along major trunk roads leading out of town. Here they would be in the company of other merchants selling everything from shoes, clothing, meat, and groceries to haircuts and motion-picture shows.

Like Main Street, these new corridors of commerce thrived on traffic. Occasional horse-drawn delivery wagons (now relics from an earlier age), mothers from the houses and apartment blocks crowded along nearby streets, and children walking home from school formed only part of the parade of potential customers passing before the shop fronts. In addition this already hectic scene was interrupted every few minutes by flashes of bluish white light, the sharp crackling of electricity, and the clanging of a bell as a streetcar trundled into view. Soon the car came to a scraping stop, pneumatic doors folded open, and waves of people poured into the street.

The road in front of the stores was also alive with the newest vehicles to join the cavalcade of urban traffic—automobiles. Cars could be seen everywhere—their horns honking, weaving around trolleys and pedestrians, lining up by the curb with doors opening and people climbing out, or stopping under a gas-station canopy waiting for a fill up.

The evolution of shopping streets, like the one just described, began in the second half of the nineteenth century when many cities started expanding, in long fingers of development, into the surrounding countryside. As cities spread, truck farms and outlying villages were engulfed by the ever-widening urban infrastructure. The first prime mover in this process called "metropolitanization" was the horsecar. Even before the Civil War, in older cities such as Philadelphia, New York, and Boston, horsecar lines advanced from the town centers, and residential areas sprang up on either side of them. Late in the century, in some of the largest urban areas, elevated railways further extended the range of these new neighborhoods. But for most places, it was really only after the appearance of electric trolleys, in the late 1880s, that metropolitanization came into full swing.

Twice as fast as the horsecar and with three times the capacity, the new streetcars made it possible for traction companies to link up scores of little crossroads hamlets as they extended their lines out into the country. Companies often constructed amusement parks such as White City in Worcester, Massachusetts, or Riverside in Indianapolis at the end of the line as a clever way of building ridership. However, more than mere revenue from transportation and entertainment provided incentive for extending the trolley lines. With each new stretch of track, the land along the right-of-way—which had often been bought up prior to construction by company directors and other alert investors—grew exponentially in value. Now only minutes away from the center of the city, lots within walking distance of the nearest car stop sold rapidly, and within a few years clusters of houses and apartment buildings appeared.

As a result of this process, many cities doubled, tripled, even quadru-

"Roadtown" is Edgar Chambless' futuristic alternative to the haphazard residential and commercial development spreading out along streetcar routes by the turn of the century. His solution: an endless concrete building containing housing, stores, and a subway, and roofed over by a grand promenade. (American Architects' and Builders' Magazine, August 1910.)

Trolley line; Pasadena, California; photograph c. 1898. Not long after the opening of a street railway, vacant lots such as the ones here would often be bought for more intensive residential and commercial development. (The Huntington Library.)

Brady Block, c. 1925; Boston; photograph 1928. The typical taxpayer block consisted of a row of stores united under a single roof. Taxpayers housed a wide variety of neighborhood businesses, in this case a druggist, barber, and undertaker. Thousands were built along streetcar lines, and eventually auto routes, in cities across the country, between the turn of the century and the depression. Note the mailbox, an article of street furniture unchanged to this day, and the advertising signs jerry-rigged above the parapet (far left). (Society for the Preservation of New England Antiquities.)

pled in area. Take Boston, for example. As Sam Bass Warner recounts in his definitive study, *Streetcar Suburbs: The Process of Growth in Boston, 1870–1900*, street railway construction played a major part in that city's dramatic residential expansion. Starting about 1870, pioneering streetcar lines were laid down along major roads leading out of town. Soon, adjacent vacant lots mushroomed with housing developments, and water and sewer lines, police and fire protection were extended out to these new neighborhoods. More lines were built. Other neighborhoods formed. By 1900, Boston's residential land area had increased sixfold.[7] Philadelphia, New York, Louisville, Chicago, Kansas City, Denver, San Francisco, and dozens of other cities across the nation experienced similar residential expansion from the end of the Civil War until the onset of the depression.

This boom in urban development, however, was not limited just to residential construction. The many households located along the car lines created a strong need for neighborhood stores to spare anyone wanting to buy groceries or have their hair cut from having to go all the way downtown. So by the close of the nineteenth century, alert speculators had begun erecting commercial buildings along the streetcar routes. These structures usually consisted of a single row of shop fronts, although some were capped by an additional story or two of lofts or offices. Since builders assumed that more concentrated urban settlement spreading out from the city center would eventually make land along the avenues valuable for more intensive development, they generally conceived of the structures as interim improvements designed to produce enough revenue to pay the taxes and hold the property for the future. Hence these buildings were often referred to as "taxpayers."[8]

By the turn of the century, miles of taxpayers were going up in cities across the country forming vast linear commercial corridors, or what may be called "taxpayer strips."[9] In Cleveland, for example, as one observer

Taxpayer strip; Detroit; photograph 1921. Long corridors, walled in by one- or two-story commercial blocks, plied by cars and trolleys, and punctuated by hundreds of signs, were one of the chief by-products of metropolitanization. (The Edison Institute.)

noted in *Architectural Record* in 1918, taxpayer construction was rapidly spreading up Euclid Avenue, one of the most important streets in the city:

[Recently] the last bars were let down and the trolley cars permitted to run through the exclusive section, familiarly known to the Philistines as "Millionaire's Row." The next logical step is being taken at the very time this is being written and the broad grass plots and shade trees, which added so much to the beauty of this portion of the street, are being cut away and the pavement widened to the line of the down town business section. . . . It will doubtless become a great commercial street.[10]

Meanwhile, no doubt influenced by the rapid spread of commercial development along Dorchester, Massachusetts, Brighton, and Huntington avenues, and other thoroughfares radiating out from the center of Boston, the American author Winston Churchill included this description of a taxpayer strip in his 1917 novel, *The Dwelling-Place of Light:*

The main artery of Hampton [a fictional industrial town near metropolitan Boston, is] a wide strip of asphalt threaded with car tracks, lined on both sides with incongruous edifices indicative of a rapid, undiscriminating prosperity. There were long stretches of "ten foot" buildings, so called on account of the single story. . . . These "ten foot" stores were the repositories of pianos, automobiles, hardware and millinery. . . . Flanking the sidewalks, symbolizing and completing the heterogeneous and bewildering effect of the street were long rows of heavy hemlock trunks, unpainted and stripped, with crosstrees bearing webs of wires. Trolley cars rattled along, banging their gongs, trucks rumbled across the tracks, automobiles uttered frenzied screeches behind startled pedestrians.[11]

With minor modification, this same account could have described Clark Street in Chicago, Colfax Avenue in Denver, Jamaica Avenue in New York City, Woodward Avenue in Detroit, and dozens of other booming

Above:
Taxpayer strip; Whittier Boulevard,
Belvedere, California; photograph 1924.
The auto continued to stimulate taxpayer
development where trolleys left off. (The
Huntington Library.)

Above, right:
Colfax Avenue, Aurora, Colorado, east
of Denver; photograph 1982. Taxpayer
strips such as this one, plastered over
with half a century of facade remodel-
ings, can still be found along older urban
access routes. (Author.)

commercial arteries during the early years of the new century.

For many of the businesses located in what Churchill refers to as the "ten foot" buildings along these new shopping streets—the grocers, butchers, restaurants, printers, hardware, stationery, and candy stores—the taxpayer strip offered an ideal situation. Rents were often lower than downtown, yet large numbers of people lived close by. Customers could walk, take the trolley, or drive to the shops; the street was less congested and allowed for more parking near the stores.

These same attributes proved attractive to larger businesses as well as smaller stores. Soon banks and chain stores such as A&P, Woolworth, Sears, Roebuck and Company, and Montgomery Ward opened branch outlets along the taxpayer strip, vying for choice plots on major intersections. Movie theater moguls followed suit. Soon the brilliantly lit marquee and the humpbacked roof of the cinema palace presided over major junctions along the streetcar strip in the same way that the church steeple had dominated rural crossroads of a generation before. In fact many old churches still stood at what were now key commercial intersections—a reminder of the rural villages that had been swallowed up by the city. This same pattern of visual events—blocks of little shop fronts interrupted occasionally by a church, department store, or the towering hulk of a movie theater—is still in evidence along many of the country's aging taxpayer strips.

As new businesses induced more and more customers to drive to the taxpayer strips, the demand for parking soon overwhelmed available curbside space. Before long, enterprising developers started building taxpayer blocks set back a car length from the sidewalk to provide perpendicular parking in front of the stores.

Other merchants carried convenience for the motorist even further. They paved vacant lots, cut driveways through curbs, and set up filling stations, hamburger stands, and diners toward the *rear* of their property. The long-standing tenet of Main Street commercial site planning—line the shops along the sidewalk with room for parking only at the curb—was finally cast aside.

Nowhere did the automobile have more impact on the taxpayer strip

Earl's Place; Stone and Fifth streets, Tucson; photograph c. 1930. Gas stations, lunch stands, diners, used-car lots, and other businesses requiring off-street storage of cars began to invade the taxpayer strip by the mid-1920s. (Arizona Historical Society.)

than in Los Angeles. By the late 1920s, vast new residential sections of the city primarily oriented to automobiles rather than trolleys proliferated. Many of the business streets passing through these neighborhoods skipped a step in development and began filling up almost exclusively with auto-convenient businesses instead of conventional taxpayer blocks. As critic Douglas Haskell noted in *Architectural Record* in 1937, "Los Angeles is a city built on the automobile as Boston was built on the sailing ship. [It] appears to the casual view as a series of parking lots interspersed with buildings."[12]

Since the primary incentive for erecting miles of "ten foot" buildings was to hold down land until it could be placed in more profitable, intensive use, why have so many taxpayer strips survived? Because the proponents of this strategy did not realize the extent to which the automobile would decentralize urban settlement. Instead of more concentrated development spreading out from the center to ultimately engulf the streetcar suburbs, cars made even the remotest property relatively accessible to downtown, thus causing vacant land to be developed not only beyond but in between the rapid-transit lines. Instead of becoming more densely packed, cities simply continued to sprawl. The automobile had taken over where the trolley left off.

As it turned out, taxpayer strips were zones of transition. They began with many of the characteristics of nineteenth-century Main Streets, only the distances were longer, the buildings generally squatter. By the time the nation slid into the Great Depression, these same places had been swept into the auto age and had become the evolutionary link between Main Street and the thousands of miles of bright strips of highway commerce that unfold across the landscape today.

Below, top:
National Road marker; U.S. Route 40, east of Jacksonville, Ohio; photograph 1981. (Author.)

Below, bottom left:
Locust Creek Inn; near Bethel, Vermont; photograph 1981. This inn was built in 1837 with an addition in 1860. Like the road marker, it is typical of the wayside relics that would have been encountered by motor tourists in the early years of this century. (Author.)

Below, bottom right:
Surviving stretch of "seedling mile," completed in 1915; along the old Lincoln Highway, near Grand Island, Nebraska; photograph 1974, Dr. Alan D. Hathaway. This automobile, the ten-millionth Model T to be cranked out by the Ford assembly line, is now owned by Alan Hathaway of the Lincoln Highway Rediscovery Committee. (Dr. Alan D. Hathaway.)

EARLY HIGHWAY STRIPS: WAYSIDE BUSINESS RETURNS

By the time of World War I, business was springing up in still another place, a place that was most easily reached by car. To get there, it was necessary to drive out beyond the last taxpayer, then past the old estates, amusement parks, golf courses, fairgrounds, truck farms, orphanages, and cemeteries typically near the city limits, until the road broke into open countryside. There, around the next curve, a cheery homemade sign bearing the message "fresh vegetables" beside a makeshift stand might suddenly come into view. Little did the passing motorist know that such quaint displays of native entrepreneurship were only the advance guard of a commercial transformation of gigantic proportions.

This was not the first time trade prospered along the open roadside. In colonial times and the early years of the republic, travelers could obtain food and lodging for themselves and their horses at the many wayside inns located at convenient stopping places along the trails, post roads, and turnpikes. The heyday of roadside services ended, however, with the coming of the railroad. As train travel became the preferred mode for long-distance transportation, many highways fell into disuse, while inns and other wayside services declined or disappeared altogether.

By the third quarter of the nineteenth century, rural roads were primarily used to transport goods between farm and market. As a result, each population center and rail shipping point became the hub of a star-like pattern of feeder roads that permitted the delivery of agricultural goods. The same forces of centralization that caused Main Street to prosper did not bode well for the open road. The nation's highways entered a dark age,[13] during which few improvements were made and total road mileage grew very slowly.

By the 1880s, this general apathy toward roads was being challenged

✳ *"Life's Guide to the Suburbs," 1907. This spoof suggests the degree to which, even at this early date, the automobile was changing the roadside beyond the taxpayer strip, at the outer edges of the urban fringe. The beleaguered estate behind the wall in the background would very likely have been sold, within a short time, for commercial purposes. (Life, 7 October 1907.)*

by an unlikely coalition of farmers, who had to ship goods to market, and bicyclists, who had recently taken to the open road in droves and needed a smooth surface for their fragile, two-wheeled vehicles. But it was the commercial availability of the automobile that tipped the scales in favor of improving highways.[14] From only 8,000 registered automobiles in 1900, the number jumped to 468,000 by 1910, and to more than 8 million by 1920.[15] These millions of car owners, along with automakers and petroleum companies, became a new and powerful force agitating for better roads. Other interests that stood to benefit from well-maintained highways also joined in. Producers of brick, creosoted wooden blocks, concrete, and asphalt stood to make fat profits from paving contracts, while many Main Street merchants wished to draw traffic to their communities, under the theory that in each car was a potential customer. Together they formed a powerful lobby for better roads.

One of this lobby's most effective techniques took the form of numerous private highway associations, each touting the virtues of a pet route that, if built, was certain to bring untold prosperity to communities along its path. One of the most ambitious of these efforts began in 1913, when a private association under the leadership of then president of the Packard Motor Car Company, Henry B. Joy, set out to build a paved highway from coast to coast.

With neither the financial resources nor the legal power to complete such an undertaking, the association resorted to extremely clever psychological weaponry. First, this great highway of the future needed a name. By calling the road the Lincoln Highway, Joy and his associates, for the price of a few words, bestowed upon the fledgling enterprise all the inspirational patriotic associations of a martyred president.

Then a route had to be selected. Communities across the center of the country were held in suspense wondering whether they would be touched

Highway six miles west of Orlando, Florida; photograph 1917. Although this road was paved with bricks laid up in sand filler in 1915, at nine feet wide it is still in nineteenth-century scale. Even though this is a main thoroughfare, it is almost completely free of wayside commercial development—with the exception of the paint-company sign cast in the shape of an old turnpike marker. (Florida State University Photographic Archives.)

by the magic concrete ribbon. The route finally chosen began at Jersey City (with a ferry connection to New York), ran to Philadelphia, Gettysburg, and Pittsburgh, across the Ohio, through Fort Wayne, Indiana, then around Chicago to join the old Overland Trail at Geneva, Illinois. From there it crossed the Mississippi at Clinton, Iowa, on the way to Omaha, Cheyenne, and Salt Lake City; and finally it took the old Pony Express route to Ely, Reno, Carson City, Sacramento, and San Francisco.

Even with a route in mind, the association still faced a major obstacle: how to make a three-thousand-mile highway materialize out of little more than rhetoric. Its ingenious solution was the concept of the "seedling mile."[16] First the association selected a mile of unimproved rural road, often at the midpoint between two towns along the route. Then, with financial backing from concrete manufacturers, they would grade and pave the rutted byway to a standard never before seen by the local residents. Soon word leaked out that the road was finished, and before long a contingent of local motorists would struggle through the mud and bumps to the new highway, whiz along at thirty or forty miles an hour for a couple of minutes, only to run off the end of the pavement and back into the mire. Once intoxicated by the speed and smoothness of the ride, nearby communities were more than ready to raise funds to extend Main Street out to the seedling mile.

During the same period, other associations laid out a whole series of routes—the Dixie Highway, the Jefferson Highway—using similar methods of persuasion. It was not uncommon at the time to see telephone poles festooned with the colorful markers of four or five different highway associations along stretches where their routes overlapped.

Above, left:
Automovile Saloon; Ranchos de Taos, New Mexico; photograph 1913. This enterprise was an early, makeshift attempt to cash in on the auto trade. (Arizona Historical Society.)

Above, right:
Ramsey Garage sign; Grand Junction, Colorado; photograph 1917. A pioneering example, this giant roadside ladder sign was built expressly to catch the attention of passing motorists. Such signs were quite rare when this photograph was taken. Modern variations now soar over the roadside commercial landscape. (Colorado Historical Society.)

As effective as these private initiatives were in garnering public interest and local investment in better roads, the general cause of road building received its greatest boost when finally backed by the authority and funding of the federal government. With the Federal-Aid Road Acts of 1916 and 1921,[17] large sums of federal dollars became available for building a national network of primary, hard-surfaced, two-lane highways. Four years later, in 1925, these roads were assigned their now-familiar numerical designations—odd numbers for north-south roads, and even numbers for east-west roads. The days of competing markers and unclear jurisdictions came to an end. The coast-to-coast, all-weather highway network, as we know it today, had been firmly established.

To what extent did this highway renaissance revive roadside commerce? Until the time of World War I, business concentrated along Main Street and the taxpayer strip, and little if any new commercial activity appeared along the open road. Relics of another era persisted, however, as many newly improved highways followed the same right-of-way as older routes—routes that once supported a thriving roadside trade. Often, elderly commercial artifacts survived along these routes too, awaiting rediscovery by curious motorists. This fact did not go unnoticed by the writers of contemporary highway guidebooks. Exploring roadside history became a favorite pursuit, as evidenced, for example, in guidebook writer Robert Bruce's 1916 descriptions of relics encountered while motoring along the old National Road: "On the left, only a short distance west of Ellicott City, there stands an old toll-gate. . . . Now and then we pass an old, low, square signpost ____M. to Baltimore, the figures and letters often difficult to decipher at speed. . . . On the near right-hand corner is the Eagle Hotel. . . ."[18]

Amid artifacts from waysides past, motorists occasionally came across harbingers of what the roadside would look like in the not-too-distant future. Bruce recounted, with little enthusiasm, the discovery of one such early ancestor of the motel, between Hagerstown and Cumberland, Maryland; he described it as a "rough unpainted wood building, with a home-made sign, 'Meals and Lodging.'" He conceded that while "ordinarily it is not very attractive to the motor tourist," it "might be useful in case of a breakdown. . . ."[19]

Bruce's ambivalence toward this flickering of hucksterism aimed exclusively at the motorist was understandable. Pioneering auto tourists ventured out across a settlement pattern long shaped by the railroad, which concentrated goods and services in towns and cities. At nighttime motorists either headed for the nearest town to find a hotel or simply camped out by the side of the road. Wayside services for car travelers were at best an unproven novelty.

By the 1920s, this climate had changed. Driving had become a potent form of mass entertainment, and the automobile elevated to a much-sought-after cultural icon. Next to a home, a car was a family's most expensive purchase. For many people, especially those living in rented quarters, it was psychologically as well as economically their single most important possession. The number of registered cars more than tripled during the 1920s, to an astonishing 23 million by 1930.[20] Assaulted by advertising, goaded by peer pressure, and lured by the installment plan, many people of limited means made the leap; once it was made, they were anxious to find as many things to do with their cars as possible. Each weekend thousands of potential consumers on wheels rolled out of the nation's cities—all ripe and willing targets for new diversions and activities. At the same time, motortrucking, another by-product of the auto age, enabled the swift delivery of everything from gasoline to hot dogs to any point along the highway.

Given this favorable economic and psychological climate, it is not surprising that what had recently been only a windshield vision of considerable rarity was becoming commonplace. Businesses by the thousands germinated along the 1920s roadside. New entrepreneurs—from farmers and factory workers to teachers and retirees—built refreshment stands, restaurants, stores, cabin camps, and other wayside emporia, while petroleum

Below, left:
Highway construction; Burlington, Vermont; photograph 1928, L. L. McAllister. By the end of the 1920s, the nation's basic system of two-lane, numbered interstate routes had been substantially completed. (University of Vermont Special Collections.)

Below, right:
Central Ohio; photograph 1938. A symbol of prosperity in an era of economic adversity, the flamboyant hucksterism of the roadside entrepreneur was looked at with considerable fascination in the 1930s—in this case by photographer Ben Shahn, on assignment for the Farm Security Administration. (Library of Congress.)

companies made their products available beyond the limits of Main Street and the taxpayer strip. Standard Oil boasted of this progress in its 1925 New England tour guide: "When you advance the throttle and glide through 'SOCONYLAND TOURS,' you will be agreeably surprised to find a service station 'just where you need one.'"[21]

By 1927, wayside businesses had become so prolific that even the established business community began to take notice. That year the *Magazine of Business* reported:

Wayside stands along almost every strip of road in the country are reaping a harvest from the millions awheel. These are mainly operated by farmers and villagers, selling fresh fruits in season, canned stuff, vegetables, soft drinks, candy, tobacco, souvenirs, magazines, newspapers, books, maps, and what have you. It is very hard to get authentic information concerning the operation of such places, but the owner of two such stands just south of Milwaukee claims a net profit of $6,000 a season.[22]

The onslaught of roadside commercialism roared on through the remainder of the decade. Even after the depression had devastated most sectors of the economy, wayside business continued to flourish. This surprising trend sparked considerable contemporary speculation as to why highway commerce, long considered to be ephemeral, continued thriving while mighty industries faltered. *Harper's* in 1933 offered this somewhat tongue-in-cheek answer:

There's gold in them shacks—so long as the cars keep rolling by. And they are still rolling by. The depression hasn't stopped them at all. On the contrary. People who used to travel by train can no longer afford three or four cents a mile. Graduates of our thousand colleges, unable to get jobs, sponge on the family, club together to buy an old Ford, and point its radiator toward the great open spaces. Salaried men who have lost their jobs but saved something (or often almost nothing) say goodby to the landlord and take their families off to see the world before it blows up. Farmers who have failed or been dispossessed crank up the last thing which a good American surrenders—his car—and push off into a possibly happier nowhere. And then the great army of incurable wanderers, prosperous or poverty-stricken, who are always yielding to the restless, pioneer, gypsy streak that lies at the bottom of most Americans, roll back and forth, to the Lakes in summer, to California or Florida in the winter, with less reason than ever for settling in one place. And all of them must find some place to eat and sleep.[23]

A year later, *Fortune* carried this insight further. It observed how, by the 1930s, the automobile had sharpened "probably the profoundest and most compelling of American racial hungers"—the hunger for movement.[24] Roadside businesses were successful because they were able to capitalize on this craving:

The automobile became the opium of the American people. After the autoist had driven round and round for awhile, it became high time that people should catch on to the fact that as he rides there are a thousand and ten thousand little ways you can cash in on him en route. Within the past few years, the time ripened and burst. And along the great American Road, the Great American Roadside

Polarine Oil and Greases advertisement, 1918. Oil companies were among the first corporations to realize the economic potential of selling by the roadside using buildings designed and positioned to attract maximum attention when viewed from a speeding car. (Mobil Oil Corporation.)

Above:
Resort strip along Route 24, east of Manitou Springs, Colorado; photograph 1981. By the late 1920s, an assortment of cabin camps and gas stations (a number of which miraculously survive to this day) had sprung up to accommodate the flood of motor tourists visiting nearby Pikes Peak. Visible (far left) is an arch of iron trusswork marking the entrance to the village, a late-nineteenth-century resort spa. A new limited-access highway, which bypasses the older strip, can be seen in the foreground. (Author.)

Above, right:
Cartoon of resort strip, 1933. (Roadside Merchant, July 1933.)

sprang up prodigally as morning mushrooms, and completed a circle which will whirl for pleasure and for profit as long as the American blood and the American car are so happily married.[25]

The fact that the love affair with the auto endured the depression is borne out by other indicators as well. While automobile production sagged in the early thirties and later made a mild recovery, many used cars were kept in circulation, and passenger-car registrations inched up to 27.5 million by 1940.[26] Highway building—an excellent way to put people back to work—also continued at almost full tilt.

With the basic primary road system in place, the 1930s brought a period of improvement and expansion. Key roads (especially at the approaches to cities) were widened and congested areas bypassed. Bridging over railroads and highways and building traffic circles eliminated dangerous intersections, while larger metropolitan areas undertook construction of limited-access highways to relieve traffic.

At the same time, a number of places along this ever-changing web of highways emerged as favored locations for selling to this nation of "incurable wanderers—the most obvious being resort areas. By this time, the car had opened up vacation spots across the country that once had provided escape for only a few. Waves of tourists overwhelmed these resort areas, demanding not only accommodations and amusements that were less expensive and more informal than those offered at more traditional summer hotels, but lodging for the family car as well.

A good illustration of the way private enterprise cashed in on the summertime armada of vacationing motorists is Manitou Springs, Colorado. Located near Pikes Peak, this Victorian-era resort spa once received most of its visitors by railroad. By the late 1920s, it was so inundated with auto tourists that a whole new strip of gas stations and cabin camps soon mushroomed up on the outskirts of town.

Highways not only stimulated commercial development around existing scenic attractions but also helped to create new ones as well. Because of the complete mobility of the auto traveler, vacations no longer had to be confined to a small area surrounding a railroad station. Whole regions and their inhabitants were now open to tourism—a prospect not always looked upon with great enthusiasm.

In 1929, for example, the Canadian government built a highway around the Gaspé Peninsula along the south shore of the Gulf of St. Lawrence that was accessible to motorists from nearby metropolitan areas. This provoked Boston landscape architect Arthur A. Shurtleff to write a thoughtful protest:

Winding roads which were previously used by slow-moving carts, sledges, horseback riders, and travellers afoot have been straightened, widened, and rebuilt for

Resort strip near Provincetown, Massachusetts; photograph 1981. In 1931, builders created this exceptionally dense and linear cabin scape to squeeze the most profit from a narrow belt of water frontage on the left side of the highway. (Author.)

Hi-way Bar, c. 1940; Interstate 80 (former Route 30), Wamsutter, Wyoming; photograph 1981. Roadside cafés, gas stations, motor courts, truck stops, and souvenir stands became the mainstays of the oasis strip. This particular building, once the railroad station in nearby Red Desert, was moved and remodeled for use along the highway. (Author.)

Above:
Welcome Inn Truck Stop, c. 1950; south of Winnemucca, Nevada (bypassed by an interstate highway and closed about 1973); photograph 1982. Merchants often had to resort to visual theatrics—in this case a giant semi outlined in neon— to lure motorists off desolate stretches of highway even if their gas gauges did not read empty. (Author.)

Above, right:
Billboard advertising Boone, Iowa; photograph 1980. An event of long standing on bypass strips is the chamber-of-commerce billboard, erected by downtown businessmen in hope of enticing traffic to take a detour down the old road to Main Street. Often such signs telegraph more information about the self-image of the surrounding community than intended. In this instance, a touch of heritage ("Mamie Eisenhower Birth Place") and the phrase "The City Beautiful," coupled with an uncitylike image of a sad-eyed Bambi in front of hills more typical of the Southwest than Iowa, raise this question in the mind of the discerning driver: "Does Boone know what Boone is?" (Author.)

swift motor pleasure travel. Changes in the appearance of these quaint villages . . . may be expected to follow with nearly equal swiftness. . . . [With the highway will come] the inevitable tin can, the hot dog and clam stand, the gift shop, camp ground, advertising sign, and the debasement of those who are tempted to make traffic with these commodities for the tourists. We all know these villages are destined to lose their distinction and become like all other villages which have been overtaken by the tourists who put their foot to the gas.[27]

Such warnings had little effect. Vacation regions, from Cape Cod and the Adirondacks to Florida and the California coast, succumbed to the very fate described by Mr. Shurtleff.

Stopping places along desolate stretches of highway were also ideal sites for wayside businesses. At these locations, entrepreneurs often erected entirely new villages of cafés, restaurants, souvenir shops, and hostelries where none before existed. Numerous examples of this type of highway oasis are still common, especially in the West. It is impossible to travel any distance along U.S. Route 30 or old Route 66 between the Mississippi and California without coming across a barrage of signs urging motorists to fill up, buy trinkets, eat, or stay over at some "meteor city," "rattlesnake village," or "Little America."

Not all highway oases were built from scratch, however. Sometimes wayside services simply overran existing crossroads villages. The sight of an old house or row of false-fronted commercial blocks engulfed in a glut of gas stations, motor courts, and other roadside emporia is a good clue that an older town was swallowed up in an onslaught of roadside development.

Bypass roads offered still another choice site for wayside enterprise. During the second quarter of the century, the idea of rerouting traffic around congested business districts gained considerable popular support. Parkway advocate Charles Downing Lay championed the motorists' point of view: "There is nothing so gratifying to long-distance motorists as a byway or by-pass for every city and village, for the difficulty of going through towns congested with local traffic, pedestrians and parked cars is the great cause of low average speeds on long runs."[28]

Kalama, Washington; photograph 1984. This view is an aboveground archeological exhibit of the history of highway transportation along the busy corridor between Portland and Seattle. Visible at far right, lined by corniced Main Street buildings, is the old Pacific Highway— the first paved highway between the two cities. At center is a bypass road built in 1946, now used as an access road for the interstate highway at left, which was completed in the late 1960s. (Author.)

Other proponents, such as Gilmore D. Clarke, dean of Cornell's School of Architecture, felt strongly that bypasses were the salvation of Main Street. In 1941 he exhorted: "How much longer are we going to allow the motor car to continue . . . to destroy the character of our cities and villages? As long as we route through traffic over Main Street, we delay the day when our communities may function in a normal, orderly way. . . ."[29]

Bypassed highway; Wareham, Massachusetts; photograph 1980. The old, faded miniature-golf sign (left) is still oriented to the former main road (trailing off at the center of the photograph). Thousands of similar ghost images of roadsides past lurk at the margins of highways coast to coast. (Author.)

The first bypasses were usually created by arrows rather than carved out by bulldozers. Highway officials simply posted signs to direct traffic around Main Street along existing roads. Unless prohibited by zoning, the rerouting presented an ideal opportunity for new businesses to move in. Soon garages, gas stations, motor courts, and snack stands began taking over vacant lots along the new route, forming a secondary business district oriented to through traffic a block or two over from Main Street.

Before long, this detour, too, grew overcrowded, and eventually still another bypass scheme appeared. These second-generation bypasses were usually new roads, rather than reroutings, designed to circumvent not only Main Street but the older bypass as well. Unless a community restricted commercial development along the new highway, land beside this express route usually filled up with yet another lineup of motor courts, restaurants, and gas stations within a few years after the ribbon-cutting ceremony. In some places a third bypass was built, and even a fourth, each new road leaving the businesses along the last bypass economically stranded.

Today the history of the American bypass is well illustrated in communities throughout the country. A parallel road to Main Street is laced with the remains of elderly filling stations; another road farther out of town is lined by once-prosperous motels whose peeling signs now advertise "Rooms by the Week"; and farther out still is a much wider and busier thoroughfare where McDonald's and Holiday Inn have set up shop—all are physical reminders that the game of bypass leapfrog had once been played in town.

While resorts, oases, and bypasses all represented popular locations for wayside selling, probably the most ubiquitous commercial strips appeared along busy highways, beyond Main Street and the taxpayer strip, at the

*The great approach strip, Route 99
North, Fresno, California; photograph
1982. (Author.)*

outer fringes of the city. During their formative years, between the mid-
1920s and World War II, these strips developed into the city gates of the
auto age. Here merchants were assured of having a first crack at inbound
trade as well as the final chance to flag down outgoing cars. As the home
of everything from dairy bars selling homemade ice cream to stands dispensing fresh produce, "approach strips"—a term that may be applied to
these linear urban commercial portals—catered to Sunday drivers, the
flocks of urban locusts on their ritualistic weekend exodus from the city,
as well as to the tourist. Today many of these approach strips have
evolved into the gauntlet of businesses, signs, and parked cars one still
has to pass through when driving into town, or between towns in cases
where two approach strips have merged into one continuous strip.

In less than three decades, roadside strips were well on the way to
becoming the undisputed marketplace of the motor age. Roadside business had evolved from a fleeting apparition through the windshield to
widespread "nickle and dime stores of nomadic America."[30] The "rough,
unpainted wood building, with a home-made sign, 'Meals and Lodging,'"
which Robert Bruce had spotted along the National Road a quarter of a
century before, proved to be only the first glimmer of a commercial transformation that would eventually grow to gigantic proportions, but not
without some minor bumps on the road ahead.

THE SUBURBAN STRIP:
MAIN STREET MOVES TO THE MIRACLE MILE

World War II posed the first real setback for wayside commercial development. Not long after the outbreak of hostilities, the federal government
imposed restrictions on the very commodities essential to the roadside

*Van Buren Street (lengthwise center),
Phoenix; photograph 1982. Once an isolated approach strip lined with motor
courts, the street is now engulfed by metropolitan Phoenix. Many of the major
routes that divide this former desert into
large squares turned into commercial
strips as the city grew up around them.
(Landis Aerial Surveys.)*

economy—cars, rubber tires, and gasoline. Production of motorcars ceased in 1942, gasoline rationing went into effect, tires grew scarce, and consequently, most nonessential driving was curbed for the duration.

Even with motorists in short supply, the vigorous highway economy did not completely suffocate. While a good number of gas stations and restaurants were boarded up and mothballed until war's end, highways near military bases bristled with honky-tonks and other distractions poised to cash in on reveling servicemen, and motor courts near defense plants doubled for workers' housing.

After the war, new cars again glistened in auto showrooms, gas flowed freely at the local service station, and lively trade flourished once more along the highway. However, with renewed prosperity, the postwar boom also brought fundamental change to the nation's roadside strips, especially to the approach strips at the metropolitan limits. A half-century before, streetcar development had gobbled up little hamlets and village centers at the outskirts of town. Now it was the roadside strip's turn to be absorbed by urban expansion; only this time the city was spreading out on rubber tires instead of rails.

Soon farms, fields, and open lands that once brought pastoral solace to legions of Sunday drivers disappeared into tract developments of hundreds of look-alike houses. Like the taxpayer strip before it, the nearby approach strip became the logical location for businesses serving these new communities. Supermarkets, auto dealers, and a wide range of other retailers, from hardware stores and dry cleaners to clothing outlets and florist shops, intermixed with the older hot dog stands, filling stations, produce stands, souvenir booths, and motor courts. This time around, however, the newcomers adopted the same site plans as many of their older roadside neighbors. For them the old Main Street tradition of building along the sidewalk was finally cast aside, and setbacks became the rule. Customers now arrived in cars, not by foot or trolley. Large and convenient parking lots became more of a commercial bonus than an attractive shop window. As a writer in *Architectural Forum* observed in 1950: "When widespread automobile ownership liberated the customer from the fixed path of the mass transit lines . . . the shopper could be pulled almost anywhere . . . by what the downtown district so signally lacked—a place to park the car."[31]

Now, along the same roads where travelers once rented cabins to avoid the downtown hotel, and families on a Sunday outing stopped to pick up fresh corn at the farm stand, postwar motorists cruised for a place to buy groceries or a suite of bedroom furniture. The old approach strip had clearly changed. The postwar roadside was now the all-purpose, intense, high-speed linear commercial corridor described in this account of a typical drive out of town in 1956:

Streaming out from the central city, through fringetown and all across the country, a gaudy honky-tonk slowly filled up the great American road. At first it was limited to wayside gas stations and restaurants needed by the traveler. But then came his lodging shops and entertainment to recapture him. Market St., Front St., Times Square and Coney Island all exploded into the country and took roots on a broader scale than ever possible in the city. The new motorized fairyland offered something for everyone: frozen custards, pizza pies and foot-long hot dogs; golf, baseball, shooting ranges; wild animals, snake pits, frontier villages; Kozy Kabins and lush Hollywood Motels; drive-in movies; drive-in banks, drive-in churches; steak palaces, gin mills, burly shows. Bigger merchants, too, saw the mood of the new moving market and came out to flag it down. The scale of disorder grew with supermarts, used-car lots, seat-cover showrooms, outdoor furniture stores, do-it-yourself centers, discount houses, pipe-rack clothing chains.[32]

In many cities, this almost instantaneous transformation of some stretch of highway at the edge of town into a bustling shopping corridor was viewed by a society long conditioned by depression and war as an economic event of miraculous proportions. Taking their cue from the now-famous stretch of Wilshire Boulevard in Los Angeles called the Miracle Mile because of the way it boomed with interwar commercial development, speculators and town fathers across the country were often quick to celebrate their own example of commercial magic. Soon the term "Miracle Mile" became the local synonym for busy roadside trading places from Manhasset, Long Island, and Pittsfield, Massachusetts, all the way to Phoenix, Arizona.

Of all the new efforts to "flag down" the moving market, nothing did more to transform the Miracle Mile from an odd mélange of miscellaneous little businesses to a serious and respectable commercial zone than the shopping center. The evolution of the modern roadside shopping center originated with a discontent with Main Street that appeared after World War I.[33] By this time, the addiction to the seedling mile had begun to take hold on a grand scale. To a population rapidly succumbing to the opiate of high-speed travel down manicured highways, driving down Main Street with its stop-and-go traffic and bumpy pavement was becoming an annoyance. As one irate motorist complained in 1921: "You drive for miles through open country over a velvet highway. Suddenly you are jounced and jerked over a dilapidated brick pavement, or pitched into and out of deep holes in prehistoric macadam, or made to vibrate to the alternate sharps and flats of a 'block' pavement of which no two adjacent blocks by any chance strike the same level. No sign is needed to identify this as the city."[34]

The lack of convenient parking and the traffic overload found in big-city commercial districts added fuel to this discontent. Market forecasters and developers soon took notice. In 1926, for example, a report prepared by Harold H. Dunn, engineer of the New York–based Beeler Organization, concluded that "growing traffic congestion in cities is making it increasingly difficult for the suburban customers of city stores to reach these stores and shop in leisure and comfort. Surveys show that these people are reducing the number of their shopping trips to the stores in the congested centers. . . . A larger and larger proportion of their buying is being done in stores within their own suburban area."[35] A similar study, undertaken in 1929, on the shopping habits in New England's largest city showed that 24 percent of families living outside the corporate limits of Boston but within fifteen miles of the city preferred not to shop

EVOLUTION OF THE NEIGHBORHOOD
SHOPPING CENTER:

Above:
*Taxpayer block, c. 1930; Route 1, Col-
lege Park, Maryland. Taxpayer blocks,
set back from the street to allow for
parking out front, were the forerunners
of today's neighborhood shopping centers.
(Author.)*

Above, right:
*1 Stop Shopping Center, c. 1950; Wash-
ougal, Washington; photograph 1974,
Richard Longstreth. Take a contemporary rendition of the old one-story taxpayer block, attach a supermarket, and
wrap the result around a parking lot—
this was the most common recipe for
building neighborhood shopping centers
along the post–World War II suburban
strip. (Richard Longstreth.)*

in town.[36] Obviously Main Street had to be brought to the suburbs, a
realization that helped spawn the development of the shopping center.

From the very start, the shopping center's family tree developed along
two parallel branches. The first, the neighborhood shopping center, owes
its ancestry to a phenomenon on the taxpayer strip that was observed in
Baltimore as early as 1907. There developer Edward H. Bouton constructed "an architecturally unified building for stores set back from the
street."[37] Originally a grass lawn and carriage drive graced the area in
front of the structure. It was only a matter of time, however, before the
auto trade superseded the carriage trade, and the building's owner impro-
vised accordingly by "paving the front grass area and the carriage drive"
to create a customers' parking lot.[38]

In the 1920s, as described earlier, speculators began building setback
taxpayer blocks with similar off-street parking out front, and by the early
1930s, they began expanding the idea. They purchased lots on the outer
reaches of the taxpayer strip, increased the setbacks to provide more parking, added supermarkets, gas stations, and even small department or five-
and-dime stores to the formula—and the neighborhood shopping center
was born. Dey Wilcox's Shopping Center, which opened in 1938 in Battle
Creek, Michigan, is an excellent example of this new twist in the taxpayer
scheme. According to its designer, Leland F. Champlin, the complex was
"built for temporary use until such a time . . . as more stable conditions
in the neighborhood may justify a more permanent building"; this particular supermarket, with its string of attached stores, was arranged on an
"L-shaped plan, which provides adequate parking space for shoppers'
cars."[39]

From the early years of the depression to the outbreak of World War
II, a scattering of similar neighborhood shopping centers appeared in a
variety of cities, including Los Angeles; Washington, D.C.; and Birmingham, Alabama. After the war, their number and distribution shot up dramatically; only now these drive-up marketplaces were located along suburban strips rather than closer to town. Here builders took advantage of
the bigger lots and the demand for stores to serve the hundreds of nearby
subdivisions, and they erected larger centers, with vastly expanded super-

markets, more attached stores, and bountiful parking. While the size, lay-out, and architectural embellishments vary, this basic formula for neigh-borhood shopping centers has changed little to this day.

Local shopping centers helped bring neighborhood business to the strip, but it was through the development of regional shopping centers and malls that Main Street was finally transplanted in entirety to the roadside. Although enclosed arcades existed for many years in Europe, and nineteenth-century American examples could be found in such cities as Providence and Cleveland, the modern history of the regional shopping mall can be traced back to 1922, on the outskirts of Kansas City, Mis-souri. There, real estate entrepreneur J. C. Nichols constructed a novel shopping facility, called Country Club Plaza, as the commercial hub for a large residential district he was developing nearby.[40]

A forerunner of the modern highway shopping mall, Country Club Plaza embraced a variety of retail services, from small shops to depart-ment stores and filling stations. The plaza provided off-street parking in lots screened by walls that lined the street frontage and in multilevel ga-rages. However, Country Club Plaza still adhered to the Main Street tra-dition of having shop fronts face streetward along the sidewalk.

Developer Hugh Prather carried the planned regional shopping com-plex one step further. In 1931 he planned and built Highland Park Shop-ping Village in Dallas, generally regarded as "the first unified commercial development having its stores turned away from the access street."[41] By the early 1950s, this innovation was tested on a grand scale with the construction of two huge shopping complexes, Northgate in Seattle (1950), designed by John Graham and Company; and Shoppers' World, in Framingham, Massachusetts (1951), by Ketchum, Gina and Sharp.[42] In Northgate, businesses flanked each side of a fifteen-hundred-foot-long in-terior street open only to pedestrians, while at Shoppers' World two tiers of stores surrounded a grassy interior common. A giant lot around the perimeter provided parking for several thousand cars.

The metamorphosis from Main Street to roadside shopping mall en-tered its latest phase in 1956 with the construction of Southdale in Min-neapolis, designed by Victor Gruen and Associates. In this complex, the central common, or mall, was roofed over, creating an "air-conditioned outdoors,"[43] indoors. Free of vehicles, protected from the weather, with a department store instead of a church or courthouse as central focus, Main Street had been successfully condensed, repackaged, and transported to the Miracle Mile.

Back in 1932, architect Frank Lloyd Wright, then one of the country's more vocal decentrists, predicted the existence someday of a "great archi-tectural highway with its roadside markets, super-service stations, fine schools and playgrounds, small, integrated, intensive farming units, great automobile objectives and fine homes winding up the beautiful natural features of the landscape into the Broadacre City of the Future."[44] Forty years later, the highway had become the center of the city of the future, albeit not as the carefully planned, mixed-use vision that Wright had fore-cast. Nevertheless, from a collection of fly-by-night businesses hastily erected at the edge of the city, the suburban roadside strip had matured.

**EVOLUTION OF THE ROADSIDE
SHOPPING MALL:**

Right:
Country Club Plaza, begun 1922; Kansas City, Missouri; photograph c. 1930. A very early attempt to recreate Main Street in new form at the outskirts of town, this pioneering shopping center included ample off-street parking in both surface lots and multilevel garages. (Kansas City Public Library.)

Right, bottom:
Shoppers' World; Framingham, Massachusetts; photographed shortly after opening day in 1951. The next step toward the enclosed shopping mall, this complex consists of two tiers of stores ringing a grass-covered common. Parking was handled in a giant six-thousand-capacity car lot at the perimeter. (University of Louisville Photographic Archives.)

Below:
Southdale, Minneapolis, 1956. Victor Gruen took Shoppers' World one step further. His firm designed a shopping complex with a roofed-over common area, creating what is widely regarded as the prototype for the modern shopping mall. Soon downtowns nationwide faced a formidable rival—the all-weather roadside Main Street. (Gruen Associates.)

Its gas stations, fast-food restaurants, auto showrooms, motels, supermarkets, countless stores, and shopping centers together formed a high-speed linear Main Street through the nation's sprawling suburbs. As city planner Robert Riley observed in *Architectural and Engineering News* in 1968: "[Now] the vast majority of its businesses are the identical ones found downtown or in any neighborhood commercial area or any new shopping center. Its motels are the meeting places of the local civic clubs, its drive-ins the congregating places for local teenagers. . . . It is a healthy response to new patterns of living and it is not going to go away."[45]

FRONTAGE STRIP AND INTERCHANGE CLUSTER: SELLING BY THE SUPERHIGHWAY

The latest stage in the evolution of the wayside marketplace began when still another transportation network was imposed upon the landscape, the road carried to its ultimate expression—the superhighway. The dream of tearing along an endless ribbon of silken roadway, free of stop-and-go dangerous intersections and traffic signals, is almost as old as the auto itself. Back in 1908, for example, the Vanderbilts constructed a private motor speedway (the remains of which are still visible) from the borough of Queens all the way out to Lake Ronkonkoma, Long Island. Within a quarter of a century, the public sector followed suit. By the 1930s, metropolitan areas such as New York were busy building park-

El Cajon, California; photograph 1960. The interstate highway under construction (left) now bypasses the busy approach strip (note used-car lots and miniature golf course) at right. Superhighways disrupted and rearranged the pattern of wayside commerce. (California Department of Transportation.)

Above:
Junction Route 209 and Interstate 70, Cambridge, Ohio; photograph 1982. Wherever an interstate highway crossed an older artery, the surrounding land became extremely valuable as the best location for a high-speed highway oasis. Today clusters of giant corporate logos looming up by the side of the interstate signal to motorists that an interchange is rapidly approaching. (Author.)

Above, right:
New York State Thruway under construction; Yonkers, New York; photograph 1955. The Howard Johnson's (built 1940) here was completely cut off by boulders being pushed up to form an embankment. The restaurant and other nearby businesses survived because of an access road built alongside this stretch of thruway to form a frontage strip. The restaurant can still be seen, in somewhat altered form, on the west side of the thruway, just north of the New York City line. (Howard Johnson's.)

ways to speed the flow of urban traffic, while the opening of the Pennsylvania Turnpike, in 1940, presaged a postwar boom in the construction of state-owned toll roads, including the Massachusetts Turnpike and the New York State Thruway. However, development of a truly national network of superhighways, while first planned by the federal government in 1944, did not materialize until 1956, when Congress authorized funding to help complete a nationwide interstate highway system.

This forty-thousand-mile network of four-lane speedways, in addition to eating up thousands of acres of land and ripping through the historic cores of countless cities, also did much to alter the pattern of roadside commercial development. Each new interstate tended to siphon off traffic from older parallel trunk roads. In Connecticut, for example, the old Berlin Turnpike, between Meriden and Hartford, once boasted so many gas stations per square mile that it was the battleground for some of the Northeast's most cutthroat price wars. Then Interstate 91 opened in 1966, and with it went the bulk of the long-distance through traffic. From a roaring thoroughfare, the old turnpike was reduced to a far more docile road.

U.S. Route 41, between Kennesaw and Cartersville, Georgia, just north of Atlanta, underwent a similar transformation. By the early 1970s, this stretch of old Dixie Highway had the distinction of being the last bottleneck along the entire span of Interstate 75 from Michigan to Florida. Traffic poured off the interstate at either end, clogging the road with upwards of fifty thousand vehicles a day, and thousands of motorists were greeted by this amazing spectacle as they inched their way along: "Chenille sellers . . . stringing their peacock-emblazoned bedspreads and bathrobes on clothesline for display. Plywood-fronted fruit stands . . . [offering] Georgia peaches, mountain cider, boiled peanuts. . . . Diners broadcast the virtues of pot likker and cornbread. . . . Filling station attendants grinned and drawled polite 'sirs' and 'ma'ams' when they took your money. . . ."[46]

This fleeting contact with the Southern heartland came to an end on 15 December 1977 when, with the snip of a ribbon, Interstate 75 became a continuous concrete pathway stretching from Sault Sainte Marie to

A BRIEF TRIP BACKWARD ACROSS THE
ROADSIDE COMMERCIAL TIME LINE
FROM MIRACLE MILE TO MAIN STREET
ALONG CENTRAL AVENUE (OLD ROUTE
66) IN ALBUQUERQUE (ALL PHOTO-
GRAPHS 1983):

*Suburban strip; looking west from Inter-
state 40. Here motels and other services
for travelers are intermixed with everything from war surplus stores and auto
dealerships to convenience groceries and
shopping centers. (Author.)*

*Farther in is a modest taxpayer strip
lined with older residences and one-story
shop fronts built along the sidewalk, interspersed with newer motels. (Author.)*

*Finally, the tall, densely packed build-
ings of the downtown shopping district
come into view. (Author.)*

SEARS MOVES FROM MAIN STREET TO
MIRACLE MILE:

Sears (opened 1929, closed 1968); Lo-rain, Ohio; photograph 1968. At first the company's retail outlets were located in rented space in Main Steet commercial blocks. (Sears, Roebuck and Company.)

Sears (opened 1928, closed 1976); Gra-tiot Avenue, Detroit; photograph c. 1930. Beginning in the late 1920s, Sears started to build much larger stores, with sign towers at key intersections along the taxpayer strip to attract the attention of approaching motorists. (Sears, Roebuck and Company.)

Sears (opened 1962); Oakbrook, Illinois; photograph 1962. In the postwar era, Sears became an anchor store in large shopping centers. (Sears, Roebuck and Company.)

Tampa. A year later, *Atlanta Magazine* examined the fate of this once-prosperous commercial carnival: "Roadside ecology has moved fast to obliterate the knowledge of what was there even a year ago. . . . Vacant filling stations and lonely signs look like an abandoned studio backlot. Many remaining businesses have changed hands or found other uses."[47] A similar destiny befell many of the businesses once crowded along Route 9 in the Adirondacks, the great Airline Highway in Louisiana, and hundreds of other older strips across the country.

The coming of the interstate, however, did not always spell economic hardship for nearby Miracle Miles. In a number of cities, older strips continued to flourish as so-called business routes, and some even gained new status as "frontage strips" for the superhighways they paralleled. This latter development has made it possible for motorists to conduct high-speed scans of the businesses flashing by without having to leave the new highway. If a glimpse of a Holiday Inn or Mexican restaurant seems compelling, one simply takes the next exit and doubles back.

In fact, being visible from the super road is now a commodity of considerable value. Today the sight of glass-box office buildings or earth-tone condominiums lined up beside the interstate has become rather commonplace. At first glance (despite excellent access to the highway), with all the air and noise pollution, this would appear to be a less-than-desirable location in which to impress clients or cook steaks on the patio. Yet from an advertising standpoint, it is superb, for every motorist knows the exact location of these "executive squares" and "life-style estates." In Houston one office building even has expansive plate-glass display windows specially designed to face the interstate. When the building is lit at night, motorists are cleverly afforded a windshield view of people working out on Nautilus machines in the health spa on the upper floor. Once pedestrians strolled casually along Main Street; now it is possible to window-shop at fifty-five miles an hour.

The areas around interchanges have also proved to be prime targets for roadside commercial development. Since businesses were prohibited from having direct access to interstates, land around the interchanges became highly sought after and extremely valuable—so valuable as to be priced beyond range of all but the wealthiest roadside merchants. Consequently, the big winners in the interchange land rush were the shopping-mall developers, oil companies, and the national franchise organizations that dominated roadside business by the mid-1950s.

Today the interchange has become both town center and oasis. Once trolley lines from all over the city brought thousands of shoppers downtown. Now the interstate makes it possible to speed out of the city, exit the interchange, veer into a giant parking lot, and then stroll along a climate-controlled, indoor Main Street at the mall. At this same place, exiting travelers are fairly certain to find a knot of competing fast-food, gasoline, and lodging chains. It is no longer necessary to cruise the strip; all wants can be satisfied in this one section along the Miracle Mile. A forest of skyscraper signs bearing familiar national trademarks has become the visual signature of this newest highway marketplace and the last stop, for now, along the road from Main Street to Miracle Mile.

There is an ironic postscript to the saga of the super road. From the mid-1950s to the early 1970s, interstate highway construction slashed through thousands of acres of streets, houses, stores, schools, factories, churches, and parks to bring the spirit of the seedling mile to downtown. At the same time, urban-renewal programs continued the demolition of neighborhoods near the city center. At the core of these new urban clearings stood the remains of Main Street—its face, which once beamed prosperity, now revealed the ravages of a half-century-long trade war with the roadside strip. The solution: a massive dose of J. C. Nichols and Victor Gruen with a dash of historic preservation.

Millions of dollars became available to revive Main Street. The very same source of funds (the federal government) that built the highways could now be used to resuscitate an economic casualty of three quarters of a century of unrestrained road building. City officials banished cars from Main Street; hired designers to cover its surface (where once horses trod and streetcars rumbled) with fancy paving blocks, trees, sculpture, and a panoply of doodads from overhead canopies to giant flowerpots; turned the road over to pedestrians; restored old shop fronts; and filled up the surrounding renewal clearings with parking.

To get downtown by car, it was once necessary to poke along the entire length of the taxpayer strip. Now it is possible to leave the suburbs, streak along a superhighway, exit at Main Street, pull into a parking garage, and go shopping in the "new," "restored," "historic" Main Street shopping mall. Main Street, once the heart of the city, has in reality become another regional shopping center along the interstate.

Seldom does the road in real life reveal such a neatly wrought pattern of development as the one presented here. Instead, the outline of the story builds with gaps and flickers, broken by renovations, demolitions, and makeovers of roadside businesses, rerouting and destruction of old highway networks, and varying local conditions. Yet it is possible to piece together a framework from the evidence that remains, peeling back layer after layer to recognize an original core.

With this new information, the visual clues speeding by during the automobile trip described at the opening of this chapter can now be sorted out and decoded. Beginning out in the country this time, there is the little village of tourist cabins that once flourished as an oasis strip. Farther in, the K Marts and 7-Elevens intermixed with older roadside businesses, such as the Nite-O-Rest Motel and Star Cafe, are a good indication of an old approach strip swallowed by suburbia. The next episode is an interchange cluster, with its shopping malls, Holiday Inns, and yellow arches set high in the air. The fork where the road now narrows is the place where the bypass meets the old highway into town. Trolley tracks and rows of one-story shop fronts, a classic taxpayer strip, are brick-and-mortar testaments to the era of metropolitanization. Finally the trip ends at Main Street, the point of beginning.

Each drive down the highway then is a trip along a vast linear time line in three dimensions, each passing scene a clue for unraveling the larger puzzle of how and why twentieth-century society has chosen to reorganize its civilization around the highway.

I M A G E

Architecture for Speed-Reading

Now THAT the episodes of the movie through the windshield have been located in time and space, it is time to review the cast—the thousands of commercial structures designed to capture the attention of an audience passing by at high speed.

On a drive along a major artery from Main Street through the taxpayer strip, or along the suburban strip to the outer limits of the urban fringe, one commonly encounters roadside buildings cloaked in a wide variety of guises. Take the gas station, for example. Some gas stations look like little cottages, or big white boxes; others have soaring canopies reminiscent of a jet taking off from a runway or are festooned with wood shingles. Nearly all roadside building types, from motels and restaurants to auto showrooms and supermarkets, over the years have been wrapped in a similar array of garments designed to promote business.

Is there any pattern to this seemingly confusing wardrobe? When and why were particular costumes for wayside selling in vogue? To what extent, if any, does the ornament and imagery of roadside buildings reflect the values and priorities of the age in which they were built? A look at the general phases in the evolution of roadside commercial imagery can begin to answer these questions.

SHEDDING THE IMAGE OF MAIN STREET

Not surprisingly, the evolution of roadside commercial building imagery begins at the very same place where car first met commerce—Main Street. Here, by the turn of the twentieth century, a tradition for designing business structures had so firmly taken hold that any new enterprise setting up shop was simultaneously forced to conform to a rather rigid mold and to break it.

The mold took form in the mid-nineteenth century when industrialization had spawned thousands of new retailers, each in need of sales space.

To be interested in the popular culture of contemporary America is to be interested in our popular architecture; the architecture of those buildings in which we live or work or enjoy ourselves. They are not only an important part of our everyday environment, they also reveal in their design and evolution much about our values and how we adjust to the surrounding world.
—J. B. Jackson
*The Necessity for Ruins
and Other Topics*

39

The oversize, gable-roofed house with ground-floor shops, still the most common template for commercial building design at the time and a conceptual throwback to the colonial era, no longer provided an adequate prototype for business structures. Since the retail economy now depended on distributing output from factories rather than merely showcasing a trickle of wares crafted by artisans, the legions of new shopkeepers needed commercial structures that could be built in a variety of sizes and internal configurations while adhering to prevailing aesthetic sensibilities.

Over the next several decades, architects, developers, and speculators responded with a generation of business structures neatly tucked behind facades usually designed according to one basic prescription—shop fronts along the sidewalk, surmounted by several stories of flat wall, capped by a large ornamental cornice. Whether detailed in Greek Revival, Italianate, Romanesque, or other stylistic appliqués fashionable at various times during the period, this basic three-part formula prevailed well into the new century and became virtually synonymous with the image of Main Street. These tripartite stage sets, however, covered up more than the structures in back of them. A mélange of establishments—department stores, restaurants, livery stables, hotels—also competed for business from behind the assemblages of columned storefronts and heavily ornamented windows.

As might be expected, given this weight of precedent, the first businesses catering exclusively to the auto trade also conformed to the established Main Street mold. Ironically, most downtown garages, showrooms, and curbside gas stations, although built to serve a radical new machine that would eventually transform almost every facet of twentieth-century life, exhibited dutiful adherence to the cornice, wall, and storefront regimen. Only the sight of curbside gas pumps, garage doors filling voids where storefronts otherwise would have been located, cars rumbling in and out, and the message on the business sign distinguished these edifices from neighboring buildings.

This conformism in commercial building design actually proved a boon to early auto merchants striving to evoke a respectable image for an indus-

Below, left:
Union Mercantile Company; Cheyenne, Wyoming; lithograph 1884. Note the three-part format of storefront, wall of upper stories, and cornice—a prescription well established for design along Main Street by the dawn of the auto age. (American Heritage Center, University of Wyoming.)

Below, right:
Auto Livery; Merna, Nebraska; photograph c. 1910. Many of the first structures built to serve the auto conformed to the Main Street look and blended in with neighboring structures. (Solomon D. Butcher Collection, Nebraska State Historical Society.)

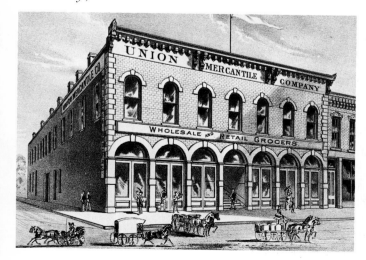

try still considered fly-by-night.[1] Nevertheless, even these new entrepreneurs were unwittingly caught in the same dilemma that had confronted merchants for decades—Main Street architecture, while designed for civic propriety and current fashion, contributed far less to the other task for which it was intended: assisting in the process of selling goods and services.

The tension between business and building actually extends back at least to the mid-nineteenth century to the very same time Main Streets across the country began to be lined by business blocks rather than oversize houses. Although the builders of these new structures lavished attention on everything from decorative brickwork to cornice brackets, they rarely allotted more than a narrow signboard strip, in addition to the storefront window, for advertisement. Keenly aware that trade would be lost if they could not capture the attention of the many pairs of eyes passing before their stores, merchants soon rebelled against prevailing architectural convention. With assistance from local sign makers, Main Street shop proprietors took matters into their own hands.

As a result of this collaboration, by the 1840s and 1850s Main Streets were alive with signs.[2] Signs covered windows and spandrels, blanketed exposed walls, projected out from the building facades, and jutted up from roofs high above the cornice line, not only advertising businesses within, but hawking products of other companies as well. Ironically, the rigid architectural mold for Main Street produced a situation where the buildings that fit in so aptly gradually disappeared under a growing thicket of blatant commercial messages.

The speed of passing vehicles played a role in this trend for more and larger signs. Trolleys, especially the fast-moving electric streetcars in operation at the close of the century, carried passengers who could, in the few seconds of their passing, catch only the most vivid and arresting advertisements. Commercial touts learned that public transit brought potential customers in quick succession; hence they directed their efforts at this market. Still more aggressive commercial messages appeared on Main Street in the form of billboards hawking brand-name biscuits, beverages,

Above:
Woodward Avenue, Detroit; photograph c. 1905. By the turn of the twentieth century, Main Street was often decked out in as many signs as a roadside strip today. (The Edison Institute.)

Above, right:
Times Square; New York, New York; photograph c. 1930. The "Great White Way" was the ultimate expression of the visual tug-of-war between sign and building along Main Street. (Coca-Cola Company Archives.)

and a host of other products; outdoor advertising companies, a corporate outgrowth of the bands of bill posters who had gone about randomly plastering broadsides on any available surface only a few decades before, erected these billboards.[3] And incandescent bulbs began to illuminate signs so that even at night, when the buildings were shadowed in darkness, the utterances of commerce clamored for attention.

By the beginning of the twentieth century, Main Street was more than the hub of trade and the backdrop for civic life and urban ceremony; it had become the site of a full-scale visual tug-of-war between traditional building styles and bold commercial signs—the need to be appropriate versus the imperative to sell.[4] Nowhere was this visual battleground more obvious than in the nation's largest city. As author John C. Van Dyke describes in his 1909 work, *New New York:*

The brilliancy of certain streets and spots like Herald Square, or Times Square, or the shop portion of Fifth Avenue, is materially augmented . . . by the prevalence everywhere of the electric sign . . . [which] now goes along with every place of amusement, and is frequently flashed at night from large commercial houses, hotels, railroad sheds, and steamboat docks. . . . Roof lines are their favorite locations, though doorways, arches, chimneys, vacant wall-spaces, are all utilized. Letterings, patternings, arabesques, figures of birds, beasts and men, are outlined by small electric globes, and the whole thrust upon the night in giant proportions. Sometimes there are changing letters and different readings, or flash lights that keep blinking and going out in darkness like miniature lighthouses. . . . All told, the glitter and glare of these signs make up a bewildering and . . . brilliant sight.[5]

What role did the automobile play in the development of this new commercial overlay? Although environmental critics and historic preservationists today often blame the superimposition of advertising over architecture on the automobile,[6] Main Street was already clothed in signs from cornice to curb by the dawn of the auto age. The presence of cars on Main Street simply accelerated the already well-established trend toward larger, more visually aggressive signs.

Along Route 25A, Kings Park, Long Island; photograph 1982. Two giant ice-cream cones and a church steeple are architecture for speed-reading from two different eras. (Author.)

However, outside the central business districts, the new vehicles prompted a marriage of architecture and advertising, a blend of building and sign, far beyond any sales campaign ever envisioned downtown. In fact by opening up vast expanses of roadside beyond the urban fringe to commercial exploitation, the automobile helped stimulate not only a new kind of landscape but also a commercial architectural revolution. As landscape theorist J. B. Jackson emphasized in *Landscape* magazine half a century later: "Never before had there been so total and dramatic a transformation of a portion of the American landscape, so sudden an evolution in habits, nor such a flowering of popular architecture."[7] With fewer, if any, legal restrictions—health laws or zoning regulations—outside of town, there was room to innovate and license to experiment. Unlike Main Street, these decentralized marketplaces usually carried little tradition for civic propriety and less imperative to "fit" the rest of the community. They became, instead, an ideal spot for a new breed of entrepreneurial pioneers to try their luck at snaring the mobile trade.

Who were these new highway merchants? Some represented large corporations such as oil companies seeking new outlets. Others were seasoned business people. A large majority, however, were amateurs in retailing—retirees, farmers, clerks, factory workers, and others of relatively modest means looking for extra, sometimes part-time or seasonal, income.[8]

Nevertheless, whether novices or professionals, all wayside entrepreneurs faced the same formidable commercial challenge: selling to customers enclosed in fast-paced vehicles. A roadside merchant needed not only to grab the attention of the speeding motorist in a very short period of time, but also to prompt the critical decision to stop and purchase. To catch the passing motorists' attention in this brief "flash time," the merchant had to resort to anything that would make his business visible

*Frozen Custard Stand; Washington,
D.C.; photograph 1940, Jack Delano.
The challenge facing early roadside merchants was to devise a sequence of visual
tricks to snare the passing motorist. (Library of Congress.)*

(signs, lights, shapes, heights, colors) and to devise a message (something
intriguing, fun, comforting, unusual, or just promising cheap goods) that
would draw them in without fail.

In the beginning, neither the problem nor its solutions were clear cut.
Merchants began by converting existing buildings for wayside selling—
old mills into tearooms, farmhouses into tourist homes—or by constructing rudimentary structures or shacks. Often the job of stopping traffic
was relegated solely to a sign or billboard—a technique borrowed from
Main Street. However, as competition increased, by the mid-1920s the
pressure was on to involve roadside buildings themselves actively in the
sales effort. Roadside retailers were forced to address the problem that
had plagued Main Street for almost a century—to forge a union between
building and sign.

In making the building an effective sales tool in its own right, highway
merchants, or their contractors and architects if they did not do the job
themselves, faced the same challenge as amusement-park builders, motion-picture producers, and advertising designers: finding images embedded in the public's consciousness that would have broad popular appeal.

DOMESTIC IMAGERY

Of all the images used in roadside commercial building during the
interwar years, that of a house, cottage, or cabin was probably the most
prevalent, for the concept of home held deep-rooted symbolic value.
When roadside business began to boom in the 1920s, for example, the
nation was in the grip of the jazz age, a full-scale rebellion against Victo-

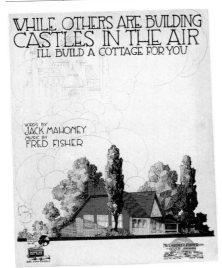

Above, left:
Sheet-music cover for "Castles in the Air," 1919. In the decade following World War I, "normalcy" and "home" were virtually synonymous. (Fisher Music Corporation.)

Above, right:
Journal Roadside Stand; Graves & Epps, architects; 1932. In the early 1930s, Ladies' Home Journal proposed a series of designs to correct what it perceived to be the "hideous American roadside spectacle." Domestic imagery was most palatable to early critics of roadside architecture. (Ladies' Home Journal, August 1932.)

rian values that had lingered into the twentieth century. But along with the popularity of flappers, cigarettes, and speakeasies, a strong societal longing for tradition continued—a yearning so powerful that the country elected a president whose vague but appealing slogan was "A Return to Normalcy." No symbol better personified normalcy than home.[9]

Middletown (1929), the pioneering study by Robert and Helen Lynd of daily life in Muncie, Indiana, underscored this fact. In Muncie, although the automobile had made inroads as the most-sought-after material possession (prompting one person interviewed to declare, "We'd rather do without clothes than give up the car"[10]), residents consistently regarded home ownership as "a mark of independence, of respectability, of belonging, a sentiment strengthened by the lag in house building during the war years."[11] During the depression era, the house took on even deeper, more emotionally charged meaning as something that everyone longed for, but fewer could afford. Herbert Hoover echoed these heightened sentiments at the Conference on Home Building in 1931. "Every one of you here is impelled by the high ideal and aspiration that each family may pass their days in the home which they own; that they may nurture it as theirs; that it may be their castle in all that exquisite sentiment which it surrounds with the sweetness of family life. This aspiration penetrates the heart of our national well being. . . . There can be no fear for a democracy or for self-government or for liberty and freedom from home owners no matter how humble they may be."[12]

Imbued with this degree of cultural symbolism, the image of home was therefore ideally suited for exploitation by the roadside merchant. Purely utilitarian reasons existed for the choice as well. Houses were small buildings and readily adaptable for roadside selling. Plans for a variety of small residences—from bungalows to Tudor cottages—were widely available, and ready-made components could be purchased through catalogs such as the one from Sears, Roebuck, from mail-order houses that specialized in build-it-yourself blueprints,[13] or from the local lumberyard. From the

Above:
Sandwich shop; Los Angeles; photograph c. 1930. By naming their business the Bungalow, the owners exploited the domestic appeal of their building to the fullest. (The Huntington Library.)

Above, right:
Lone Star Inn; Fresno, California; photograph May 1939, Dorothea Lange. The clapboarded, hipped-roof box, vaguely reminiscent of a bungalow, was an extremely popular all-purpose roadside-building form for everything from motel cabins to refreshment stands from the 1920s until about 1950. (Library of Congress.)

1920s well into the postwar era, such designs were adjusted to serve thousands of roadside businesses—from restaurants to motor courts and gas stations.

To flash the maximum dose of domesticity at the passing motorist, a roadside business had to showcase those characteristics that the public most closely associated with home. In *Middletown*, for example, the Lynds identified a number of features that symbolized home for the workingman with a little extra money: "a tidy frontyard . . . a bungalow or cottage . . . geraniums in the front windows."[14]

These and other such popular cues of the period were frequently transposed into stage sets for wayside vending. The illusion of a tidy yard, for example, might be created by planting grass at the perimeter of a parking

area and surrounding the lot with a picket fence. A small garden with bright flowers was another way of landscaping a business to achieve a homelike atmosphere.

By resembling interwar suburban houses, such as picturesque half-timbered "English cottages" with overshot eaves, the design of wayside commercial structures often traded on familiar domestic imagery. However, with roadside selling, exaggeration was usually the rule. Structures were often garnished with oversize roofs, nonfunctional shutters and dormers, and extra-large chimneys—all features exuding domesticity. Finally, the entire composition was frequently executed in diminutive scale, not only to save costs, but also to appear as charming, quaint, and inviting as a gingerbread house in a storybook. As if this were not enough, the house image could further be commercially exploited simply by erecting a sign reading "Kozy Kottage" or "Bungalow Tea Room" to hammer home the point.

This orchestration of assorted domestic symbols into an appealing display along the highway came quite naturally, for many early roadside merchants shared the same background, values, and aspirations as the highway travelers to whom they wished to sell. Though often lacking in retail experience, they usually had gained a great deal of practical expertise from their various trades and professions; they were part of the growing ranks of Americans who could now afford houses, cars, and appliances yet did not have the extra capital to hire help to fix a roof, overhaul the engine in the Model T, or rewire an electric fan. Instead they turned to "do-it-yourselfism," a philosophy well codified by the early twentieth century in the pages of national magazines such as *Popular Mechanics* and *Popular Science*.[15]

This combination of limited capital, shared dreams, and basic know-

St. Albans Bay, Vermont; photograph c. 1948, L. L. McAllister. Modest scale, scrupulous maintenance, an aura of informality, and the visual results of dozens of do-it-yourself improvement projects (from picket fences to roadside fantasy gardens) became hallmarks of the handyman aesthetic. (University of Vermont Special Collections.)

Giant cash register built to record Liberty Bond sales; downtown Dayton, Ohio; retouched photograph 1918. Mimetic buildings were used to attract attention years before the emergence of the roadside strip. (Popular Mechanics, December 1918.)

Conversion of giant wooden bottle (moved from an amusement park) into a summer cottage; Pine Island, New Hampshire. (Popular Mechanics, April 1921.)

how resulted in the development of what might be called the "handyman aesthetic." This aesthetic characterized the thousands of little quaint roadside cottages, where everything from jams and jellies and gasoline to a night's rest was sold amid landscaped settings that were outlined in borders of marigolds and petunias and replete with homemade goldfish ponds and lawn furniture. Modest in scale and scope, with buildings and grounds that could be kept by one family, these roadside ensembles were executed in materials that could be easily purchased, then assembled according to one's particular fancies. The best examples of this aesthetic combined scrupulous maintenance, naïveté in design, and an aura of friendly informality. In effect the merchant served as steward of a visual invitation beckoning motorists to spend a few moments in a mutually shared dream castle à la Hoover, with all its "exquisite sentiment."

Roadside selling—and buying—with domestic imagery points up the curious fact that the process of enjoying the highway demanded a certain measure of imagination from its participants. Since a business is clearly not a home, and customers were of course aware of this, a collusion existed between merchant and customer to join in a fantasy constantly being played along the road. The illusion, which became an essential part of the roadside experience from the 1920s until the early postwar years,[16] required a suspension of disbelief similar to that expected at Coney Island[17] or the local movie palace.

FANTASTIC IMAGERY

By the late 1920s, motorists also found themselves mesmerized by the sight of giant milk bottles, watermelons, dogs, and root-beer barrels poised along the side of the road. These surreal images were not jazz-age hallucinations, but yet another strategic weapon in the roadside merchants' developing arsenal of selling tricks—the lure of the bizarre.

Customarily the shapes of these unusual structures physically illustrated the name or nature of the business or the merchandise sold inside. Thus a building in which dairy products were sold might appear in the form of a giant milk can, while a gigantic toad would predictably house a business with a name such as the Toad Inn. Over the years, structures disguised as other objects have been classified under a variety of labels—mimetic or programmatic architecture, the French *architecture parlante*, or simply "duck," after the famous roadside duck built in Riverhead, Long Island, in 1931.[18]

As larger-than-life sculpture and absurd objects that surprise us by their unexpected shapes and materials, such fantastic designs have a long history as a notable form of artistic expression. Their roots reach at least as far back as the sculptured fountains and grottoes of ancient Rome, extend into the Middle Ages when "a tooth-puller was represented by a tooth the size of an armchair, a glover by a glove with each finger big enough to hold a baby"[19] along fourteenth-century Main Streets, and are linked as well with the Renaissance art of topiary, eighteenth-century garden follies, and the iconic work of French visionary architects.[20]

Above, left:
The Dog refreshment stand; Route 99,
Oregon; photograph 1939, Dorothea
Lange. (Library of Congress.)

Above, right:
The Big Duck, 1931; Riverhead, Long
Island; photograph 1982. Probably the
most publicized mimetic building in the
country, the Big Duck was pictured in
Peter Blake's God's Own Junkyard *as*
an eyesore and in Robert Venturi, Denise
Scott Brown, and Steven Izenour's
Learning from Las Vegas *as an exam-*
ple of the successful use of popular sym-
bolism in architecture. Designed as a re-
tail outlet by William Collins for then
Long Island duck magnate Martin
Maurer, it measures twenty by thirty by
fifteen feet. The portland-cement stucco
over wire lath structure was moved to its
current site on Flanders Road in 1941.
(Author.)

The mimetic tradition continued to flicker in the nineteenth century. Along Main Street, merchants freely exploited a variety of easily recognizable images of everyday objects, from clocks to teapots, for their commercial value. Giant watches hung above jewelers' shops, mortars and pestles graced druggists' doorways, and oversize boots announced to passersby that a cobbler was close at hand. By century's end, buildings—such as the sixty-five-foot-high elephant built in 1881 by James V. Lafferty in Margate, New Jersey, as a real-estate promotion scheme—became attractions at a growing number of resort and amusement areas.

Thus during the preceding centuries, the public had become conditioned to associate this kind of representational giantism with both recreating and spending money. It was only a small step for roadside merchants to turn the public's positive feelings about mimetic imagery to their advantage. If giant dogs or ducks prompted motorists to turn into the parking lot, part with cash, and enjoy themselves a bit in the process, then fantastic buildings were sure to appear along the road, which by now was becoming a combination of Main Street and amusement park.

The largest concentration of these fanciful structures seems to have been in the Los Angeles area—which architectural historian Reyner Banham suggests was due in part to the proximity of the movie industry, "a peerless school for building fantasy as fact."[21] Even so, from the 1920s to World War II, reasonable numbers could be found as well near many cities with more prosaic reputations. Only a handful of the earlier examples survive, although a few new mimetic structures are still being constructed to this day.[22]

Wherever and whenever built, mimetic forms combined advertising and architecture into an ingenious and unified commercial package. With this combination, early roadside business pioneers had achieved what more-traditional merchants had failed to do on Main Street: create a total synthesis of sign and building—evocative, compelling, and effective in the quest to attract, hold, and sell.

Alvarado Hotel, 1901–1902; Albuquerque; photograph c. 1903. One of the Mission Revival–style Harvey Houses, this hotel was built along the Santa Fe Railroad. (Albuquerque Museum Photoarchives.)

REGIONAL AND HISTORICAL IMAGERY

Stimulating associations with places other than home made good commercial sense also. Since tourists usually had well-formed notions about what they should find in a particular part of the country—seafood in New England, cowboys and Indians in the West—businesses could benefit from the reservoir of romantic ideas the public held regarding a historic site or geographic region. By anticipating these preconceptions, the creative owner of a roadside business could pull together a potpourri of references—through landscaping, architectural features, or simply an evocative name and picture on the sign in front—that would convey the appropriate image with all its corresponding associations.

Tempting travelers with stereotypes was a commercial technique that began well before auto touring became a national pastime. Starting in the late 1890s, in order to capture the passenger trade in the Southwest, Fred Harvey, for example, began building his famous trackside hotels and restaurants in the style of Spanish missions and Indian pueblos.[23] During the same period, railroads such as the Canadian Pacific erected stations cast in the form of French châteaus—the very types of buildings the tourists expected to see. A generation later, the switch from trackside to roadside offered even more possibilities for this brand of commercial costumery.

The most commercially exploitable historical and regional images were, in the broadest sense, those widely recognized "pictures" that had stirred the popular imagination—from log cabins to tepees—already embedded in

Mission Revival tourist cabin, El Colorado Motor Lodge, 1927; C. E. Thomas, architect; Manitou Springs, Colorado; photograph 1982. (Author.)

the public's mind by dime novels, Wild West shows, travel brochures, postcards, stereopticon views, advertising, museums, and finally the movies. Most commercial proprietors mined their own visual memories for the most effective imagery to sell their services and merchandise. Once an idea came to mind, handyman instincts often took over, and everything from old wagon wheels to lobster traps was scrutinized for its decorative potential.

Popular images that had acquired the additional weight of cultural symbolism provided especially rich source material that could be turned to commercial advantage. Colonial imagery serves as a particularly long-lived case in point.

By the early 1800s, colonial architecture, considered outmoded and old fashioned, had generally fallen out of favor. However, by midcentury, colonial buildings began to take on new prestige as symbols closely identified with the Founding Fathers. This return to respectability was fostered in part by the preservation of Washington's Headquarters in Newburgh, New York, in 1850; his home Mount Vernon in 1859; and with the celebration of the national centennial in 1876. By the turn of the twentieth century, a Colonial Revival was in full swing. Houses sprouted hipped roofs and porticoes; cupolas capped town halls. Historical societies and patriotic organizations also contributed to the new popularity of all things colonial by restoring ancient structures as house museums.

Eventually newly rich industrialists got into the act, with Henry Ford's 1923 acquisition of the Wayside Inn, built in 1702 in Sudbury, Massachusetts. The crescendo of colonial mania came with John D. Rockefeller II's reconstruction of colonial Williamsburg, begun in 1927. By the 1930s, the

Dad Lee's; near Carlin, Nevada; photograph 1948, T. W. Kines. Dad Lee employed a battery of regional stereotypes—from ox yokes and tepees to buckboards—to catch the motorists' attention. (National Archives.)

Hooper's Chocolates, c. 1940; Oakland, California; photograph 1971, Richard Longstreth. The colonial look could be relied on to unleash a cache of stored associations including the Founding Fathers, neatness, quaintness, and tidiness. Once more the idiom was generally regarded as aesthetically respectable, making it ideal for commercial exploitation. (Richard Longstreth.)

sight of a little white or brick building with a broken pediment over the doorway and a small-paned window sash could be depended on to call forth a cache of predictable associations—New England, East Coast, quaint, pure, Ye Olden Times, simple living. The colonial had acquired the patina of age, the sentimental aura of nostalgia, and probably most important, the wholehearted endorsement of elite culture. It had become a cliché and therefore suitable for selling on the roadside. (So powerful are the public associations with both colonial and Spanish colonial that the idioms have persisted in roadside architecture to the present day.)

Other types of images beyond the regional or historical were transplanted to the roadside marketplace and used effectively. National, patriotic symbols, such as the Capitol, widely understood by the motoring public became old favorites for highway businesses. Chinese pagodas, Dutch windmills, and other international stereotypes were also relied upon to attract attention, whether on a restaurant in Maine or a gas station in Wisconsin.

Capitol Motel, 1946; La Cienega Boulevard, Los Angeles; photograph 1982. National symbols such as the dome of the Capitol were also popular attention-getting motifs. (Author.)

In addition to being used separately, it was also possible to find all these categories of images—from house to duck to Spanish mission—scrambled in unpredictable combinations. A restaurant built to look like a house, for example, could also have a coffeepot mounted on its roof and a cactus on the lawn. Harnessing more than one type of evocative imagery was the wayside merchant's form of insurance that the speeding motorists' eyes would be arrested, if not by one visual lure, then by another.

While a cozy little cottage, a restaurant shaped like a hat, or a miniature Mount Vernon appear very different, collectively these images had much in common. All, including those with high-art roots, had filtered through the popular culture and had already been certified within society as acceptable visual triggers for evoking expected emotions; all were literal rather than abstract in content. Together they represented a powerful yet safe vehicle for inducing a generation of Americans to cruise, stop, and buy along the nation's highways–cum–amusement parks.

MODERNE AND MODERN IMAGERY

Popular images invested with vivid and reliable associations were not the exclusive source of costumery for roadside services. Beginning in the late 1920s, other architectural imagery appeared along the nation's budding commercial strips as well. This new wardrobe of wayside selling disguises had its origins in a growing dissatisfaction, within avant-garde design circles, with the iconography of classicism and its most recent reinterpretation in the Beaux Arts, Neoclassical, and Colonial Revival styles.

Architects and designers, in Western Europe as well as the United States, began searching for a visual vocabulary that, instead of being rooted in antiquity, expressed the fast-paced technological excitement of their own times. During the interwar years, several new systems of design and decoration emerged from this search, including Art Deco, or Zigzag Moderne; the Streamline Moderne;[24] the Modern; and after World

*Commercial block; La Brea and Wil-
shire, Los Angeles; photograph c. 1930.
Miles of taxpayer blocks were etched with
the repetitive geometry of the Art Deco
style. (The Huntington Library.)*

War II, exaggerated forms of the Modern which will be codified later in
the chapter. As each of these design trends became linked in the public's
mind with being progressive and up-to-date, sellers along the American
roadside borrowed and exploited them.

ART DECO

Art Deco was the most traditional of these new forms of imagery. Although it has been touted as a reaction to Beaux Arts Classicism, which
had heavily influenced building design during the late nineteenth and
early twentieth centuries, Art Deco was in reality more an exercise in the
substitution of machinelike ornament for classical ornament than a radical
approach to design. Its new decorative vocabulary consisted of a variety
of geometrical forms in low relief—from highly stylized floral motifs to
circles, segments, zigzags, and chevrons. These motifs, which were frequently used in repetition to evoke the spirit of the manufacturing plant
and assembly line,[25] epitomized the machine age.

Popularized by the Exposition Internationale des Arts Décoratifs et In-
dustriels Modernes held in Paris in 1925, by the late 1920s Art Deco had
become the favored style for detailing a host of downtown buildings—
from skyscrapers and movie theaters to banks, post offices, and department stores. The style also affected the appearance of the streetcar strip,
as builders etched miles of new taxpayer blocks with the repetitive geometry of the new style.

Although employed extensively in urban areas, the use of Art Deco

Art Deco–style gas station, c. 1930; San Francisco; photograph 1972, Richard Longstreth. (Richard Longstreth.)

along the roadside was more sporadic—limited to an occasional gas station or auto showroom. The style simply came along too early (in the late 1920s, at a time when popular imagery predominated) to be widely adopted in its pure form. By the mid-1930s, when roadside merchants, along with other businesses, did begin to embrace the Moderne, the Streamline rather than the Zigzag was in vogue, although some elements of the latter were often incorporated into the newer look.

STREAMLINE MODERNE

In contrast with Art Deco, which was generally a machinelike appliqué, Streamline Moderne developed from the processes of designing and selling machines themselves. Back in the nineteenth century, when the nation hungered for mechanical devices to ease the task of settling a continent, mechanics and engineers generally devoted the bulk of their efforts to making machines work, not to how machines looked. Once a mechanical design had been successfully tested, it was then decorated with ornament and placed in production. Fluted Greek columns graced weighing scales; scrollwork and brackets festooned locomotives; even the massive bulk of bathtubs was poised on diminutive ball-and-claw feet.[26]

By the early twentieth century, so many competing products had flooded the marketplace that how an item looked now became as important as how well it worked. In the late 1920s, a new group of professionals called "industrial designers"—with backgrounds ranging from theater design to mechanical engineering—spotted a potential market in assisting manufacturers to develop products with greater visual appeal. The idea caught on slowly until an event that devastated the rest of the economy—

Streamlined motel and streamlined trailer, both c. 1950; Manitou Springs, Colorado; photograph 1982. (Author.)

Below, left:
PCC trolleys; Toronto, Ontario; photograph 1977. Trolley cars were one of hundreds of kinds of vehicles, structures, machines, and objects redesigned during the depression years. (Author.)

Below, right:
Stuarts Club Grill; Houston; postcard c. 1940. This streamlined roadhouse sported a round, illuminated central sign pylon designed to be seen easily through the windshield of a speeding car. (Kathlyn Hatch.)

the Great Depression—ironically helped to launch the new profession.

As the nation slipped deeper into hard times, manufacturers, alarmed about plummeting demand for their products, turned to industrial designers in the hope of stimulating sales by enlivening the appearance of their products.[27] Manufacturers challenged these new designers to develop a visual idiom capable of telegraphing such positive thoughts as "up-to-date," "technologically advanced," "the shape of things to come" into the mind of a buying public beset with uncertainty—an idiom that could be flexible enough to be applied to a wide spectrum of objects, from refrigerators to trolley cars.

Most leading industrial designers—from Henry Dreyfuss and Norman Bel Geddes to Walter Dorwin Teague and Raymond Loewy—became fascinated with the visual celebration of the essential characteristic of all machines: motion through the reduction of friction.[28] They were influenced by forms expressing movement, from the rounded corners and undulating

facades of European Modernists such as Eric Mendelsohn to the teardrop-shaped cross section of airplane wings.

The teardrop shape, which neatly parted the air into smooth streams rather than turbulent eddies, became a favorite motif of the industrial designers; central to their visual vocabulary, it was known as "streamlining." From the early 1930s until well after World War II, streamlining was the rallying cry for the redesign of scores of objects from automobiles and locomotives, which could benefit from aerodynamic design, to thousands of perennially static objects, such as radio cabinets, furniture, and pencil-sharpener cowlings.

Although it began as a futuristic wrapper for mechanical products, streamlining soon became a prominent form of architectural expression. Buildings were designed with rounded corners and detailed with lines of flow suggesting motion, and modern materials enhanced the effect. Structural glass and porcelain-enameled metal panels, once used for bathroom partitions and advertising signs, made walls smooth and gleaming; stainless steel—a bright, silvery alloy that looked more like steel than steel itself—provided futuristic accents; and glass blocks were built into huge, glowing, translucent yet structural windows.

What made the Streamline Moderne so commercially viable? While bright, curving, smooth shapes may have had some subconscious appeal to a society in the throes of economic turmoil, the conceptual link between streamlining and a prosperous future was not left to chance—too many businesses were counting on it. Instead the connection was jackhammered into the public's consciousness. Railroads called their sleek new trains "streamliners." Advertisements extolled the virtues of streamlined irons and streamlined toasters. The word even became a popular synonym for "modern," as trade magazines encouraged merchants to engage in streamlined merchandising and to streamline their operations.[29] But probably the greatest marketplaces of modernism were the Chicago Century of Progress Exposition and the New York World's Fair. Planned since the late 1920s, the former, which took place in 1933–1934, still bore the machine-made look of the Art Deco; while at the latter, held in 1939–1940, visitors were greeted by exhibits depicting the streamlined World of Tomorrow, crafted by the nation's leading industrial designers.[30]

As a result of this massive indoctrination campaign on behalf of Moderne imagery, industrial designers and their clients succeeded in establishing a visual vocabulary that bridged the gap between style and sales by telegraphing the dual message: "I'm modern, the latest scientifically designed object—buy me." As a result—although this new vocabulary was abstract, as opposed to a literal reference such as "duck"—the Streamline Moderne could be relied upon to evoke exciting, positive associations that could be exploited for wayside selling.

By the late 1930s, streamlined imagery began to permeate roadside commercial design. Corporations hired industrial designers and architects to prepare prototypes for their roadside outlets, and the idiom also trickled down to the mom-and-pop outfits as well. Do-it-yourself magazines and trade journals doused merchant handymen with advice on streamlining their buildings,[31] and before long everything from hot dog stands to motor courts sported smooth surfaces and rounded corners.

However, roadside architecture continued to be a mélange of whatever imagery seemed to work. Zigzaggy Art Deco elements were often mixed in with the Streamline Moderne, since the former still held modern connotations. Moreover, although streamlining symbolized the future—and hence contrasted with the images of home, fantasy, and the romance of the past that were still very popular for roadside buildings—it was not uncommon to find, for instance, quaint cottages with glass-block walls. The strip-side loyalty was not to pure architectural style, but to sales.

MODERN

The third new source of twentieth-century imagery to be commercially exploited along the roadside during the depression was the work of European Modern architects which became known collectively as the International Style. This new movement was first popularized in this country in 1932 at the Museum of Modern Art's International Exhibition of Modern Architecture, assembled by Henry-Russell Hitchcock and Philip Johnson, featuring buildings by its leading proponents, including Le Corbusier, Walter Gropius, and Ludwig Mies van der Rohe.[32] Its influence changed from theory to reality on this side of the ocean with structures such as Howe and Lescaze's Philadelphia Savings Fund Society building, completed the same year.

After an initial period of high controversy, the International Style was parlayed into broad public acceptance through the efforts of a very committed following. These individuals saw to it that the scattering of buildings that served as bricks-and-mortar object lessons appeared frequently, not only in design journals but also in daily newspapers and popular magazines. By the late 1930s, the most obvious visual clichés of the International Style, from corner windows to flat roofs, began to be absorbed into the pool of features—both Art Deco and Streamline Moderne—constituting the Moderne look. This infiltration of International Style elements in the Moderne vocabulary manifested itself in places such as Miami Beach, where during the great hotel building boom at the end of the decade, Art Deco geometrics, Steamline curves, and International Style ribbon windows were blended into a showy surface modernism.

This intermingling of design elements could also be seen along the roadside by the late 1930s. For example, a whole new genre of gas stations[33] combined the International Style white box with the streamlined corners and flow-line accents, while alternatives to the little rustic motor-court cabins were built in the form of corner-windowed cubes.[34] Occasionally roadside structures of the period even reflected a strong adherence to the International Style, untainted by the Moderne.

But the greatest impact of the Modern movement, as the International Style eventually became known, was in the area of doctrine rather than decoration. Young architects grew infatuated with manifestos such as Le Corbusier's *Toward a New Architecture* (1923), translated from the original

Sales office; Spokane, Washington; photograph 1984. By the close of the 1930s, the influence of the International Style (stark cube forms with corner windows) began to show up along the commercial strip. (Author.)

French to English in 1927. He encouraged them to study modern objects from grain elevators to airplanes,[35] not necessarily to mimic their shapes but to apply the process that had been followed in establishing their design. The purpose of a ship, for example, was to carry cargo or passengers rapidly through the water. The nautical engineer took this program, combined it with the latest material—steel—and designed a vessel that would part the oceans most efficiently with maximum speed. Le Corbusier implored architects to do away with reliance on historical styles for packaging buildings and instead permit a good plan, executed in the latest materials and expressed with the designer's own skill and talent, to ultimately determine a structure's form.

To ensure that their message would be perpetuated, Modernists became involved in the education of young designers—in America this dissemination of Modern ideas received a boost with the appointment of Walter Gropius as head of the School of Architecture at Harvard University shortly after he fled Nazi Germany in 1937. In time most American design schools switched over to teaching the tenets of the International Style, conditioning a new generation of architects to cast aside historic styles; to work in glass, steel, concrete, and other modern materials; and to seek innovative design solutions expressive of the building's particular function. This reprogramming of the way that architects approached their practice would have a profound impact on the course of architecture; ultimately it helped transform roadside commercial design.

EXAGGERATED MODERN

After the bombing of Pearl Harbor, the federal government instated a strict wartime economy. Driving was curtailed by gas rationing, the manufacturing of consumer goods was severely limited by the shift to war production, and much nonessential construction was banned. These measures helped dampen the expansion of roadside business, though wayside commercial activity, including restaurants, motor courts, and roadhouses, continued to flourish near defense plants and military installations.

Although much new building, and therefore new design, had to be shelved in the war effort, the promise of a modern and mobile tomorrow still loomed bright. In fact, the same dreams of a future of prosperity through technology promised by designers and manufacturers to lift the nation out of the depression were called on now as a form of psychological weaponry for winning the war. To keep their products prominent in the public eye for the duration, corporations bombarded the home-front populace with advertisements predicting a wonderful postwar era full of better houses, railroad trains, radios, stoves—the rewards for a successful war effort.[36]

However, when the war was over and millions of Americans began to take to the road, move to the suburbs, eat out, watch movies at drive-ins, and shop at the supermarket, the world of tomorrow that had finally arrived had the Streamline Moderne look of yesterday. Manufacturers, having spent the preceding four years on the war effort, had not had a chance or the resources to redesign their commercial products in any noticeable way. Consequently, everything from automobiles to fountain pens during the early postwar period was often a warmed-over version of old prewar designs.

The same held true of early postwar roadside buildings—prewar imagery dominated. Many wayside structures still took the forms of little houses and regional stereotypes or were decked in Moderne wrappers to look up-to-date. By the close of the decade, however, this aging wardrobe of sales costumes rapidly became passé. Domestic, historic, and other popular imagery, as well as the zigzags and curves of the Moderne, began to disappear. Utilitarian, plain, and boxy, only the Modern idiom survived as the up-to-date look for roadside building.

Visually understated when seen from the windshield of a passing car, Modern nevertheless served as an adequate wayside selling medium in the halcyon days after the war when, following years of pent-up demand, mere newness drew the customers in. However, as competition along the roadside increased, so did the demand for more eye-catching imagery. Roadside merchants turned toward the architectural community to come up with designs that would be attention getting yet modern.

Only two decades before, prior to the depression, designing cabins, dining spots, and gas stations generally was of little interest to architects, and architectural publications took scant notice of the potential for commissions presented by these new building types. Shortly after the stock market crash, this attitude changed. For a profession now fallen on hard times, the possiblity of roadside commercial commissions became more attractive. As early as 1931, *Architectural Record* suggested to its readers: "Increasing traffic on the highways . . . has created a demand for filling and service stations, roadside inns and refreshment stands. . . . The architect can well undertake this work."[37] In the following year, the ground-breaking introduction to the International Style at the Museum of

Modern Art included a design for a gas station among its exhibits,[38] suggesting that, among the avant-garde at least, roadside work was respectable. Although the roadside was not yet considered a prime showcase for design talent, during the 1930s architects took on wayside business commissions for everything from gas stations to drive-in restaurants when they could find them and could earn suitable fees.

During the war, many architects and builders viewed highway development as an important source of postwar employment, and professional publications featured a good number of proposals for drive-in restaurants and other roadside businesses.[39] By the late 1940s, an increasing number of architects were involved in designing wayside commercial structures, because roadside developers had fewer do-it-yourselfers within their ranks and more professional business people who were willing to contract for design services.

Yet, since Modern doctrine had become deeply implanted in the practice of postwar architecture, the prospect of designing a roadside business posed a very interesting philosophical dilemma: how could a building be Modern, express its function, and yet sell a product along the highway without resorting to applied imagery?

One solution to the problem was the "visual front," a concept that began to surface in the mid-1930s for downtown architecture but did not gain widespread application along the roadside until after the war. A visual front was created by completely glazing the front, and sometimes the sides, of a commercial building, so that the interior of the structure, especially when lit at night, would provide visual appeal for the exterior. The glass was sometimes canted inward, to cut down on glare and provide visual variety. In this novel way of handling a favored Modern material, glass, architects devised sleek-looking buildings that both answered the demand to attract attention and, by showcasing the inside on the outside, exhibited "function," therefore conforming to Modern architectural dogma.

Another particularly effective way for architects to attract attention, while at the same time adhering to the Modernist dictum of functional expression, was to exaggerate a building's structural components. In this form of overstated functionalism, concrete, glass, plywood, steel, plastics, and other industrially produced building materials were crafted into displays of technological exhibitionism, designed for effect more than for structural requirements. Long practiced by Frank Lloyd Wright, the technique became popular in the postwar years with an increasing number of architects wishing to widen the vocabulary of visual expression of Modern architecture beyond the basic strictures of the International Style. Roofs were one building feature most often exaggerated. Marcel Breuer, for example, departed from the Modernist flat roof by popularizing the "butterfly" roof in 1949; Ulrich Franzen the "airplane" roof in 1955; and Eduardo Catalano the soaring "hyperbolic parabola" roof the same year. Similar oversize roofs (along with huge signs and canopies soaring at raking angles), V-shaped columns, and visual fronts were among the hallmarks of a new genre of roadside commercial images that may be grouped under the term Exaggerated Modern. As Herbert Smith of the *Architec-*

Above:

Bea's Sandwiches, 1963; Methuen, Massachusetts; photograph 1982. Large raking roofs with wide overhangs, visual fronts, and prominent roof-mounted signs are all typical roadside commercial design features from the late 1940s to the mid-1960s. (Author.)

Above, right:

Shopping Center, c. 1960; Tucson; photograph 1982. Undulating canopies like the one here shielding a visual front were another common feature of the rock-and-roll roadside. (Author.)

tural Record proclaimed in 1951: "The era of concrete dogs and oranges is fortunately on the wane. Frank expression of the structure and its purpose can often make an arresting design."[40]

Exaggerated Modern appears to have first taken hold along the roadside marketplace in the Los Angeles region as early as the late 1940s. Here, in

International Cafe, 1965; Yermo, California; photograph 1980. The Exaggerated Modern—as exemplified in this structure with its multiple roof planes and raking, exposed structural supports—was extremely popular for the design of West Coast coffee shops. (Author.)

Liberty Motel sign, 1953; Van Buren Street, Phoenix; photograph 1982. By the mid-1950s, popular imagery was often relegated to signs. Here, perched on a raking pedestal, a rendition of the famous statue lifts her neon-outlined torch to flag the passing travelers on the busy Van Buren Street strip. (Author.)

the mecca of the car culture, owners of coffee shops,[41] drive-in restaurants, discount gas stations, and other wayside emporia faced stiff competition on the strip earlier than their counterparts in many other regions of the country; they began hiring architects to design structures with massive displays of visual razzle-dazzle.[42] Soon the idiom was catching on in other parts of the country, and the flamboyant, intensely developed strip took its place beside the ranch-style suburban house, the patio, the barbecue, and casual living as a California export.[43]

By the mid-1950s, when car designers scrapped the last remaining streamline curves in favor of tail fins, and the smooth veneer of swing music had bowed out in favor of the beat of rock and roll, the nation's roadside strips were rapidly evolving into the vision that the American pop-culture writer Tom Wolfe would describe a decade later: "Endless scorched boulevards lined with one-story stores, shops, bowling alleys, skating rinks, tacos, drive-ins, all of them shaped not like rectangles but like trapezoids, from the way the roofs slant up from the back and the plate-glass fronts slant out as if they're going to pitch forward on the sidewalk and throw up. The signs are great, too. They all stand free on poles outside. They have horribly slick dog-legged shapes that I call boomerang modern."[44]

The visual theatrics of the Exaggerated Modern turned out to be exactly the kind of energetic look needed along the commercial strip. The style was a good attention getter, for it made a very memorable sales pitch. For architects it offered a workable formula for the roadside's programmatic necessity—effective advertising—and even a professional rationale, for they could "make a virtue of this mundane function as earlier modernists made virtues of factories, steel and concrete. . . ."[45]

Dinnies Restaurant sign, 1963; Richmond, Indiana; photograph 1981. In the years following the launching of Sputnik *in 1957, satellite forms became a common roadside commercial motif. (Author.)*

While Exaggerated Modern became the banner look of the late 1950s and early 1960s, it was not the only mode of expression on the commercial strip. During this period, a new genre of popular imagery, inspired by science and technology, also appeared. Some of these new images were abstract, such as amoeboid-shaped signs borrowed from biological models.[46] Others were representational in nature. Soon after the launching of *Sputnik* in 1957, for example, shining globes bristling with antennae so as to resemble space satellites began to protrude from buildings and signs throughout the country, while sign makers crafted advertisements in lenticular shapes reminiscent of flying saucers.[47]

Amid the amoebas, stars, atoms, and rockets, older sources for popular roadside imagery—from little houses to regional stereotypes—were still being mined for their intrinsic and well-proven attention-getting ability as well. It was not uncommon during this period to discover a huge canted visual-front building—exhibiting its insides like a giant television set, with luminous scenes of people waiting at motel desks or eating hot dogs at counters—flanked by a gigantic pulsating sign formed of an oversize colonial pediment or cactus, and then capped by a star or rocket or miniature *Sputnik*. Despite Modernist philosophy discouraging historical references, the roadside continued to be a great linear exhibition of cumulative emotive imagery.

THE ENVIRONMENTAL LOOK

With the coming of the 1960s, a ground swell of disillusionment began to build—disenchantment with the "world of tomorrow" promised during the depression and the war and put into practice in the late 1940s and early 1950s. A public that for three decades had been bombarded with the message "new is better" by everything from advertising to architecture was losing its faith in newness for its own sake. Their disappointment grew in the wake of influential manifestos that revealed the darker side of progress.

In *The Death and Life of Great American Cities*, published in 1961, city planning critic Jane Jacobs decried the leveling of large portions of American cities to make way for superhighways and high rises sitting in a sea of rubble-strewn grass. She insisted that "there is nothing economically or socially inevitable about either the decay of old cities or the fresh-minted decadence of the new unurban urbanization."[48] For Jacobs the total-clearance projects, resulting from the urban-renewal programs of the 1950s and 1960s, had been a costly error for cities, an error based on a widespread mistaken valuing of the completely new over all else.

A year later, pioneer environmentalist Rachel Carson, alarmed over the atomic and chemical pollution of the planet, published her profoundly influential *Silent Spring*, in which she cautioned: "Along with the possibility of the extinction of mankind by nuclear war, the central problem of our age has therefore become the contamination of man's total environment with such substances of incredible potential for harm—substances that accumulate in the tissues of plants and animals and even penetrate the germ cells to shatter or alter the very material of heredity upon which the shape of the future depends."[49]

Architect Peter Blake, among others, took on the postwar suburb and its inevitable by-product the commercial strip. In *God's Own Junkyard* (1964), he complained that the outskirts of the nation's cities had become "interminable wastelands dotted with millions of monotonous little houses on monotonous little lots and crisscrossed by highways lined with bill-boards, jazzed-up diners, used-car lots, drive-in movies, beflagged gas sta-tions, and garish motels."[50] Roadside development had long pricked the aesthetic sensibilities of many of the country's pundits, who like Blake derided the penchant for magnifying popular imagery in a blatant appeal for sales. *God's Own Junkyard*, on the other hand, went a long way toward identifying the commercial strip with a litany of environmental problems: overpopulation, overdevelopment, and national mobility.

Over the next decade, public policy gradually addressed the complex issues of environmental pollution and urban preservation with such mea-sures as the National Environmental Protection Act of 1969. Programs for everything from cleaning up the country's rivers and streams to combat-ing air pollution evolved in an attempt to rectify many of the problems Jane Jacobs and Rachel Carson had exposed.

However, the most readily perceived causes of visual pollution—such as intrusive highway billboards and cars rusting beside run-down houses— became the immediate targets of what would be a continuing struggle for reforming the environment. The crusade against all that was thought to be ugly in America received a boost from the widely publicized White House Conference on Natural Beauty in 1965. At that meeting, which covered an array of topics from installing utility cables underground to banning billboards from the interstate highways, the chief organizer, Lady Bird Johnson, called for "pleasing vistas and attractive roadside scenes" to replace "endless corridors walled in by neon, junk, and ruined landscape."[51]

Why were highway strips condemned along with more obvious forms of visual pollution such as junkyards? Certainly roadside strips were cha-otic, confusing, and often dilapidated, and they gobbled up hundreds of miles of prime frontage land; however, this growing discontent with the aesthetics of the strip most likely had a deeper underlying cause.

From its very beginnings, roadside commercial architecture had gener-ally mirrored the longings and preferences of the population at large. Most recently the Exaggerated Modern visually encoded a nation that had been hot-rodding over the landscape, polluting the environment while ex-hausting valuable natural resources. It is not surprising that this vocabu-lary of images for wayside vending would be criticized, denounced, and rejected by a society beginning to challenge the values of the postwar period.

This shift in public mood and aesthetic preference could not go unnot-iced by entrepreneurs, especially the large corporations that by this time owned or franchised some of the most visible roadside businesses—gas stations, motels, and fast-food restaurants. Exterior sales displays that

Commercial block, 1882, with cosmetic mansard, c. 1969; downtown Marion, Ohio; photograph 1982. This building has become a visual battleground between images of commercial appropriateness from two different eras. (Author.)

would be both acceptable to the passing motorist and palatable to the surrounding community seemed essential to their economic survival. This shift in the industry mood is typified by advice given to McDonald's chief, Ray Kroc, by one of the fast-food giant's regional real-estate executives in the mid-1960s: "How can we go into these towns and propose to put up these slant-roof buildings, which are absolute eyesores?"[52] By the mid-1960s, tail fins had disappeared from cars, the primal beat of rock and roll had been infiltrated and softened by folk music, and the Exaggerated Modern began to fade from the Miracle Mile.

The new national mood demanded a radical shift in style, a new vocabulary that would mute the blaring statements of the 1950s and early 1960s and convey to the viewer a softened presence, one perceived to be compatible with the environment instead of aggressively confrontational. The staple feature of this visually quieter style, the mansard roof, has become one of the most ubiquitous architectural elements along the roadside even to this day. Unlike the Victorian mansard, the modern versions are usually cosmetic appliqués rather than integral parts of a structure's roof.[53] Whereas the nineteenth-century ancestors were often sheathed with slate, their 1960s offspring generally consisted of cedar shakes, vacuum-formed plastic, or tiles.

The new mansards proved extremely versatile disguises for toning down the visual persona of wayside vending. Not only could they be included easily in new building designs for fast-food restaurants as well as supermarkets, drive-in banks, and gas stations, but they could also be deftly applied as instantaneous visual cosmetic to existing roadside buildings. For instance, a Dunkin' Donuts tucked away in Nonantum, Massachusetts, which had managed to survive with its old flat roof and visual front intact until 1981, was updated in less than a day through the application of specially made plastic mansard sections along its roofline. Mansards also had a totally functional purpose—they hid the mechanical system of vents and fans perched atop roadside hamburger factories and similar emporia.

By 1965, mansards began appearing in *Sweet's Catalog*, the compendium of building materials available to the nation's architects and builders and an excellent telltale for shifts in architectural winds. By 1970, mansard roof components were regularly featured in the publication, while V-shaped columns, the building blocks of the Exaggerated Modern, vanished from its pages, going the way of the streamlined materials of more than a decade before.[54]

By the late 1960s, mansards dominated the roadside, adorning everything from the roofs of fast-food stands owned by industry giants such as McDonald's to shopping-center canopies, auto-showroom parapets, and miniature-golf clubhouses. They were even tacked up over the ornamental cornices and decorative storefronts of nineteenth-century commercial blocks along Main Street.

Mansards were not the only manifestations of this environmental aesthetic. By the early 1970s, the rustic vocabulary had expanded to include brick walls or walls made of diagonal or board-and-batten unpainted wood siding, smaller signs using less neon and more acrylic or carved wood, and low-maintenance landscaping, in which very hardy plants (or plastic imitations) were set out in beds of bark mulch encased by several railroad ties, rechristened "landscape timbers." All provided popular vehicles for telegraphing the new commercial message: "We're for the environment; we don't pollute; we fit in; buy here."

By the Arab oil embargo of 1973–1974, the woody and the earth toned had made substantial inroads into the residue that had accumulated over the years from the many ingredients of roadside imagery. However, historical imagery as a source for roadside architecture was far from defunct. During the late 1970s, an energetic renewal and expansion of more-literal commercial imagery took place, influenced by two parallel developments: the historic preservation movement and Postmodern architecture.

Below, left:
Hank's Hangout, 1975; Panola, Texas; photograph 1982. Unpainted board-and-batten siding and mansard roofs (here in the handyman version) are the quintessential hallmarks of the Environmental Look. (Author.)

Below:
Kentucky Fried Chicken, remodeled 1982; Cambridge, Ohio; photograph 1982. The chain has replaced its old Exaggerated Modern striped roofs from the 1950s and 1960s with earth-tone metal mansards. The diminutive likeness of the old roof (above the sign) has been incorporated into the new design for its trademark value. (Author.)

THE OLD BUILDING LOOK

For many years, only a handful of historical styles—from colonial to mission—had been deeply enough implanted in the public's consciousness to be relied upon as selling costumes for commercial enterprises. Historic preservation, a concept that began to receive broad public support after the passage of the National Historic Preservation Act of 1966, helped change this situation. In addition to preserving old buildings and helping to invigorate dying cities, the movement accomplished something it has yet to be fully credited (or blamed) for: helping bestow commercial value upon a far greater spectrum of historical visual references. This was accomplished by a concerted campaign to link in the public's mind the image of clean, sparkling, restored old buildings with status, the availability of unusual merchandise, and economic gain.

Young professional couples who would have snapped up a new ranch house in a remote subdivision just a few years before, now chose old urban row houses. Families that at one time would have cruised the strip to eat at the local burger palace and watch movies in the drive-in now started to flock downtown to the local version of Quincy Market or Ghirardelli Square to eat quiche, oysters, and Chinese food and buy flowers and designer clothing. Developers, who once viewed old buildings solely as obstacles to be cleared from a construction site, by the mid-1970s were clamoring to grab hold of them. Due to federal tax incentives, coupled with the popularity of "restored" old structures as backdrops for housing and commerce, investors began scouring the nation's cities for old mills, warehouses, and commercial blocks. Any structure certified as "historic" by a listing in the National Register of Historic Places was an especially likely candidate for conversion into apartments, condominiums, and retail or office space.

Thus the historic preservation movement aided in the overthrow of the massive Moderne and Modern indoctrination campaign of the 1930s and 1940s. As *New York Times* architectural critic Paul Goldberger observed, "Suddenly to be modern is to be old-fashioned and to be old-fashioned is to be modern."[55]

While the move to make the old new changed popular tastes and patterns of real-estate investment, the Postmodern movement helped amend the very doctrines that had guided design for half a century as well. The Le Corbusier of the movement, Robert Venturi, in two works, *Complexity and Contradication in Architecture* (1966) and *Learning from Las Vegas* (1972), (coauthored with Denise Scott Brown and Steven Izenour), shook the already tottering foundations of the Modern movement as he urged architects to shed the dogmatic ties to expressing function and to be freer in the use of architectural symbolism from the past—particularly symbolism with proven popular appeal.

Venturi and his contemporaries made official in the world of architecture what roadside merchants had proven more than fifty years before—borrowing popular imagery attracts attention. A generation of architects

Former service-station sign, c. 1950, after gentrification; Mystic, Connecticut; photograph 1981. (Author.)

Big Yellow House restaurant, 1978; Reno, Nevada; photograph 1980. A by-product of historic preservation and Post-modernism, the Old Building Look had become popular along the roadside by the late 1970s. (Author.)

once trained to shun historical references began to festoon new buildings with everything from classical columns to Queen Anne Style shingle work.

As a result of these shifts in both popular taste and architectural doctrine, just as the smooth, curving Streamline Moderne could be relied upon to provoke associations of futuristic promise during the depression, by the late 1970s the sight of a structure overflowing with brackets and

Jelly Mill Commons, 1984; John Haines, architect; Shelburne, Vermont; photograph 1984. (Author.)

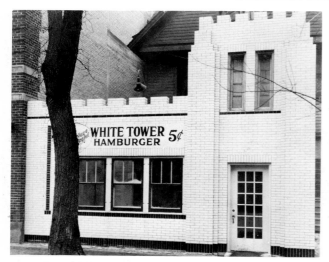

CHANGES IN THE COMMERCIAL IMAG-ERY OF THE WHITE TOWER CHAIN:

Above:
White Tower, Detroit; photograph c. 1930. The chain's earliest towers were built of brick with crenelated parapets; note that the structure is located on the former front lawn of the house behind it. (*John and Eugenie Fauver.*)

Above, right:
White Tower; New York, New York; photograph c. 1935. By the early 1930s, the chain began building stylish Art Deco towers. (*John and Eugenie Fauver.*)

CHANGES IN THE SIGN IMAGERY OF HOWARD JOHNSON'S, 1935–1973:

Right:
Howard Johnson's sign; North Weymouth, Massachusetts; photograph c. 1935. The chain's earliest roadside signs were designed with a broken pediment and urn motif to cash in on the public's positive associations with all things colonial. (*Howard Johnson's.*)

Far right:
Howard Johnson's sign; Forest Hills, Massachusetts; photograph c. 1957. By the 1940s, when this sign was erected, the company had streamlined the colonial motif with rounded corners and Moderne lettering. Note that a neon-outlined Simple Simon and the Pieman trademark has been added at the top. (*Howard Johnson's.*)

gewgaws, painted Victorian colors, and identified by a carved wooden sign became a trustworthy visual trigger to convey the fact that something very au courant was within, perhaps a nouvelle-cuisine restaurant or a boutique, encased in bare brick and oak trim.

Thus what may be called the Old Building Look—a hybrid of the literal historical expressions growing out of historic preservationism coupled with the more abstract arrangement of symbolic historic forms by Postmodernists—has become, in its turn, ripe for commercial exploitation. Surveying the roadside in the mid-1980s, one finds shopping centers that look like Victorian villages, roadside restaurants that resemble Main

Street commercial blocks or Queen Anne Style houses. Ironically, many of the same motifs that Main Street merchants masked with giant signs in order for better selling potential at the turn of the century were now sufficiently invested with commercial associations to sell themselves.

THE HIGH-TECH LOOK AND BEYOND

The American roadside today is more than a cacophony of the aesthetic howlings of competing enterprises—it is a visual museum containing dozens of exhibits that mirror swings in the national mood. Although increasingly rare, businesses—from motor courts to gas stations—can be found that still display the handyman aesthetic and the deep-rooted popular im-

Above, left:
White Tower; Richmond, Virginia; photograph c. 1957. In this design from the late 1950s, the tower motif has been superseded by an Exaggerated Modern visual front, undulating rear canopy, and trapezoidal sign. (John and Eugenie Fauver.)

Above, right:
White Tower; Toledo, Ohio; photograph 1984, Gloria Scott. The most recent towers feature the bare-wood Environmental Look. (Gloria Scott.)

Far left:
Howard Johnson's sign; Needham, Massachusetts; photograph 1956. In the mid-1950s, Howard Johnson's switched to an Exaggerated Modern trapezoidal sign with flashing arrow. (Howard Johnson's.)

Left:
Ground Round sign; Anaheim, California; photograph 1973. The carved-wood Environmental Look was adopted in the early 1970s for the chain's Ground Round subsidiary. (Howard Johnson's.)

ages of home, fantasy, and history, first pressed into service for wayside selling duty during the jazz age. Structures bearing geometric decoration or the smooth flowing lines of the hopeful Moderne of the depression years survive as well. And many examples of Exaggerated Modern—reflecting the faith in technology and rapid expansion of the car culture of the two decades following World War II—still gleam, soar, pulsate, dazzle, and blast off to attract the motorist's attention. Emporia costumed in the bare wood and earth tones of the Environmental Look, or disguised with the Old Building Look, are everywhere. Thus the roadside is both a visual bellwether of the prevailing popular mood and a storehouse of the emotive imagery of preceding generations. Can it also portend the future?

As of the writing of this book, there are signs along the highway of a switch over to still another system in roadside imagery—one that might be called the High-Tech Look. Once used to give a professional, reflection-free appearance to cameras and stereo equipment, the look made its debut on the road in the mid-1970s. It first showed up on cars in the form of matte-black bumpers and trim instead of the traditional shiny chrome accents, then buses with dark-tinted windows that on the outside appeared to be gaping black voids.[56]

Esso self-service filling station, c. 1982; Montreal, Quebec; photograph 1985. The High-Tech Look, as exemplified by this gas station—where even the wooden-tub planter (an Environmental Look holdover) has been painted black—is the most recent genre of commercial costumery to appear along the North American roadside. (Author.)

The trend is surfacing in architecture, as well. Gas stations and drive-in banks are being trimmed with black or muddy gray, outlined in iridescent red or green, while billboards and business signs also seem to be switching to a black background. Is this a harbinger of a coming aesthetic—an aesthetic with appeal for a nation increasingly infatuated with the black void of space, Star Wars, and the black matrix and bright images on video-game and computer screens? Or it is just a passing fad? If it captures the public imagination, and that appeal translates into sales, it will hold, or be absorbed into some later aesthetic during the closing years of the twentieth century.

T Y P E

Auto Showrooms

Auto showrooms have played an essential role in the commercial ecology of the roadside.[1] Nearly every car that has ever cruised the nation's highways made its debut as a gleaming newborn industrial artifact at an auto showroom. In addition to being the maternity wards of the motor age, showrooms have also served the roles of wedding chapel, where driver and new car are first united; hospital, where ailing cars receive treatment; and funeral parlor, where owners and their elderly vehicles part company at trade-in time. What are the history and evolution of the places that have served as a backdrop for these emotional and expensive twentieth-century rituals?

STORES FOR SELLING CARS

When automobiles first came to market at the turn of the century, car manufacturers needed to make considerable outlays of capital to tool up their factories, while simultaneously developing national retail networks quickly and at minimum cost. This was most easily accomplished by granting selling rights to local entrepreneurs.

These first dealerships (or "agencies," as they were sometimes called) were eagerly snapped up by Main Street businessmen, especially those already engaged in selling and servicing horse-age transportation. Horseless carriages went up for sale at livery stables, blacksmith shops, and carriage and bicycle stores across the country. It was not long, however, before the volume of auto sales began to overwhelm this existing retail infrastructure.

As business boomed, some dealers dropped other product lines or services and turned their buildings over completely to automotive commerce. Such was the case with the old Columbus Stables in downtown Bridgeport, Connecticut. Built in the mid-1870s, the four-story, red-brick structure was used exclusively as a livery until its owners began selling auto-

mobiles as a sideline in 1909. Five years later, a budding industry trade journal, *Horseless Age*, reported how "the automobile venture prospered" so that the building was "thoroughly renovated and remodeled to meet the requirements of the exacting automobile trade . . ."; a new electric sign, with "garage" outlined in incandescent bulbs, was installed over the main entrance to announce that this former "carriage and wagon repository" had truly entered the motor age.[2]

Many auto merchants, however, did not resort to renovation, opting instead to construct entirely new buildings in which to house their operations. Not suprisingly, these early motor marts were built along the lines of the older commercial blocks they superseded, with conservative modification. While facades of the new buildings usually adhered to the storefront, upper-story, cornice format—long a tradition on Main Street—the storefronts were generally larger so that passersby could catch a better glimpse of the cars displayed inside. On structures without side or rear access, a large front doorway was included so that automobiles could be driven in and out.

Existing commercial-block design influenced interior organization as well. Many early showrooms were laid out like any large retail shop. The structures still had the customary store space behind the shop front. However, instead of being filled with carriages, hardware, or dry goods, it now functioned as a salesroom for cars, accessories, clothing, and technical literature. Long a retail-store mainstay for everything from stock storage to restaurant kitchens, the back room was reincarnated as a repair shop with workbenches, lubrication pit, wash rack, and turntable (if the site did not permit sufficient turnaround space). If a building was more than one story high, upper floors, rather than containing offices or apart-

Hartman Bros. Ford agency, under construction; Montrose, Colorado; photograph 1909. Facades of first-generation auto salesrooms usually adhered to the storefront-cornice format. (Hartman Brothers.)

ments, were instead portioned out into inventory and storage areas made accessible by a heavy-duty freight elevator. If a showroom was located on a major touring route, the dealer sometimes used one of the upper stories to provide space for lockers, baths, and showers for chauffeurs, just as livery-stable operators had done for coachmen.

R. W. Whipple's thirty-three-thousand-square-foot garage, which opened in downtown Binghamton, New York, in 1904, was one example of hundreds of such dealership buildings built in the early years of the century exhibiting most of these exterior and interior elements. The four-story structure—featuring large plate-glass display windows divided by ornamental columns, upper-story windows set into paneled-brick recesses, and an ornate, bracketed cornice on top—could look right at home on any Main Street. Inside, the street end of the ground floor was "elaborately fitted up as a showroom, the ceiling being of ornamental steel and all partitions of glass," while the garage occupied "the entire rear portion . . . [and included] lockers for automobile owners. . . ."[3] The structure was also equipped with "an Otis Elevator, with a platform 16 × 8 feet," which ran from the basement to the top floor, where "second-hand automobiles" were sold.[4]

SALON SHOWROOMS AND AUTOMOBILE ROW

However ingenious these nascent sales facilities may have been, they could not keep pace with the industry exploding around them. In 1900, factory automobile sales amounted to only about 4,100 units nationally. Just ten years later, this number had shot up dramatically to 186,000.[5] From a curiosity, cars were rapidly becoming a serious means of transpor-

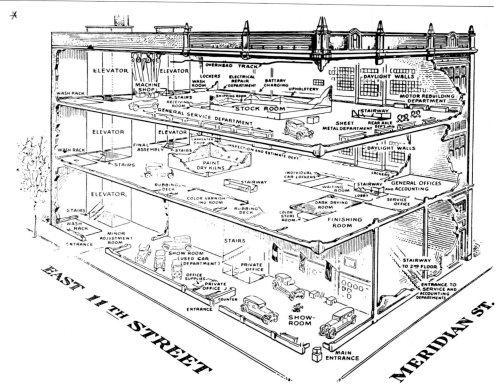

Nordyke & Marmon Factory Service and Retail Sales Building; Indianapolis. This interior organization was typical of <u>multistory urban auto sales salons</u>. Note beflagged first-floor salesroom, straddled and topped by utilitarian factory space that was used for everything from charging batteries to the final assembly of new cars. (Motor Age, 14 August 1919.)

tation. Automobile-dealership buildings were no longer considered merely places where a fad was merchandised; now they were the point of contact between the public and a rapidly expanding industry, consisting of scores of manufacturers. Nagging questions plagued the early-twentieth-century car buyer. "Should it be a Gray, Dodge, Autocar, Studebaker, Oakland,

Mechanic with wrench, detail of interior column capital; former Noyes Buick building, 1919 (now Boston University School for the Arts); Arthur H. Bowditch, architect; photograph 1981. Showrooms were frequently decorated with automotive motifs interwoven in capitals, cornices, and other traditional architectural embellishments. (Author.)

Regal, Chandler, Gordon, Packard, or Ford?" "Will the company be around in ten years?" "Will parts continue to be available?" Producing good cars and convincing advertisements was one way to inspire public confidence. Building impressive and attractive showrooms was another.

No longer content to leave showroom design up to the whim of individual dealers, manufacturers began to demonstrate how they wished the buildings to look. They did this by building "object-lesson" salesrooms in highly visible locations near business districts of large cities such as New York, Boston, Chicago, and Detroit.[6] Instead of being patterned after ordinary Main Street commercial blocks, these model showrooms were crafted to resemble the most impressive office buildings, banks, and railroad depots so they would instantly be perceived as civic assets. Exteriors often sported bas-reliefs, grand ornamental cornices, and entrance porticoes, while inside cars were sold in elegant surroundings in large, opulent sales salons.

Improvements did not stop at appearances. Many early auto showrooms were not designed to stand up under the ever-increasing load of cars, engines, repair equipment, batteries, tires, and myriad parts, nor were they constructed to take the constant pounding and shaking caused by moving automobiles. They were also susceptible to fire. With gasoline

Main salesroom, Ford Motor Company; Albert Kahn, architect; New York, New York; photograph 1917. Kahn's interior displays the full range of devices commonly used to give the auto showroom a level of repectability similar to a bank, hotel, or apartment-house lobby of the period. (Albert Kahn Associates, Inc.)

Neo-Gothic auto showroom, 1925; Denver; photograph 1982. During the salesroom building boom of the 1920s, auto showrooms were designed in a wide variety of architectural styles. Inside the structure here (now Gart Bros. sporting goods), ramps that once permitted cars to be moved between floors are now used to take customers, via golf cart, to a rooftop tennis court. (Author.)

and electricity in close proximity, one misplaced spark could quickly turn early motor marts, with their wooden floors and ceilings, into blistering infernos.

The new object-lesson showrooms were designed to correct these deficiencies. Builders accomplished this through the widespread use of reinforced-concrete construction. Pioneered by Ernest Ransome,[7] Thomas Alva Edison, and a long list of others, this technique for literally pouring buildings into place around bars of steel, still in the experimental stages in the early 1900s, was rapidly gaining favor for constructing everything from railroad bridges to auto factories. Capable of supporting large loads, vibration resistant, and relatively fireproof, reinforced concrete made an ideal skeletal system for structures designed for the selling and servicing of cars.

In 1907 architect Albert Kahn designed one of the first company-built prototypes to embody these sundry exterior and interior improvements for Packard at Broadway and Sixty-first Street in Manhattan. Kahn was a logical choice for the commission. He had recently designed the company's manufacturing plant in Detroit and was becoming nationally recognized for constructing large, fireproof industrial buildings using reinforced-concrete girders and columns.

Kahn cleverly applied his experience in building factories to Packard's showplace in the nation's largest and most influential city. He gave the three-story structure a skeleton of reinforced concrete and then camouflaged the whole in a respectable, Neoclassical facade faced in terra-cotta. This disguise was so effective that only the cars exhibited in the oversize plate-glass display windows at the gound floor divulged the secret—the structure was an auto showroom, not an office building.

Inside, an expansive salesroom—two stories high and illuminated by

Former Don Lee's Oldsmobile/Cadillac dealership, 1921 (now San Francisco Lincoln Mercury); Weeks and Day, architects; photograph 1982. This opulent salesroom trimmed with carved-wood paneling is still in use today. (Author.)

huge pendant-shaped chandeliers—was designed to appear as grand as a fashionable hotel lobby; however, its lofty setting was intended to show off cars rather than provide a backdrop for crowds. Along the back wall of the showroom, Kahn located an office that was "a finely finished apartment, with wood mosaic floors, covered with heavy rugs."[8]

Above and behind the salesroom, the character of the facility changed abruptly (a change not unlike that which a railroad passenger experienced when leaving the sumptuous waiting room of a train station to enter the train shed with its paved platforms and soaring trusses). Here, between massive concrete columns, the company placed the inventory of shiny new cars, plus spare parts and repair shops needed to keep cars running after being purchased.[9]

→ *revolutionary of waiting rooms.*

Other automakers undertook similar efforts. In 1912, for example, a "Model Garage and Salesroom," designed to "furnish object lessons to visiting Studebaker dealers in window display, floor arrangement, repair economy and a score of other details," opened in Detroit.[10] The same year, Rambler christened what *Horseless Age* called "one of the most imposing sales and service buildings in Boston."[11]

It was not long before these model facilities were having the desired effect. By the second decade of the new century, dealers began pouring their own money into lavish new facilities. Within ten years, fashionable showrooms were going up by the hundreds, and auto-showroom construction had become a game of visual one-upmanship. Now architectural imagery was used not just to give credibility to fledgling companies, but also to symbolize the power of well-established corporations and the prosperity of successful dealers.

To create these corporate status symbols, auto companies and their dealers scrambled to obtain the services of prominent architects. Along

Remains of Chicago's automobile row; Michigan Boulevard, south of the Loop; photograph 1981. Note that the large dealership buildings are interspersed with smaller showrooms built by speculators. Automotive Main Streets such as this flourished in the 1920s along major avenues at the fringes of downtown commercial districts across the country. (Author.)

with Albert Kahn (who went on to design factories, salesrooms, and office buildings for Ford, General Motors, and other giant automakers), firms such as Morgan, Walls and Clements[12] and Smith, Hinchman and Grylls[13] tried their hand at designing automotive sales palaces. Facades were treated in a variety of styles from Gothic and Neoclassical to Spanish and Georgian Revival, while interiors sported oriental carpets, carved wood tables, chairs, fountains, grand staircases, potted palms, coffered and vaulted ceilings, fireplaces, and gargoyles.

These luxurious stage sets, however, were more than an outpouring of commercial braggadocio. As William F. Wharton observed in *Architectural Forum* in 1927:

> The keen rivalry in creating automobile show rooms that shall be imposing from their sizes and their fitness for the adequate display of the cars . . . cannot by any means be set down to mere vainglorious "swank" . . . . The one aim apparently common to all who have embarked upon the broad program of embellishing their show rooms has been to invest them, as far as possible, with an air of luxury and leisurely detachment from any insistent suggestion of mere commercialism. The patrons, who presumably are accustomed to and appreciative of luxury, and who are looking with fastidious eyes at the qualities of the cars

before them, are to be welcomed amid congenial surroundings. They are to be entertained,—not hurried,—in their inspection. The technicalities and formalities of sale and purchase are not to be over-emphasized by an obtrusive array of desks, typewriters, filing cabinets and other office paraphernalia.[14]

This philosophy of exhibition held true, not just for expensive cars, but for Detroit's more utilitarian offerings as well. In New York City, for example, even Model T Fords were exhibited in a salesroom, built in 1917, that boasted high-coffered ceilings, plush armchairs, oriental rugs, chandeliers, potted palms, walnut paneling, and a grand staircase.[15] The automobile salon was not strictly an urban phenomenon either. Dealers in smaller cities throughout the country, from Colorado Springs and Greenwich, Connecticut, to Sioux Falls, South Dakota, and Oil City, Pennsylvania, built their own scaled-down sales palaces as well. Through the creation of an environment that offered leisure and luxury, companies, dealers, and their architects had developed an effective backdrop, a stage set for selling automobiles.

Along with the development of these lavish set pieces for auto vending came the birth of a new type of commercial district—automobile row. The evolution of these marketplaces for motorcars usually began when a dealer—often motivated by company object lessons, along with a desire to forsake high rents or taxes and cramped quarters in the central city—relocated along a main road, farther out of town. Before long another dealer moved in nearby, then another. Soon speculators built small, one-story showrooms in the gaps between the larger, more impressive sales buildings. These in turn were rented by agents of smaller, lesser-known automakers. Within a few years, a whole new Main Street was born, lined by walls of buildings whose shop windows, instead of being crammed full of jewelry, clothing, hardware, or groceries, showcased a single product—automobiles. By walking, driving, or riding a trolley down the street, shoppers could survey the latest cars available, while

more visible.
less functional .

Window display, Brewer Bros. Inc.; Pittsfield, Massachusetts; photograph 1925. At night automobile row was transformed into a series of incandescent showcases. (Brewer-Perkins, Inc.)

gaining an impression of dealers and the companies they represented from the appearance of their buildings.

Even today, in cities across the country, it is still possible to spot the remains of these early automobile rows. In Boston one can do so by riding the Green Line west, from where the streetcar emerges from the darkened tunnel at Kenmore Square, down the center of Commonwealth Avenue. Lining both sides of this broad thoroughfare for the next mile or so are block after block of substantial buildings—some several stories tall, many just a single story. The majority of these structures bear the outline of once-large display windows, since reduced in size or entirely blocked in. These traces, along with other telltale clues—an occasional bas-relief cast in the image of wheels and tires, an inscription of a long-defunct motor company over a doorway, one or two lone car dealers, and a scattering of auto supply houses—reveal that this stretch of avenue was at one time the city's premier automobile row.

The district was founded by Alvan T. Fuller, once Boston's key distributor and dealer for Packard (also Cadillac) motor cars. Fuller began selling automobiles shortly after the turn of the century in a bicycle shop on Columbus Avenue and soon moved to larger quarters in a building actually named the Motor Mart—an oversize taxpayer block shared by a number of auto merchants. Sales climbed rapidly, and before long Fuller again needed expansion room, so he decided to build a new showroom farther out of town.

The site he chose was on Commonwealth Avenue (near the junction with Brighton Avenue), a broad boulevard planned by Frederick Law Olmsted. The recently completed avenue was only sparsely developed, taxes were low, and land was cheaper than comparable property downtown. Fuller's lot had room for expansion. It was also near a railroad—the steel highway linking factory to showroom—and fronted on what was rapidly becoming a main streetcar-and-auto route to the city's western suburbs.

Having secured this excellent spot, Fuller commissioned Albert Kahn,

EVOLUTION OF THE SHOWROOMS OF ALVAN T. FULLER, FOUNDER OF BOSTON'S COMMONWEALTH AVENUE AUTOMOBILE ROW:

Below, left:
Motor Mart; photograph c. 1908. (Peter Fuller.)

Below, right:
New showroom, 1910; Albert Kahn, architect; photograph c. 1917. (Peter Fuller.)

who had recently completed Packard's New York showroom, to design a model sales-and-service building. Completed in 1910, the structure had a sales salon on the ground floor, while the remainder of the building was given over to functional assembly, storage, and repair facilities—thus fulfilling the dichotomous architectural program of stimulating sales while providing for service, all under the same roof.

So successful were both building and location that other dealers followed Fuller to Commonwealth Avenue. In 1912, for example, the architectural firm of Gay and Proctor was commissioned to build a showroom for Kissel Kars, while nearby, Clinton J. Warren designed a showroom for the White Automobile Company in 1913. This migration reached new proportions in the boom following World War I. In the blocks between Fuller's first showroom and the Cottage Farm (now the B.U.) Bridge, more than ten new salesrooms mushroomed up in 1919 alone.

During the 1920s, the street bustled with activity, and thousands of autos seen darting about the Bay State in the jazz age had begun as exhibits in Commonwealth Avenue showrooms. Business was so good that after first expanding his building in 1916, Fuller made another addition in 1928. He also remodeled his entire complex, installing a new showroom with high ceilings and fluted columns, lit by elegant hanging fixtures and a barrel-vaulted skylight. The space was furnished with large comfortable chairs surrounding a baronial-looking table, an ensemble straight from an apartment-house lobby of the period. By entering this or other similar enclaves along this stretch of avenue, customers could bask in the prestige of a grand interior space, relax, and survey the cars exhibited around them.[16]

Similar automobile rows crystallized in other cities as well. In Portland, Oregon, for example, about the time of World War I, the Rubin Motor Car Company (along with a number of other dealerships) was forced to move due to a new city ordinance that declared that "no automobiles, trucks, or other vehicles using gas or distillate, could be stored, kept or repaired in a building of frame, or having wooden floors. . . ."[17] After

Below, left:
Naturalistic display of Cadillacs and La Salles; photograph c. 1928. (Peter Fuller.)

Below:
Clark and White Lincoln Mercury showroom; Alvan T. Fuller's 1928 addition, shortly before interior features were obliterated in a condominium conversion; photograph 1981. (Author.)

a "traffic check," the company's president, B. W. Rubin, purchased a one-hundred-by-one-hundred-foot lot containing "an old, ill-smelling, dilapidated barn" at the corner of Broadway and Hoyt Street along a major artery leading out of town.[18] By 1919 the company had erected a new building with a fifty-by-fifty-foot showroom with a "terranza [terrazzo] floor, massive fireplace, [and] beamed ceiling."[19] Soon after its opening, Rubin declared, "Since starting our building every shack and vacant lot and old building in the neighborhood has been leased . . . some of the largest automobile dealers are coming on this street and it is now being heralded as 'automobile row.'"[20] Similar districts sprang up in Chicago, on Michigan Avenue south of the Loop, while in San Francisco, several great sales parlors towered along Van Ness Avenue. Even smaller cities such as Huntsville, Alabama, and Burlington, Vermont, had their own lineup of diminutive showrooms strung out along some road or other threading out of town.

MODERNIZING THE SHOWROOM

The depression, and the sharp drop in new-car sales that accompanied it, brought an abrupt change of fortune along automobile row as many once-proud owners of elegant sales palaces suddenly found themselves overburdened by their grandiose facilities. Some sales structures continued to be built on a grand scale like Albert Kahn's 100,000-square-foot, Art Deco–style General Motors showroom at the 1933 Chicago Century of Progress Exhibition.[21] As the crisis wore on, however, many automakers, to save their sales networks from the economic maelstrom, began to urge dealers to adjust their physical plants to the new commercial realities.

This time companies tried a powerful, yet less expensive, means of influencing their agents. Rather than merely building model showrooms, as had been done in the past, they began to publish manuals—optimistically written guidebooks outlining steps toward a brighter economic future. One panacea widely touted in these paper object lessons, and adopted by some dealers who could afford it, was to relocate on a large lot farther out of town, put up an oversize rendition of one of the modern gasoline service stations that were springing up everywhere, and wait to add on more space if the economy improved. In its 1936 publication, *Modern Buildings for Modern Automobile Dealers*, Oldsmobile, for example, presented a number of designs for what it called "super service stations." These were boxy, flat-roofed, one-story buildings (often of less-expensive load-bearing masonry construction)—composed of a string of service bays radiating out from a small showroom—laid out in an L or U shape around a bank of gasoline pumps.[22] While a considerable number of these cousins to the gas station were built, economic conditions forced many dealers to make the best of their existing facilities rather than build anew.

With this in mind, manufacturers' design manifestos also promoted an alternate course of action—the same basic solution being proffered to depression-weary Main Street merchants by numerous trade and architectural journals—modernize! Soon hundreds of old showrooms across the

country were streamlined with sleek new porcelain-enameled metal or
structural glass facades and translucent walls of glass block.

Inside, buildings were given a new look as well. With new-car trade
lagging and used-car sales increasing, showrooms were reduced in size
and <u>more space given over to marketing secondhand vehicles</u>. To better
profit from the millions of motorists trying to make do by keeping their
old cars running, parts departments were given more visibility, and drab,
grease-spattered service areas were glamorized. In 1938 an industry trade
journal, *Gas Station, Garage and Motor Car Dealer*, marveled at how far
some dealers and their designers went to "streamline the service bay":

Accustomed as they are to ultra-modern "sets" on the movie lots and sound
stages, the boulevardiers of Hollywood, Calif., get a real eye-opener when they
drive their motor cars into the newly designed lubrication department at A. E.
England's Pontiac Agency, 6032 Hollywood Blvd., which features Hyvis Modernized Lubrication.

The paneling which creates the modern, streamlined setting for service, is
banded with glistening chromium-plated metal and the Pontiac Indian Head is
silhouetted against indirect lighting which also illuminates the oil hi-boys. A
wide band of scarlet extending the entire length of the backboard separates upper
and lower panels of yellow. "Porthole" windows give a nautical air and the cosy
waiting room with its modern furnishings provides the comfort of a swanky
club.[23]

The rush to modernize was temporarily dampened by World War II.
New-car production ceased altogether, drivers were forced to keep even
old cars patched up, and demand for spare parts and mechanical work
skyrocketed. Although service business boomed, with nonessential construction severely curtailed and materials and labor in short supply, most
dealers scrapped their building plans for the duration.

At war's end, a new era of opportunity opened up for the auto industry
at long last. The nation's automobile fleet was aging and decrepit, pent-up
demand was unleashed, and people wanted to buy. At first new cars were
scarce as plants took time to retool. Soon, however, motor vehicles

Above:
Broadway Chevrolet; Louisville, Kentucky; photograph c. 1945. This is a relatively rare example of a showroom built in wartime. The 1943 structure, with its lozenge and porthole windows, showroom with rounded corners, and projecting sign pylon, was quintessentially Streamline Moderne. (Broadway Chevrolet.)

Above, right:
Same Broadway Chevrolet building after streamlined detailing was removed in the 1960s; photograph 1981. (Author.)

streamed from the assembly lines, and companies and their dealers renewed the push for more eye-catching showrooms to keep a competitive edge. A decade before, many automakers had advocated drastically smaller sales buildings and remedial fix ups to save dealers from extinction. Now they renewed their campaign for dealer modernization with vigor; only this time, they geared it toward taking advantage of a boom rather than cutting losses in a down slide.

The war had barely ended, for example, when General Motors—no doubt wishing to influence the way an estimated 450 million dollars would be spent on new showrooms over the next few years—held a "Design Competition for Dealer Establishments." This was appropriately chaired by Timothy Pflueger, a master of commercial architectural illusion, as demonstrated by his design for the Oakland Paramount Theater, built in 1931. *Architectural Forum* made this pronouncement on the results in October 1945:

The shoddy allusiveness of the twenties and thirties has disappeared from the facades. Gothic arch and Classic frieze are no longer achingly stretched to span the horizontal voids of 20 ft. plate glass windows. Tapestry brick and marble facings no longer stop in transparent falsehood 6 in. off the street front. Instead, there is every evidence that both modern structure and modern display techniques have been studied and largely mastered by the contestants.[24]

A second flood of design primers also issued forth from the automakers. Studebaker did not even wait for the war to end to send a tome entitled *Post-War Housing and Facilities for Studebaker Dealers*, published in 1944, to its dealers. Ford followed with *Plans for New and Modernized Sales and Service Buildings* in 1945; General Motors issued a voluminous study, *Planning Automobile Dealer Properties* (including many of the designs from its earlier competition), three years later.

Several common threads ran through these and similar competition's design manuals—concepts that effectively have influenced not so much the appearance, but the basic organization, of dealership buildings right up to the present day. First was the matter of location. Automakers again exhorted dealers to leave the old automobile rows, if possible, to relocate on larger lots farther out of town, where room for sprawling (preferably) one-story buildings existed. They selected sites with more precision than they had in Alvan T. Fuller's day. For example, the far side of an intersection on the homeward-bound side of a major commuter highway was touted as the best place for a dealership. Forcing the drivers to contemplate the building while stopped at the traffic light made them more likely to pull in on impulse when the light turned green. Also, under less time pressure, motorists were more likely to stop on their way home than when inbound for work.

After location came the issue of exterior treatment. In contrast to the older salon showrooms, where buildings were designed to convey prestige and credibility, the street facade of the modern dealership was viewed as a sequence of visual events for rapidly communicating to passing motorists what was sold inside—yet another example of architecture for speed-reading. The focal point in the sequence was the new-car display, a large, glare-free window through which a gleaming car was presented at its most flattering angle, almost as if appearing on a huge television directed at the traffic stream. Sometimes the parts department also had its own display window, although smaller and visually subordinated to the new-car display.

Next came the service wing. Usually the largest part of the building, its sheer bulk, along with broad driveways leading up to the service bays, helped to visually telegraph the message: "Service is a priority here, drive right in!" The final exterior element was the used-car lot—a special display challenge. Because older vehicles varied so widely in make, age, and condition, one or two examples did not suffice as an exhibit, with the rest out of sight in inventory space. Each car had to sell itself. As a result, dealers usually displayed secondhand autos in an open lot next to the showroom, with the most attractive cars arranged facing front along the street. Besides the cars themselves, a second essential ingredient in the used-car presentation was a broad canopy. Connected to the showroom and extending above the procession of round headlights and shining grills, this ingenious and low-cost visual trick made the used-car display appear to be part of the building.

Signs further underscored this play of distinct, yet unified, functional parts. A sign reading "sales," "service," or "used cars" labeled its appropriate department. Outsize porcelain-enameled metal bow ties, Indian heads, or other famous trademarks surrounded in neon also came into favor for visually broadcasting, day or night, that Chevrolets, Pontiacs, or some other familiar make of car was sold inside.

The interior arrangement of these postwar auto marts was as carefully orchestrated as the facades. Showrooms continued to be small, with only a few cars displayed, although through indirect lighting and modernistic, contoured background panels, an effort was made to show each car to its best advantage. Parts departments, on the other hand, generally gained increased interior status. Gone were the days of the back room. The parts counter was now in full view from the salesroom. And in case this was not enough to attract attention, the cashier was placed near the parts window to draw customers past the accessory displays when they came to pick up their cars.

The location of the service department was not overlooked either. Since customers with failing cars provided excellent sales prospects, the service desk was located so that someone waiting to report the latest problem with the family car would have a tempting view of the sleek new vehicles in the showroom. A window looking out onto the repair floor was also placed near the service desk to assure the customer that work was actually going on. By positioning for profit, showroom designers applied to auto vending the same principles that supermarket pioneers[25] had begun to use for selling food a decade before. As Studebaker pointed out to its dealers in discussing the virtues of designs presented in its 1944 manual: "Chain stores discovered years ago that when goods or services are made easier for customers to buy, business increases."[26]

Viewed in its entirety, this genre of "showroom" attests to, as *Architectural Forum* pointed out already in 1945, "how complete has been the conquest of modern architecture in commercial buildings."[27] Showrooms that once looked like office buildings, hotels, or taxpayer blocks were now unmistakably buildings for selling and servicing cars. Moreover, by appearing as a unified whole, while composed of clearly readable parts, each building represented a clear, functional expression of its program. Through careful positioning of departments and displays, still another overriding Modernist objective was satisfied—auto showrooms now functioned as machines for selling cars.

but where the beauty's ?

While the format for dealership buildings has remained basically unchanged, exteriors have been dressed over the years in a predictable succession of architectural garments. At war's end, new showroom designs still displayed the rounded corners and oval windows of the Streamline Moderne. By the late 1940s, utilitarian Modern with plain surfaces, flat roofs, visual fronts, and ribbon windows had come into vogue. A decade later, soaring roofs, canted fronts, and other utterances of the Exaggerated Modern held sway, only to be supplanted, beginning in the mid-1960s, by the shingled mansards of the Environmental Look.

THE ROADSIDE AS SHOWROOM

While this basic format remained unchanged beneath successive exterior wrappers, by the mid-1950s events were taking place that would eventually influence the location and importance of the machine for selling cars. By that time, automobile production had reached staggering proportions. In 1955 alone, 7,920,100 new automobiles were shipped from the nation's factories[28]—the highest yearly output recorded to date—and automakers pressured their dealers to find each one of these cars a home. If they did not, they ran the risk of having their coveted company franchises taken away—a frightening prospect at a time when the number of makes of cars had dwindled from more than 2,600 in the early years of the century to 15 in 1956.[29]

Former Buick dealership, c. 1958 (now Honda Center); San Diego; photograph 1981. During the late 1950s and early 1960s, many auto-dealership buildings were constructed with exaggerated structural features and space-age motifs. (Author.)

As former auto dealer and World War II rationing chief Charles Franklin Phillips warned at a national convention of auto sellers in 1956 (as paraphrased in *Harper's*): "Gone are the postwar days of high profits and long lines of car hungry customers . . . the principles of volume selling—which were adopted in selling groceries, notions, electrical appliances—have finally hit the auto business."[30] This retailing change referred to by Phillips was being spearheaded by a scattering of independent entrepreneurs (often former used-car dealers), of similar ilk to the men transforming the gas station and supermarket industries,[31] with a sharp eye for capitalizing on oversupply. These phantom car merchants would make the rounds of out-of-state dealers until they found one with showrooms and back lots crammed full of Detroit's newest creations; they would then offer to take some of the overstock at a markup only slightly above cost. They brought the new cars home, unceremoniously parked them in rows on an open lot as if they were ordinary used cars, put up a few banners, and began selling the vehicles at discount prices. Manufacturers, eager to move their products, often looked the other way.[32] One such emporium was Jonnie Eagle's lot near Wichita, Kansas, which offered every make the owner could get, "including Plymouths, Dodges, Chryslers, Fords, Lincolns, Chevrolets, Pontiacs, Buicks and Oldsmobiles."[33]

Soon a new term appeared in the industry lexicon—the "automobile supermarket," which one contemporary account defined as any place selling large volumes of cars at drastically reduced prices and skipping "such luxuries as enclosed buildings, replacement parts, and repair shops. Generally, their principal asset is a neon sign; their biggest expense, advertising."[34] Although some such supermarkets were reported to be quite reputable, many bargain hunters became painfully aware of the true

Mort Hall Ford, 1972; Houston; photograph 1981. By the 1970s, sales-and-service buildings were relegated to the background. The roadside itself became the showroom. (Author.)

meaning of the phrase "low overhead" when they attempted to bring in a car for its first repair.

A number of lawsuits arose between dealers and manufacturers to blunt the momentum of the new upstarts; also, several bills to protect authorized dealers from oversupply and undue pressure to sell more cars than they could appeared before Congress.[35] Over the next few years, manufacturers cut production back somewhat, the controversy settled down, and authorized dealers retained their predominant position in the market. Nevertheless, the episode provided an important lesson for the industry. Cars had by now become a highly recognizable, standardized product that could be sold "off the shelf" like sticks of butter or cans of soft drinks. Auto showrooms were, by and large, superfluous. All that was needed was an open lot filled with rows of automobiles for the customer's inspection. The car itself and the price sticker slapped on the side window were the key elements in making the sale.

By the early 1960s, dealers began to rely increasingly on mass marketing automobiles in inventory displays like used cars. Selling new cars this way, however, took a great deal of open space—more space than was available either in many of the older automobile rows or in a good number of the postwar suburban locations. Thus dealers had a strong impetus to follow the general exodus of businesses to the outer reaches of the suburbs, where large roadside commercial sites were available. Soon the oldest automobile rows closest to town began to empty. Along Commonwealth Avenue in Boston, for example, former showrooms were turning over quickly. Some were bought by Boston University, whose campus was nearby, to be converted into classrooms and offices. Others were reworked into electronics shops, furniture stores, sporting-goods outlets, and a variety of other commercial ventures. By the 1960s, similar districts in cities around the country were undergoing like changes.

Meanwhile, out along the far end of the suburban strip, a new type of automobile row was germinating, where cars instead of buildings were the primary means of attracting attention. Here dealers still had show-rooms built within their sales-and-service buildings, but these vestigial exhibition areas now functioned more as reception halls decorated with cars than the fundamental sales tool they had been previously.

The entire sales-and-service building, showroom and all, is now set back far from the highway instead of being positioned close to the curb line, as had been the custom since the dawn of the century. The large open area in front of the structure is jammed with row upon row of new cars and trucks. With much of a dealer's inventory within full view from the highway, each passing motorist can scan the merchandise at high speed, like a vastly magnified trip down a supermarket aisle. If curiosity is piqued, the driver will swing into the lot and then slowly thread through the merchandise, stopping to appraise this make or that model. The sharp salesman will watch this process and, once he has a sense of the customer's interests, will make contact. Thus the salesman is still im-portant in closing the deal, but to a large degree the cars sell themselves.

Once new cars were exhibited in palmy splendor. Then they were sold in sleek streamlined display cases. Now they are displayed like a true mass-produced item, like cans on a supermarket shelf or hamburgers stacked up under the warming lights of the local fast-food stand. The sales-and-service building is today one section of a grand, freely defined, open-air sales floor. The roadside has become the showroom.

Gas Stations

*I*T IS hard to imagine an era when gasoline—a substance without which today's industrial world would shudder to a halt—was a relatively unimportant petroleum by-product and the entire American landscape was free of gas stations. Yet a little more than eight decades ago, gasoline was merely a sideline product of oil companies engaged in making kerosene for illumination and lubricants for machinery, the thousands of little buildings that now serve as fuel dispensaries for millions of motorcars did not even exist, and the now quick-and-simple task of gassing up took considerable planning and labor. Few places sold motor fuel, and the owners of the handful of cars then in existence often had to ride out to an oil distribution terminal at the edge of town. Once there they (or their chauffeurs or mechanics) lugged the gasoline in a metal can from bulk tank to car tank. It was a laborious, impractical, and somewhat dangerous ritual. However, it was relatively short lived.

Beginning in 1905, pumps began to appear on the market that allowed gas to be transferred to an awaiting car via rubber hose—quickly and safely. This improvement in doling out motor fuel helped to make the automobile a more practical mode of transportation, and the next few years heralded an explosion of interest in the new machines. Larger factories were built, car sales shot up 4,500 percent by 1910,[1] and the demand for gas skyrocketed. Eager to cash in on this new market, the nation's oil companies, including still-familiar firms such as the Texas Company and Shell and the numerous Standard Oil firms such as Socony (created when Rockefeller's giant monopoly was dissolved in 1911), boosted production. They also scoured the country for places to sell oil and fuel to the growing ranks of motorists.[2]

SELLING GAS AT THE CURBSIDE

Taking the path of least resistance, parallel to that of the automobile manufacturers, the petroleum industry began to eye existing businesses as

Curbside pumps, Cody Garage; Cody, Wyoming; photograph 1927. These units were of the visible-measure type commonly in use by the 1920s. Gas was pumped up from an underground tank until the glass graduate (here with protective wire mesh) was filled to the desired level. The gas was then released through the hose and flowed by force of gravity into the tank of an awaiting car. Pump makers introduced this innovation so as to visually reassure motorists that they got what they paid for. (American Heritage Center, University of Wyoming.)

potential product outlets. Soon hundreds of carriage, hardware, bicycle, grocery, and feed stores, as well as garages, blacksmith shops, and livery stables, began selling gasoline. By World War I, the volatile liquid could be conveniently bought along Main Streets, taxpayer strips, and rural crossroads throughout the country; and the curbside pump joined the fire hydrant and mailbox as street furniture on the urban scene.

Selling motor fuel through existing retailers had its advantages. Oil companies could make their products readily available at thousands of strategic locations around the country within a very short period of time. With buildings and staff already in place, all a company had to do was install a tank and a pump or two, and soon drivers would begin queuing their cars at the curb alongside the tall metal stalks and wait for a clerk to come out to man the pump.

Yet sidewalk gas vending had considerable drawbacks as well. Lines of waiting cars often blocked trolley tracks and created traffic tie-ups. The pumps also posed a safety hazard. Located within a few feet of passing traffic, they could easily be hit by an out-of-control vehicle, possibly resulting in an explosion or fire. By the early 1920s, municipal officials across the country, irate over these hazards, began a campaign to outlaw dispensing gasoline along city streets. In 1923 *The American City* reported on their progress in an article entitled "Curbing the Curb Pump":

Many American cities are making a vigorous fight for the freedom of their streets. One phase of this campaign has been directed against the glistening red curb gasoline pumps that are a godsend to the gas-famished motor car—and the bane of traffic officers and city planners. At present, curb gasoline pumps have been flatly forbidden in fourteen American cities from which reports have been received. Their installation has been restricted in many others by zoning and special ordinances.[3]

However, in small villages and rural areas, where there often was more frontage room and traffic was lighter, general stores continued to garner extra income by having a gas pump or two out front, a practice that survives to this day.

THE DRIVE-IN FILLING STATION

Besides selling gas at the curbside, early in the century oil companies also began experimenting with alternative locations. Soon embryonic examples of what would evolve into one of the most prolific twentieth-century commercial building species—the gas station—began to appear. As early as 1905, the Automobile Gasoline Company had built a chain of gas stations in St. Louis. Standard Oil opened their first in Seattle in 1907,[4] and hundreds more soon followed. While many of these new motor-fuel emporia continued to be built and run directly by the oil companies, other investors seized the opportunity as well. Oil distributors built and ran their own stations or leased them out to private operators, while countless individual investors bought lots, put up structures, and negotiated contracts to sell gas for oil companies; this same multilevel pattern of ownership still survives today. By the time of World War I, stations were mushrooming along the open road, vacant lots lining the taxpayer strip, Main Street gap sites, and even the lawns of homes fronting residential boulevards at a rate of 1,200 or more a year.[5]

In contrast to the curbside pumps, the gasoline station heralded a marked change in urban land use. While installation of the former required neither the demolition of existing buildings nor breaks in the curb line, drive-in filling stations required enough space for motorists to pull completely off the street and then back on again once their cars were fueled up and the attendant paid. In densely built-up areas, such as Main Street, often buildings had to be leveled to make room for the new drive-ins. Sites once containing several layers of stores, apartments, or offices now sported a small shelter for an attendant or two, some gas pumps, and

Below, left:
Central Oil and Gasoline Station; Flint, Michigan; photograph c. 1910. This corrugated-metal structure, a makeshift shed, is typical of the earliest gas station buildings. (American Petroleum Institute.)

Below:
Standard Oil Company filling station; Grande Avenue, Los Angeles; photograph c. 1920. Drive-in gas stations became increasingly common by the time of World War I. The flagpole and multi-globed electrolier gave the station an air of civic respectability. This aggrandized version of the station as a box with a canopy would reappear half a century later. (The Huntington Library.)

Above:
John Stef's home-built gasoline alley; Route 1, south of Portsmouth, New Hampshire; photograph c. 1921. (John Stef, Jr.)

Above, right:
John Stef's gasoline alley as it still exists, miraculously, today; photograph 1982. (Author.)

a sign mounted on a pole near the street. The remainder of the lot was given over to driveways and parking.

Drive-in gas stations were not confined to urban areas. Thousands sprang up along the nation's highways as well. Take, for example, the station built by John Stef, a Polish immigrant who had settled in New Hampshire in the early 1900s and had worked caulking ships during World War I. In 1919 Stef acquired a farmhouse surrounded by rolling woodland and pastureland south of Portsmouth, New Hampshire, along what is today U.S. Route 1. Realizing money could be made selling fuel to the cars streaming by, a year later he constructed a small gable-roofed cabin on the farmhouse lawn, installed a pump out front, secured a contract from Socony Vacuum, and went into business. Shortly after, Stef became annoyed that his contract allowed him to sell only Socony's gas, so he built several additional cabins, signed contracts with other companies, and formed his own one-man wayside gasoline alley.[6]

Many of the earliest gas-station buildings, as exemplified by Stef's, were rudimentary in design—little more than shacks or sheds. Soon larger structures appeared—big enough to serve as an office complete with desk, table, heating stove, and maybe a couple of chairs. By World War I, drive-in filling stations had become a new and formidable visual presence, especially in the nation's cities. In 1921 Kansas City, Missouri, alone had "an average of one filling station to every two or three blocks."[7]

Given the vast numbers of stations being built, it is not surprising that their appearance became an object of concern to the many prominent citizens, designers, and municipal officials who espoused the ideals of the City Beautiful movement. For the past three decades, this movement had promoted the development of corridors of park-lined avenues, dramatic urban vistas, and monumental buildings to bestow upon each metropolis some of the aura of the Great White City of the Chicago Columbian Exposition of 1893.[8] Its proponents were deeply alarmed by the unruly appearance of this new breed of commercial structures with their large lots, pint-size buildings, and clutter of pumps and signs. *The American City* magazine, a leading advocate of the City Beautiful, summed up the movement's attitude toward the gas station in 1921: "The tumble-down shack had no place" in the city, especially in residential areas; "it would behoove cities to include in their ordinances regulations for the erection of such buildings, limiting them to certain types, insisting that the design be in keeping with other buildings of the neighborhood."[9]

As a result of pressure generated by advocates of the City Beautiful, coupled with a desire to present the best possible corporate image, some oil companies began to build very substantial stations. Made out of brick, cut stone, and concrete, they looked like diminutive versions of banks, libraries, and city halls of the period—replete with Greek, Beaux Arts, or Neoclassical detailing. As J. F. Kuntz of W. G. Wilkens Co., Architects, enthusiastically described one such "ornamental" station built for Atlantic Refining Company in 1922:

This dainty little edifice graces one of the most popular automobile roadways in the Quaker City. . . . It is a reproduction, on an enlarged scale, of the monument to Lysicrates . . . and is surrounded on two sides by an Ionic colonnade. . . . The building is constructed of dazzling white terra cotta, and its perfect proportions will linger long in the memory. This charming reproduction of one of the finest bits of Grecian architecture extant forms a striking contrast to the great majority of buildings erected for the purpose of supplying the wants of modern charioteers.[10]

Often referred to at the time as "artistic stations," buildings of this genre emitted an aura of instantaneous respectability and were widely regarded as "civic assets."[11]

At the same time such civic monuments in miniature were becoming fashionable, inexpensive prefabricated buildings grew in popularity for less-prominent locations. These were usually constructed of metal, glazed with large multipaned industrial sash, and capped by standing seam or

Prefabricated metal, flat-top, one-post-canopy filling station, from the catalog of Michel & Pfeffer Iron Works, 1926; San Francisco. (Richard Longstreth.)

Neoclassical drive-in filling station; Pittsburgh, Pennsylvania; photograph 1917. This genre of stations was designed in the City Beautiful tradition to be instant civic fixtures. (American Petroleum Institute.)

imitation tile roofs. Optional canopies that extended from the front of the building out to columns near the pump island were available for sheltering attendants and customers.

Unlike the more elaborate City Beautiful structures, which often took considerable time to build, prefabricated stations had a decided advantage—they could be set up and bolted together in a matter of a day or two. One satisfied owner, the Pennsylvania Independent Oil Company, commented that their purchase "arrived on Wednesday, June 18th, at noon and by 5 P.M.—four men had unloaded it, hauled it about two miles and set up the four walls. Another day and we believe it will be ready for painting."[12]

Produced by independent manufacturers and available for sale through catalogs to anyone wishing to open a gas station, these tiny metal buildings came in a variety of models.[13] The most modest offerings resembled railroad-section shacks or industrial gatehouses; the grandest resembled City Beautiful stations with intricate ornamental details faithfully replicated with sheet steel and solder. By the mid-1920s, thousands of these diminutive structures, factory built like the automobiles that pulled up in front of them, dotted the American roadscape. A sprinkling can still be found today.

Whether custom made or mass produced, the most popular architectural costume for packaging filling stations by the early 1920s was that of a small, tidy house. Stations masquerading in the guise of houses had a number of advantages. They could be built by the do-it-yourselfer from

Sunoco station; Royal Oak, Michigan; photograph c. 1936. Enlarging the office cubicle and adding a hipped roof gave stations the look of a small bungalow. (The Edison Institute.)

materials readily available from the local lumberyard, and they fit in well in residential areas, yet were far less costly to construct than the monumental City Beautiful stations. The sight of a little house selling gas along the roadside could also trigger a host of positive associations—friendliness, comfort, and security—in the minds of motorists whizzing by.

The most ubiquitous domestically clad stations of the period were rectangular buildings with a hipped roof projecting out over a driveway to form a canopy supported by two columns. These structures closely resembled the little bungalows that were springing up in modest residential neighborhoods across the country, only now the front porches were filled with pumps and cars rather than hammocks and rocking chairs.

In addition to the bungalow, other domestic forms became popular. The English cottage-type stations built by the Pure Oil Company were among the most successful. These eye-catching gasoline stations were designed by C. A. Petersen, a self-proclaimed architect who received his training by apprenticing with a succession of New Orleans architectural firms after graduating high school. He then went on to work for Gulf Oil for a number of years until joining Pure Oil's engineering department in 1925. Shortly thereafter he was asked to provide a new design for the company's stations.[14] Petersen chose an English-cottage motif, with a high-pitched gable roof, tall end chimneys, and trellises. The stations were painted white with blue trim—the Pure Oil colors—and came in two models: small (eleven by eighteen feet) with office, compressor room, and toilet; and a larger size (thirteen by twenty feet), in which a grease room was added. The buildings were designed to be built either of brick or wood-frame construction, with the exterior sheathing in stucco or clapboard. Within a few years, this basic design had become almost synonymous in the public's mind with Pure Oil.

Other companies capitalized on the image of neat, safe, comfortable domesticity. Socony used a pedimented front to cash in on the positive associations ascribed at the time to all that was "colonial," while the Wadhams Oil Company in Wisconsin fashioned the roof of their station

Above, left:
Pure Oil English cottage–type station, with service bay, c. 1935; Columbus, Ohio; photograph 1971, Richard Longstreth. (Richard Longstreth.)

Above, right:
Lighthouse Service Station, 1933; Huntington, Long Island; photograph 1938. Lighthouses, windmills, and other eye-catching features were often used to embellish the domestic look of stations. (Frederick G. Frost, Jr.)

Layout for Super Service Station, from the catalog of Michel & Pfeffer Iron Works, 1926; San Francisco. Note the designer's provision for future store buildings to form a shopping center, with a filling station as the nucleus. (Richard Longstreth.)

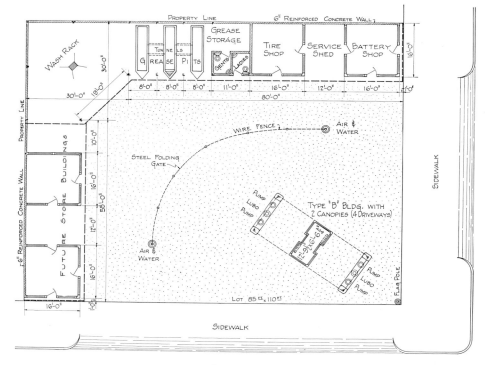

houses to resemble a Chinese pagoda, an exotic flourish guaranteed to attract attention. From the early 1920s to World War II, myriads of tiny gasoline dwellings were constructed, and in the case of Pure Oil, the company kept churning out its English cottages until the early 1950s.

THE SERVICE STATION: FROM HOUSE TO BOX

During these early decades, motorists relied upon the filling station to provide gas, oil, and perhaps a wipe of the windshield. When their auto needed repairs, however, car owners usually turned either to the repair facilities being built by major automobile companies such as Packard for servicing the cars they produced (these were first called "service stations" about 1910), or to a host of blacksmith shops and independent garages. By the early 1920s, this conglomeration of facilities was no longer able to keep up with the demand for servicing the ever-increasing number of cars on the road; filling stations began to take up the slack. Oil companies and individual owners alike added grease pits, set aside space for repairing flat tires, and began to stock a variety of routine replacement parts such as bulbs and batteries. This changeover was encouraged by trade publications such as *Motor Age*, which urged its subscribers to become "Community Service Stations" where "the Tire Shop, the Battery Station, the Mechanical Shop, the Greasing Rack, the Automobile Laundry, and the Gas Station Combined to Help Each Other."[15] By the late 1920s, the gas station was evolving into a hybrid of filling station and repair garage, and the neighborhood service station was born.

Sensing this trend, by the mid-1920s prefabricated-station manufacturers started offering a complete range of auxiliary service buildings. Along with filling stations, for example, the Michel & Pfeffer Iron Works of San Francisco listed in a 1926 catalog separate comfort-station buildings and pavilions for washing and greasing. The company even sold "Super Buildings"—service structures that combined a wash rack, grease pits, and a storage room for tires and batteries under one roof.[16]

Toward the end of the decade, these dual functions—filling and servicing—were being expressed in a combined plan, in which a single service building, often L or U shaped, formed a court around a central filling station.[17] However, by the dawn of the depression, this transitional two-building format had given way to a single service station formed by a series of service bays grafted onto the station house. Inside, a rectangular layout, containing an office, bathroom, and utility room, with the remaining space divided up into service areas, came into favor—a format that persisted as the dominant plan for the service station for the next fifty years. Other changes soon followed. Gas pumps were increasingly placed on islands away from the buildings, to keep office entrances and service-bay openings unobstructed. Because of the need to improve traffic circulation, canopies began to fall from favor, thus eliminating hazardous columns from the station yard. These porte cocheres of the motor age remained in vogue in the West, however, to help shield attendants from the sun.[18]

While a rectangular layout embracing both office and service, surrounded by a station yard with pumps rooted on little islands, became the

Former house-type station, with added-on service bays, c. 1930; North Platte, Nebraska; photograph 1980. The pumps were removed when the structure was converted for its new use. (Author.)

industry standard, the awkward juxtaposition of a tiny station house with a large garage growing out of its side did not last for long. By the early 1930s, a number of factors were at work that eventually led to a completely new image for gas stations, and the modernization of many of the nation's estimated 170,000 stations as well.[19]

First, as gas revenues slackened during the depression, oil companies became increasingly dependent on selling tires, batteries, and accessories (the key trio of products knows as TBA in the trade) as a way of generating greater income per station. Built more as eye-catching shelters than as showcases, most older stations simply were not designed with the floor area, lighting, or display windows to exhibit these new sources of revenue effectively.

Then there was a problem with the uneven quality of service. At most stations, maintenance and repairs—from a simple oil change to an engine overhaul—were usually performed by the individual station operators and thus were not under the direct control of the oil companies. Yet, in the eyes of the public, services provided—whether superb or mediocre—were linked to the oil companies and their products and reflected on those companies, for better or for worse. Improving repair facilities was seen by companies as one way to upgrade the quality of service offered at their stations.

Finally there was the question of overall product image. Beleaguered by the depression, manufacturers of everything from toasters to bathtubs were redesigning their products to look streamlined and up-to-date. Since all gasoline and oil basically looked the same, one way for oil company executives to make their liquid products appear modern was to give an exciting new look to the facilities that dispensed them.[20]

To meet these challenges, by the mid-1930s oil giants from Shell and Texaco to Socony were developing a range of new station prototypes, with the help of architects and industrial designers. These prototypes spawned a generation of gas stations designed to showcase everything from tires to motor oil, provide better service bays, and above all to present a fresh and modern corporate image to the traveling public. Toward the end of the decade, domestic gas-station imagery was being edged out by the architectural vocabulary of the International Style and the Streamline Moderne. The white, enameled-metal "oblong box"[21] with large display window, housing an office, service bays, storage space, and restrooms under one broad, flat roof, became de rigueur in service-station fashion—a functional costume that would continue to be popular for the next quarter of a century.

Some companies were quick to embrace the new look. Texaco, for example, made a rapid changeover from house to box. Dissatisfied with their current crop of gasoline emporia, the company retained the services of industrial designer Walter Dorwin Teague to restyle their stations. As reported in *Architectural Record* in 1937, a series of programmatic goals had been set for the new structures, including that they be easy to clean, contain "adequate and comfortable restrooms," provide ample display space for TBA, have "efficient" service bays, be "adaptable to different

Texaco Type EM service station, 1948; Milwaukee, Wisconsin; prototype designed by Walter Dorwin Teague; photograph c. 1950. Today this great classic of the porcelain-enameled metal-clad box stations, once a familiar sight on the nation's highways, is rapidly approaching extinction. (Texaco Corporation.)

types of country and sites," and that building, pumps, and signs together form a distinctive company trademark that would be instantly recognizable both day and night.[22]

To satisfy these programmatic objectives, Teague came up with a design that neatly fitted office, storage, restrooms, and service bays into a gleaming white box shimmering with streamlined excitement. He sheathed the walls with panels of porcelain-enameled metal steel (wood or stucco were less acceptable substitutes) so it would take only an occasional hosedown to keep the outside of the station sparkling clean. He punctuated the front elevation with a large window where everything from stacks of oil cans to processions of tires could be displayed so as to be spotted easily from a passing car. His design also called for glazing the overhead doors to the service bays so that the sight of an automobile perched high on a lift would remind passersby that the service station was more than a petroleum restaurant—it was a hospital for ailing cars. (There was also a hidden motive to making service more visible—to encourage operators to keep the repair stalls more clean and tidy.) And Teague incorporated graphic messages into the design of the stations to reinforce all visual displays. In addition to large block letters spelling "Texaco," each individual bay was labeled "lubrication," "washing," or some other word announcing the services performed within.

The overall design was united by three parallel green streamlines running horizontally across the parapet. This modernistic motif carried over into the design of the pumps that stood on islands away from the front of the building—each was elegantly wrapped in a streamlined cowl. (These pumps, incidentally, were of the new "computer type," which calculated the price as well as the amount, a feature that increased gas sales because customers began rounding off purchases to the nearest dollar rather than buying by the gallon.) The final element in Teague's design was a large, round, externally illuminated sign bearing the familiar Texaco star, mounted on a stylish, tapered pole.

These new stations were available in several models designed for varying locations and budgets. Type A was advertised as "best suited to a corner lot"; it cost about fifteen thousand dollars. Type C, one of the most popular models, featured a large office and service bays and cost between ten and thirteen thousand dollars. Even an office-only version—Type E—was available, a modest little structure cast in the image of the larger models that could be erected at a bargain price (between five and six thousand dollars).[23] Overall, the design was highly successful, and Texaco built thousands of the bold white boxes accented by green graphics over the next two decades. A fair but dwindling number of these now classic stations still exist today.

Not all companies modernized their stations as quickly as Texaco, however. Take the case of the redesign of Socony Vacuum's stations, for example. In 1934 industrial designer Norman Bel Geddes developed a prototype service station for the company. As Teague did a short while later, Geddes neatly packaged office, restrooms, and repair bays into a white box, with rounded, streamlined corners and ample display windows for tires, batteries, and accessories.[24] Unlike Teague's stations, however, only one example of the Geddes/Socony prototype was actually built. Socony and its many distributors were reluctant to embrace the concept, fearing that adoption of Geddes's design, which did not sport a classical pediment like their older station houses, would result in a loss of identity. Management backed off, preferring gradual modernization over a sudden change-over to a radically new design.

Later that same year, Socony hired the firm of Frederick G. Frost as consulting architects to work with the corporation's engineering depart-

Below, left:
Model of the service station designed by Norman Bel Geddes as a prototype for Socony-Vacuum in 1934. (Norman Bel Geddes Collection, Harry Ransom Humanities Research Center, University of Texas at Austin.)

Below, right:
Mobil station, c. 1946; Burlington, Iowa; photograph 1971, Richard Longstreth. Example of a station patterned after the Frederick G. Frost firm's drum prototype developed for Socony-Vacuum in 1940. (Richard Longstreth.)

Gulf service station, c. 1950; Scranton, Pennsylvania; photograph 1972, Richard Longstreth. Each oil company had its own version of the box. This particular design makes extensive use of Streamline Moderne vocabulary, including the wrap-around oval window, rounded corners, and flow-line neon graphics on the central pylon. (Richard Longstreth.)

ment in developing what they hoped would be less extreme designs. Frost placed his son, also named Frederick, in charge of the project, assisted by another member of the staff, Donald Dodge. The pair came up with a series of transitional designs, integrating the residual symbolism of the company's older domestic stations into a very restrained, but still more modern-looking, white box with a stepped-roof parapet. Parged with stucco or clad in porcelain-enameled steel, Frost's models could be built from scratch or created by wrapping new surfaces around existing units with a minimum of demolition.

In the second half of the 1930s, Socony built or remodeled hundreds of stations according to Frost's ideas. To please the company, at first the pediment form was retained and placed over the salesroom—a ghost image of the little station houses of the 1920s etched on the face of the newer box. But gradually all visual references to these earlier buildings evaporated. After several years of working in this transitional mode, Socony finally gave Frost's firm the go-ahead to produce a totally modern prototype. The result was the much-acclaimed 1940 drum design (the architect claims that he got the idea from the shape of an oil can), which used a half-cylinder-shaped sales-and-display room as a distinguishing motif.[25] The drum went on to become a popular Socony design in the early postwar years.

Other companies developed their own modern prototypes as well, and by the dawn of World War II, the box had replaced the house as the quintessential image for the gas station. Located on city lots or flanking highways, these sleek, utilitarian yet elegant stations served as the nation's first large-scale introduction to the functional aesthetics of the International Style, softened with the flowing lines and the rounded corners of the Streamline Moderne.

Streamline Moderne station, 1950; Kremmling, Colorado; photograph 1983. Local builders often constructed their own scaled-down interpretations of the major oil company prototypes. Note the similarities between this building and the Gulf station above. (Author.)

THE SELF-SERVICE STATION:
INDEPENDENT INNOVATION

Independent oil companies also had a pronounced impact on gas-station design during the 1930s and 1940s. The same depression-era surpluses that caused changes in scores of industries stimulated the growth of this new force in petroleum marketing. Just as an excess of food, for example, spawned the birth of the warehouse supermarket,[26] a surplus of gas encouraged a parallel phenomenon in the petroleum industry—the independently owned oil company selling large quantities of gasoline at reduced prices. Often owned by local businessmen, independents[27] usually built their own storage facilities, bought large volumes of surplus gas from the major oil companies, distributed it in their own trucks, and sold it at their own chains of filling stations under their own private brand names.[28] Throughout the 1930s, although the major brands still dominated the retail gas market, the number of independents increased steadily. Then came World War II and gas rationing, forcing majors and independents alike to reduce operations. Some stations even closed for the duration. At war's end, stations reopened, the demand for gas soared, and independents started looking for ways to capture a heftier share of the market from their gigantic and well-entrenched rivals.

Finally, in 1947, an event occurred that had profound impact not only on the design of gas stations, but on the entire way that gas was transferred from pump to car. A California independent named George Urich built what was widely acclaimed as the nation's first self-service gas station—an innovation so successful that he immediately built several more. Soon his competitors seized on the idea, and by mid-1948, about twenty-five similar operations existed in the Los Angeles area.[29]

These new serve-yourself gasoline emporia received considerable national attention. *Newsweek*, for example, enthusiastically reported the birth of the phenomenon:

Urich's stations occupy corner lots of about an acre apiece at busy intersections. The stations are of unique design, having eighteen to twenty-one pumps set on islands which are lined up at right angles to the street. Cars can pull in, in two rows twelve or fourteen abreast. Drivers can serve themselves, says Urich, in a minute and a half to two minutes, compared with five minutes at the orthodox filling station. Those who need air or water or want their windshields cleaned drive to the back of the lot and help themselves.

Five or six pretty girls in sweaters and slacks roller-skate from island to island making change and collecting. A supervisor in a glass booth directs them by loudspeaker and keeps an eye out for customers violating the no-smoking regulations.[30]

Life was equally excited, hailing the birth of the "Gas-A-Teria . . . the self-service gas station," as "California's newest contribution to the drive-in way of life."[31] The christening of serve-yourself gas, however, was not just attended by well-wishers; championing the industry view, *Business Week* held that the concept was "a strictly local phenomenon" that "could make out only in a market like Los Angeles where there is an abnormally

Fearless Farris, The Stinker: Cut Rate Gas; Salt Lake City; photograph 1954. Since their gas was not sold under a brand-name trademark reinforced by national advertising, independent dealers had to resort to visual theatrics coupled with low prices to attract customers. (National Archives.)

high concentration of motor vehicles."[32] Taking no chances—just in case the new stations did *not* prove to be a "strictly local phenomenon"—some owners of conventional stations took more aggressive measures to frighten off the newcomers. *Newsweek,* for example, offered an account of the welcoming reception arranged for Urich by his competitors. He "received anonymous letters and telephone calls threatening his life. Two of the men who replace the girls on the night shift had been beaten up by a carload of thugs."[33]

Similar vigilante actions cropped up on the East Coast as well. In 1949, one Irving Reingold was rewarded with threatening phone calls and rocks through his windows when he opened the first self-service station in New Jersey.[34] Such incidents of harassment notwithstanding, the concept of self-service gas rapidly spread. Soon motorists from as far north as Tacoma, Washington, and as far east as the New York metropolitan area were able to pump their own gas and pocket the savings.[35]

As more and more self-service stations opened, the "gas-a-terias" began to gain a measure of covert support from the industry. Because self-service outlets tended to have more pumps per station, they were of considerable economic interest to pump manufacturers. The major oil companies, while on one hand wishing to protect their own dealers, on the other also savored the extra profits generated by quietly selling off large quantities of surplus fuel to the new high-volume gasoline dispensaries.[36] Amid this climate of public opposition coupled with behind-the-scenes encouragement, many independent gas stations gradually converted to self-service during the 1950s.

Independents tended to be innovative in design as well as marketing. Since their names did not evoke the instant credibility of major brands such as Shell or Texaco—credibility reinforced by years of national advertising—as early as the 1930s some private branders resorted to building more striking stations calculated to attract attention. Along with the customary small houses and boxes, more eccentric designs began to appear. One operator in Maryville, Ohio, for example, built his station in the shape of a giant gas pump,[37] while another, near Lawrence, Kansas, crafted his station to look like a giant Indian tepee.

After the war, many independent gas-station owners, like the operators of coffee shops, drive-in restaurants, and other roadside eateries,[38] found in Exaggerated Modern the means to make their businesses more eye catching than the competition. One result was the gradual comeback of a feature that the major oil companies had dropped by the early 1930s—the canopy. Unlike the old canopies, which merely extended from building to pump in order to provide shelter from the elements, these new structures were much larger—large enough to cover not only the office but all the banks of pumps—and were designed more to grab attention than provide protection. Canopies, in fact, were becoming the centerpiece of a whole genre of station that began to emerge on the West Coast. By 1949, companies such as the California Cornice, Steel and Supply Corporation, for example, were already selling stations to independents that consisted of a small boxlike office building with multiple banks of pumps covered by a gigantic steel canopy—a type that became an industry mainstay some two decades later.[39]

REDECORATING THE BOX

While many independents were quick to embrace architectural theatrics, during the early postwar years most major oil companies followed a more conservative approach toward service-station design. As a result, the

Gulf service station, grand opening, 1 November 1952; Burlington, Vermont; photograph L. L. McAllister. Postwar stations were not the futuristic wonders predicted in the 1930s but were basically patterned after prewar designs. (University of Vermont Special Collections.)

prewar box, with minor modifications, continued to be built. Car production boomed, production and use of passenger trains and other competing forms of transportation slipped behind, suburban neighborhoods sprawled, and endless opportunities for station construction existed. So why change a format that worked?

This business-as-usual approach to station design lasted only until the mid-1950s, when, under pressure from market saturation, along with energetic competition from the independents, some companies began to rework the old designs. Following the independents' lead, they resorted to the exaggeration of once purely functional architectural features.[40] Flat roofs, for example, often gave way to rakishly slanted ones. Observing that "one school [in the industry] now holds the 'box' station [to be] outmoded and unimaginative," Richard C. Schroeder noted in *National Petroleum News* in 1958 how Shell "favors conversion to a sloped roof for the modern touch."[41] By the late 1950s, numerous attention-getting features, from jutting V-shaped canopies and expanded visual fronts to wide overhanging eaves sporting fluorescent bulbs (which reflected off shiny walls at night, transforming the structures into white luminous cubes) were being actively used to visually energize the basic box. These changes were carefully orchestrated to make stations look more modern without drastically altering their basic form—a low-cost means of updating while still conserving the inherent trademark value of the older designs.

Ironically, after a decade of trying to make the basic box more aesthetically vigorous, oil companies and their designers did an abrupt about-face. By the early 1960s, gas stations were routinely receiving bad press, joining junkyards and billboards as scapegoats in the public's growing outrage against the automobile's despoliation of the landscape. Even trade journals, which were usually an accurate bellwether of industry opinion, began to caution that a full-scale uprising was imminent if oil companies did not reevaluate their approach to station design. The influential *National Petroleum News*, for example, warned its readers in 1964 that stations had become "objectionable aesthetically because—in the public eye—there are too many of them and they are gaudy, cluttered, and made of unattractive materials"; they went on to predict a "blizzard" of restrictive zoning regulations aimed at curbing station construction and operation "unless marketers" took "timely action."[42]

Interestingly enough the new solution generally applied to this problem was in fact the reinterpretation of an old, time-tested solution. The house motif was brought back. Instead of bungalows or English cottages, however, the new domesticated box was patterned after the ranches and colonials in the postwar suburb. Low-pitched gables replaced flat or raking roofs, while porcelain-enameled panels gave way to wood, brick, and synthetic stone. Shell took the lead in domesticating the box with the introduction of a ranch-style station late in the 1950s.[43] Texaco began the shift from Teague's classic prototype to a mansard-roofed box in 1964, and other companies such as Sun Oil and Esso had introduced their own versions by the mid-1960s.[44] By the end of the decade, cosmetic mansards, cedar shakes, and bare-wood sidings—visual clichés of the Environmental

Above:

Phillips 66, c. 1960; Montevideo, Minnesota; photograph 1983, Mary M. Humstone. In this design, the basic box has been cleverly disguised with a canted visual front and soaring canopy—both hallmarks of the Exaggerated Modern. (Mary M. Humstone.)

Above, right:

Texaco Mattawan-type service station, 1965; Houston; prototype designed by Peter Miller-Munk Associates; photograph 1965. Still another reincarnation of the box, the Mattawan, with its fieldstone veneer and stylized roof, was designed to tone down the box in a time of increasing aesthetic activism against the architecture of the strip. (Texaco Corporation.)

Look—began to show up on gas stations as well. Hence the persistent box had gone through its third reincarnation. First it began as a functional yet sparkling oblong. Then, during the late 1950s, it was pumped up with visual adrenaline to become a soaring, rakish box. Now the long-familiar shape was being costumed in aesthetic palliatives chosen to telegraph the visual message: "I blend into the landscape."

Mobil (formerly Socony) was one of the only companies to counter this trend. In 1966 the company switched to a more modern rather than domestic-looking box. The prototype, designed by Eliot Noyes and Associates, kept the flat roof of the company's old box but gave it an overhang for soffit lighting, replaced the vertical piers with brick, and brightened the remaining surfaces with the contrasting colors of blue, gray, and white. A large illuminated disk bearing the flying-red-horse emblem was mounted on the front wall. Pumps were redesigned, reflecting the circular motif of the logo, and they in turn were covered by round canopies, also with the circular shape. Even the sign was reduced to a round-cornered rectangle with the word "Mobil" in bold letters.[45] Following in the tradition of Teague rather than Petersen, these stations represented the ultimate evolution of the modern box and have become somewhat of a classic along with the Texaco stations of a generation before. The hundreds of examples that to this day dot the nation's highways still appear remarkably fresh and little dated—an anomaly in the ever-changing world of roadside imagery.

HIGH-VOLUME PUMPERS AND CONVENIENCE STORES

Surface disguises—no matter how modern or homey, classic or cute—were at most a feeble panacea. Except for possibly the Noyes Mobil design, which generally received rave reviews, many of the cosmetic changes wrought in the hope of making the box environmentally compatible drew considerable fire from critics. A notable example is Wolf Von Eckardt's blast in *American Home* in 1967: "Glib folksiness may work in

First of the Eliot Noyes prototype Mobil stations to be built; New Haven, Connecticut; photograph c. 1970. At a time when other companies were disguising their oblong-box stations with false roofs and fake stone, Mobil commissioned a purely Modern design. (Mobil Oil Corporation.)

advertising; it doesn't work in architecture. It seems, in fact, ludicrously poor taste when a filling station masquerades in pseudo-colonial wrapping, selling us brake fluid and windshield wipers from a 'cutee, oldee,' miniature brick mansion with streamlined Palladian doorways. . . . Nor does the ranch-style gas station solve the problem. A place to service a modern automobile is no more a ranch house than it is an 18th century manor or the Taj Mahal."[46]

The substitution of a colonial or ranch box for a sleek white box often did not placate local officials and community activists any more than the new designs pleased the critics. Whether modern or quaint, gas stations continued to be a target of public criticism from a society wedded to the automobile yet hostile to the way it altered the environment. Finally, anti-gas-station sentiments reached a crescendo in 1971, culminating in an incident that made the industry shudder—the temporary banning of new gas-station construction by the city of Hempstead, Long Island.[47]

Fear that other localities might similarly restrict their retail operations was not the only problem facing the industry. By this time, other reasons surfaced that caused oil companies and individual station operators alike to be uneasy. With the rise in discount stores selling do-it-yourself auto parts, routine operations such as oil changes, lube jobs, and tune-ups—which used to be the bread and butter of the service-station trade—were now being performed by a growing number of motorists at home in their own driveways and garages. Franchise specialty shops, such as Midas Muffler, were also taking away much of the exhaust system, brake, and transmission repairs work. Hence the service part of the station, while still important, was slowly losing business. Then the OPEC oil embargo of 1973–1974 threatened the gas supply. The embargo's impact was immediate; it resulted in the abandonment of thousands of marginally profitable stations and hurt the independents because the oil producers often distributed what gas there was to their own stations first. By the mid-1970s, though, gas was more plentiful, and the independents rebounded to complete the conversion of most of their operations to self-service.

The major corporations, on the other hand, lacked the freedom the independents enjoyed to upgrade their facilities. They found themselves hampered by decisions made over the previous quarter of a century, such as keeping the basic box and only sluggishly adopting self-service. By the mid-1970s, they were tethered to a network of thousands of old service stations that had progressed little in concept since the mid-1930s. Designed for an attendant to dispense only moderate amounts of gasoline, these stations were often situated on sites too cramped to accommodate many self-service pumps.

Meanwhile, the independents continued to lead the way in innovations. By now many operate their own high-volume "pumpers," as they are sometimes called in the trade. Descendants of Urich's gas-a-teria, they are composed of banks of self-service pumps poised on parallel rows of islands sheltered by a giant rectangular canopy. The nerve center of these colossal filling stations is a little cubicle with a window like that of a theater box office. Enframed in this portal, a relatively unskilled attendant, capable of reading banks of remote pump meters and of making change, can preside over the gassing up of five or ten cars at a time. From an economic standpoint, such efficiency stood in stark contrast to the older service station where a higher-paid mechanic often had to pause in the middle of a tune-up to run outside and fill up a car or two.

At first the major oil companies responded with stopgap measures. Where space permitted, they added an island or two of self-service pumps. More recently they have resorted to building their own high-volume self-service pumpers.

Meanwhile—in the wake of gas shortages, a decline in the repair business, and competition from the pumpers—by the mid-1970s the oblong boxes that had worn so many disguises appeared to be headed for extinction (at least as gas stations, that is). Although a good number continued to be used exactly as they were built, hundreds of others (along with scores of earlier house-type stations) have been renovated into everything from pizzerias and insurance agencies to toy stores and ice-cream parlors. Still others have been given a new lease on life due to the discovery that

Below, left:
Self-service gas station; Sprague Avenue, Spokane, Washington; photograph 1984. The now-ubiquitous box with canopy stations, such as the one here, are reminiscent of some of the earliest gasoline stations. (Author.)

Below, right:
Former box-type gas station, c. 1950; Fort Collins, Colorado; renovation c. 1980; photograph 1981. New owners are converting surplus gas stations into many new uses. (Author.)

Floyd Ladd's filling station, 1923; Schenectady, New York; photograph 1982. Located on Erie Boulevard, which runs along the route of the former Erie Canal, this time capsule of early gasoline retailing still has its original pumps (inside the office) and a separate service building. (Author.)

old service stations make excellent convenience food stores. After a vacant or failing station is acquired, the service bay openings are sealed and covered with diagonal boards, cedar shakes, imitation stone, or metal panels painted with supergraphics. Inside, the lifts are removed and the old grease pits filled in, new floors laid down, and drop ceilings installed. Finally, with some rewiring and a coat of paint, the interior is ready to be crammed with beer coolers, grocery gondolas, and newspaper racks. Outside, a few self-service pumps are bolted down on the old concrete island, and then connected to a series of price-and-gallon meters on the sales counter. In a matter of weeks, a teenage clerk can begin selling gas, milk, and cat food and watch television all at the same time.[48]

By the early 1980s, many communities seemed to have more of these dual fuel depots for cars and humans than actual service stations. Thus the "store with gas" has returned—albeit on an asphalt-covered lot instead of along the Main Street curbside—and the evolution of the gas station has come almost full circle.

Supermarkets

ONLY A generation ago, the opening of a new supermarket was cause for celebration. Today these carefully contrived stage sets for food retailing have become so familiar a fixture of daily life that they are often taken for granted. What were food stores like before the advent of the supermarket and how did they evolve into the giant self-service food department stores of today?

THE SERVICE STORE

During the nineteenth century, most grocery stores were functionally little more than storehouses located behind commercial-block shop fronts, in generic sales spaces that might be rented out as a druggists one year, a dry-goods outlet the next. Even by the early 1900s, these archetypical food stores still conveyed an air of utility—with floors of bare wood, and light bulbs, suspended by lengths of braided wire, dangling from the ceiling. A service counter stretched rearward, and the walls were lined by towering shelves crammed with boxes and cans of food, accentuating the already long, narrow, corridorlike feeling of the salesroom.

Arriving by foot, bicycle, carriage, or streetcar, a customer pushed open a door; stepped up a high step; wandered down the center aisle, which with tall shelves looming up on either side looked like a path through a canyon lined with foodstuffs; stopped in front of the clerk; and began to read off the entries on a shopping list. The clerk plucked each item requested from the shelves, or from barrels or bins scattered about the floor, added up the prices, packed the order in a sack or carton, and handed it over to the shopper.

Except in rural areas, where many types of edibles were sold under one roof in a general store, specialization was most often the rule. A shopper usually had to stop at several stores—the grocery, the vegetable dealer, the butcher shop—to acquire all the items on the shopping list. Before

Unidentified food store; photograph c. 1927. This typical small service store interior is defined by the long, narrow shop space of a Main Street commercial block. The walls and ceiling are clad with ornamental pressed-metal—the forerunner of today's imitation brick and wood paneling. The clerk assembled the bulk of each order from the stock on the shelf behind the counter at the left. (Progressive Grocer.)

automobiles were in widespread use, people commonly traded at stores closest to home. Strong loyalties developed. Shopkeepers knew their customers and often allowed them to buy food on credit. Each household had not only a family doctor, but a family grocer and family butcher as well.

It was not always necessary actually to go to the store to fill the pantry or icebox. Local dairies could be contracted to deposit a quart or two of milk each day on the front doorstep. As more and more stores and houses were linked by telephone, orders could simply be called in from home, to arrive a while later by delivery vehicle. Nevertheless, regardless of whether an order was placed by phone or in person, the clerk usually served as the intermediary between customers and the goods they wished to purchase. The grocer gathered the canned and packaged foods; the butcher cut and wrapped the meat. Only in the produce store might shoppers be free to select their own fruits and vegetables under the watchful eye of a clerk hovering nearby.

Thousands of little stores, each with its own specialty, myriads of clerks handing over food from shelf to customer, personal service, credit, home delivery—within only fifty years, this entire system of food marketing would be drastically altered.

THE SELF-SERVICE COMBINATION STORE

Major changes first began to take place about the time of World War I, when a number of grocers across the country—in an attempt to boost sales and trim labor costs—began to test out new marketing methods that

The Manhattan Market; Central Square, Cambridge, Massachusetts; photograph 1907. This market was an early attempt to combine several different types of food stores—grocery store, fish store, produce market—under one roof in a large taxpayer block to form "An Ideal Pure Food Department Store." (Society for the Preservation of New England Antiquities.)

would eventually revolutionize the transfer of food from farm to dining-room table. One of the most influential of these experiments was conducted by a businessman named Clarence Saunders, who opened up a market in Memphis in 1916.[1] Although his operation was located in a typical, narrow, generic salesroom, Saunders substituted a radical new layout for the traditional corridor formed by walls of shelves and long counters. Customers entered his store through a turnstile, picked up a basket, and then took what he referred to as a circuitous path—an interior one-way street that led past all the groceries in the salesroom, including perishables in refrigerated cases. The path ended at a "settlement and checking department" where goods were "checked up," "billed on the adding machine," and wrapped.[2] Since the customer was free to pick his own groceries along the way, shopping was accomplished without the aid of a clerk, whose role was changed from merchandise dispenser to that of toll collector. Self-service was born.

Saunders christened his new venture, for which he was granted a patent the following year, with the unlikely name Piggly Wiggly. Whether inspired by the nursery rhyme "This little piggy went to market . . ." or by the sight of little pigs wriggling under a fence, as one industry anecdote relates, the name was chosen for calculated effect. When Saunders was asked years later why he picked such a comical name for his enterprise, he replied, "So people will ask just what you have asked."[3]

The actual invention attracted even more attention. The nation was in the throes of World War I, thousands of men had been drafted, and clerks (a predominantly male occupation at the time) were in short supply. In view of these circumstances, Saunders' self-service system, by re-

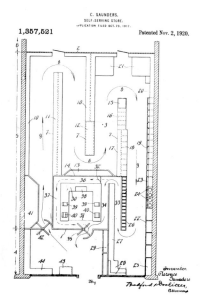

C. SAUNDERS.
SELF-SERVING STORE.
APPLICATION FILED OCT. 23, 1917.

1,357,521   Patented Nov. 2, 1920.

Plan for Clarence Saunders' "Self-Serving Store," 1917. Customers entered through the turnstile (42), circulated through a maze lined with foodstuffs, paid at the U-shaped "settlement counter," and exited through another turnstile (35). (U.S. patent application filed 23 October 1917.)

quiring less help than the traditional service store, had a decided commercial advantage. As *Scientific American* noted in 1918: "The only operatives needed are the few to handle the stock and replenish the shelves and bins, clean the building, check and wrap the purchases, and receive the cash."[4] Food retailers across the country took notice, and grocers began to purchase licenses from Saunders to convert their own stores into Piggly Wiggly markets. By the middle of 1918, only two years after the opening of the Memphis experiment, Piggly Wigglys were already in operation in Chicago, Cincinnati, Indianapolis, Houston, Dallas, Richmond, Louisville, and numerous other cities in the South and Midwest.[5]

Interest in Piggly Wiggly and self-service in general continued to grow after the war. For shoppers self-service provided a chance to select goods without interference from sales personnel. Customers by that time had become familiar with various competing brand-name products—from canned goods to crackers—and were able to make selections based on a visual scan of labels and trademarks without any help from a clerk. From a store owner's standpoint, self-service reduced labor costs—help, while more plentiful after the war, was also more expensive. It also allowed customers to shop with their eyes, which led to impulse buying and higher profits for each store visit. Faced with all these advantages, the industry as a whole began a gradual changeover to self-service by the early 1920s. However, reducing labor costs and giving customers the freedom of direct choice were not the only innovations in food merchandising taking place at the time. Equal in importance to self-service was the rise of another new development in merchandising: one-stop shopping.

Piggly Wiggly Market; Dayton, Ohio; photograph 1926. Ten years after the opening of the first Piggly Wiggly, the layout of this branch store still adhered very closely to the plan specified in Saunders' original patent. (Progressive Grocer.)

Teeter Food Market; South Bend, Indiana; photograph 1933. In this self-service market, products were still primarily stacked along the walls—a throwback to the old service-type store. (Progressive Grocer.)

During the boom following World War I, food retailing grew intensely competitive, and the industry separated into several warring camps. There still were the independently owned small service stores, long the backbone of the nation's food marketing system. However, the phenomenal growth of chain food stores was rapidly challenging the market dominance once enjoyed by these thousands of small grocery, meat, and produce markets. The chains were of two basic types. First there were corporate chains—many hundreds of groceries owned by a single company. The largest and mightiest chain at the time was A&P. Founded just before the Civil War, the enterprise exploded from only 372 stores in 1920 to more than 16,000 in 1927. By 1928 another giant, Kroger, had leapt from a single store in 1882 to almost 4,000; while the number of Piggly Wigglys, a relative newcomer to the field, swelled to over 2,600 by the end of the decade.[6] Faced with this stiff competition, some independents banded together to create a second, voluntary form of chain—an affiliation of small grocers formed to help members buy in quantity, thus obtaining the same wholesale price discounts as their corporate rivals. Founded in 1926, the Independent Grocers Alliance (IGA) became one of the country's largest "voluntary chains," expanding to 5,000 stores over the next twenty-five years.[7]

At first most chains sold only canned and packaged groceries. Anxious to increase their share of the market while reducing operating costs, they began to expand into meat and produce, areas once usually the province of the individually owned markets. Since the stores resulting from these efforts combined a grocery, produce stand, and butcher shop under one roof, they came to be known in the trade as combination stores.

While some combination stores operated on the old system of having a clerk wait on each shopper, most had as much self-service as possible incorporated into their merchandising plan. However, in contrast to the carefully laid out maze of products that shoppers were guided past in the Piggly Wiggly, in the self-service combination store, customers had the

Automarket; Louisville, Kentucky; photograph 1928. In this experimental market, customers threaded their automobiles along a narrow track, were handed merchandise by a series of curbside salesclerks, and paid at the exit—all without ever having to leave their cars. (University of Louisville Photographic Archives.)

Same Automarket, interior; photograph 1928. (University of Louisville Photographic Archives.)

freedom to wander about from one section of the store to another as well as the advantage of a wider selection to choose from. Groceries could be taken directly from low shelves along the walls, and produce was selected from bins and tables. Only at the meat counter was it necessary to ask an employee for a product rather than to simply pick it up and place it in the basket provided by the store. After roaming the store as long as they liked, customers then took their items to a checkout counter to be totaled up and packed.

To house a greater selection of food items while permitting shoppers to amble freely about, self-service combination stores required more space than the older service-type operations. Companies often had to rent two or three adjacent shops in a Main Street block or taxpayer building and then remove the walls separating them in order to provide enough floor area for the new markets. Closing off unused doors, and extending a sign across the length of the storefronts, made the outside appear as a single visual entity. Sometimes, in a higher budget conversion, owners replaced the individual fronts with a single new front consisting of two large plate-glass display windows flanking a central entrance. Inside, bare-wood floors gave way to colored linoleum, and dangling bulbs to more-permanent-looking fixtures with globes.

In some cities where ample land existed for commercial development, new stores were built on vacant lots as freestanding, one-story buildings. Los Angeles in particular became known for its large market buildings, which had distinctive open-air fronts made practical by the warm, sunny climate of Southern California. Since this region was more dependent on the automobile than most other parts of the country at the time, free parking was often provided either in front or at the side of the store—a harbinger of changes that would eventually take place in food-market design nationwide.[8]

Whether housed in an enlarged rented shop space along Main Street or the taxpayer strip, or in a freestanding structure specially built to be a market, self-service combination stores were extremely popular. Shoppers

Above, left:
Hallett's Market; Redwood City, California; photograph 1940. This combination store occupied two shop fronts of a taxpayer block and belonged to the voluntary chain Red & White. (Progressive Grocer.)

Above, right:
Open-front A&P supermarket; Long Beach, California. (The Huntington Library.)

liked to serve themselves from a greatly expanded inventory of goods, as well as to do all their shopping at one store rather than several. Owners and industry observers were equally enthusiastic. Not only were the combinations popular with the public, but fewer stores were needed to serve a given area. This was especially important to the chains, for it allowed them to replace several smaller stores with one larger one. Combination stores represented such considerable operational savings over the smaller service stores that by the late 1920s a substantial combination-store boom was well under way. Take A&P, for example. In 1925 the company owned 15,000 small groceries scattered about the country. By 1932, 4,500 out of a total of its then 15,700 markets were combination stores.[9] *Business Week* praised this changeover, observing that "the great granddaddy of all food chains" was switching from "obscure but efficient hole-in-the-wall groceries" to "prominently-located, handsomely-fixtured general food markets."[10] Many smaller chains and some individually owned markets followed suit.

THE SUPERMARKET: EXPERIMENTATION TO STANDARDIZATION

While the prosperous years of the late 1920s heralded the switch to combination stores, the depression era was the real watershed for food marketing. Hard times created an ideal climate for innovation. Slackened demand resulted in a food surplus, and everything from canned beans to sides of beef could be purchased in large quantities at bargain prices. Business after business failed, and buildings could be bought or rented at reduced cost. Unemployment was high, and people were looking desperately for ways to cut expenses. If truckloads of goods could be purchased cheaply, piled in a building bought or rented cheaply, and then sold at prices lower than those at the local service or combination store, would consumers be willing to hop in their cars or take a bus or trolley several miles to shave a few dollars off the shopping bill?

A number of innovative entrepreneurs around the country began to ask themselves this question. Probably the most famous of these was Michael Cullen. In 1930 Cullen suggested to his employer, the Kroger chain, that they open a number of huge self-service markets (several times larger than the typical four- to six-thousand-square-foot combination store), which would sell great quantities of goods at low prices and with a minimum of overhead expenses.

In his proposal, he cajoled Kroger to invest in his concept: "I would convince the public that I would be able to save them from one to three dollars on their food bills. . . . Can you imagine how the public would respond to a store of this kind? . . . Nobody ever flew the Atlantic either until Lindbergh did it."[11] Despite his enthusiasm, Kroger turned him down; so that same year, to test his marketing theories, Cullen rented a building on Jamaica Avenue in Queens, New York, filled it with truckloads of groceries, meats, and produce that had been bought at high volume at reduced cost, called it King Kullen, and passed the savings on to

*An early King Kullen supermarket;
Queens, New York; photograph c. 1934.
(Progressive Grocer.)*

his customers. He also reinforced the lure of "rock-bottom prices" with forceful advertising, proclaiming himself "King Kullen—world's greatest price wrecker."[12] Shoppers mobbed his first store, which was so successful that by the time of his premature death in 1936, he had expanded his chain to fifteen outlets in the New York metropolitan area.

Two years after the grand opening of King Kullen, in nearby Elizabeth, New Jersey, Robert M. Otis and Roy O. Dawson converted a vacant building in the Durant Automobile complex into Big Bear, "the price crusher."[13] Several times larger than Cullen's first store, the fifty-thousand-square-foot, "circus-like emporium" consisted of a high-volume, cash-and-carry, self-service food market as its hub, surrounded by eleven specialty departments selling everything from paint to radios.[14] King Kullen and Big Bear were not alone. In the opening years of the new decade, dozens of similar operations sprang up around the country.

About the same time, a word began to appear in the trade journals and the popular press to describe these new food outlets—"supermarkets." Although its exact origin is obscure, an industry source claims that the term was first coined in Los Angeles by an enterprising grocer eager to capitalize on words such as "super" and "stupendous," the vocabulary of gala picture premiers.[15] According to M. M. Zimmerman in his 1955 work *The Super Market:* "All evidence thus far indicates that the first user [as an official corporate trademark] of the term 'Super Market' . . . was Albers Super Mkts., Inc.," in Cincinnati in 1933.[16]

Despite the widespread use of the word by the mid-1930s, no exact definition of what constituted a supermarket existed at that time. Nascent examples of the new food marts were generally larger and sometimes disheveled versions of the combination stores that had preceded them. Floor areas were often greater, quantities of stock at lower prices were scattered on tables and in piles rather than neatly tucked in shelves, and some of the customers came a considerable distance to shop. On the whole, however, the difference between combinations and supers stemmed more from ballyhoo than format. Supermarket advertisements crammed local newspapers and radio airwaves, boasting how the latest "price destroyer" was practically giving food away. But even more important than the Barnumesque hucksterism was the very word "supermarket" itself. To a public dispirited by the depression, the ability to shop at a place called "supermarket" rather than just a plain old grocery or food store was to participate in the future, now. The very use of the word was enough to give the illusion that profound advances had taken place.

While the public was very enthusiastic about the new markets—Big Bear's opening day, in fact, "made history in food distribution; all records were shattered for attendance and volume"[17]—their growing presence began to alarm existing food retailers. Some, such as Ralph's and Alpha Beta in Los Angeles or J. Weingarten's in Houston, had, years before the depression, developed large combination stores that were for all practical purposes supermarkets except in name.[18] However, to many independents, and chains such as Kroger or A&P composed of many hundreds of small service and combination stores, the supers represented a considerable competitive challenge. In 1933, *Business Week* summed up the generally negative reaction of the industry to the "cheap jack cash and carry" invasion:

Four walls—crude floors—bare ceilings—flimsy fixtures—glaring lights and gaudy signs—merchandise piled everywhere and apparently any old way—that's the inside of a typical cheapy in the food field.

They establish themselves in low-rent locations on the fringe of thickly populated sections, on the outskirts of cities, or in déclassé neighborhoods where the owner of an abandoned warehouse or a deserted department store is willing to accept starvation rentals for large floor space.

Cheapness is their motto and the outside, generally including the show windows, is invariably plastered with posters that proudly proclaim the price-wrecking proclivities of the proprietor. . . . Maybe they are just a depression phenomena that will vanish as times get better. But only the optimists are sure.[19]

Some chains and independents simply proceeded with business as usual, hoping that the supermarket scare was just a passing fad. Others took more drastic measures, such as organizing advertising boycotts against local newspapers that carried supermarket ads. In Detroit an alliance of 850 irate food retailers even collected under the stirring name the Home Defense League and attempted to prevent supermarkets from opening in their area.[20] But the "fad" did not evaporate. The new stores steadily increased their volume at the expense of many of the older chain and independent outlets. As the owners of the "cheapies" grew prosperous, they began to upgrade the image of their businesses. Soon the warehouse markets gave way to gleaming new supermarkets crammed with great expanses of discounted food.

Soon it became obvious to most in the industry that supermarkets were too potent a force to be curbed with defensive measures. The choice was

The Trading Post; Kansas City, Missouri; photograph 1933. The typical warehouse supermarket of the early 1930s was a jumble of cans, packages, counters, and signs. (Progressive Grocer.)

clear—in order to survive, those established food merchants who had not already done so had to begin building supermarkets themselves. A good illustration of how competition forced this changeover is the battle that took place between A&P and Streamline Stores for the dominant share of food sales in the Pittsburgh area. The very names of the two enterprises epitomized the conflict. The Great Atlantic & Pacific Tea Company (from which came the name "A&P") reflected the confidence and boosterism of the Victorian era in which the company was founded. On the other hand, the word "Streamline" in Streamline Stores was the current slogan for all that was modern and up-to-date. The upstart food chain was founded by a local jobber who, after analyzing several supermarket prototypes including King Kullen and Big Bear, opened up the first sleek new Streamline supermarket in 1935. Business was so successful that it quickly spurred A&P to begin building their own supermarkets in the area.[21] This scenario was repeated in countless cities throughout the country. By the mid-1930s, a full-fledged supermarket explosion was under way.

Trade publications such as *Progressive Grocer*, which rallied its readers to jump on the supermarket bandwagon, hastened the switch over in part; their pages overflowed with suggestions for building new stores and converting old ones into modern, high-volume self-service cash-and-carry markets. This advice was often couched in the jargon of modernization embraced by many branches of the retail trade during the depression era; grocers around the country were told that they could convert their old market into a "scientific food store,"[22] for after all, "the efficient self-service food store is a machine."[23]

What changes in store design did this transformation entail? On the inside, vertical wall shelves were considered obsolete. As their replacement, banks of shelves called "gondolas"—which are long and narrow and can carry a full payload the way a Venetian gondola or gondola railroad car can—came into vogue. So did gondola end displays—those familiar piles of marked-down merchandise that are still found at the ends of supermarket aisles. Open-topped display tables also grew increasingly popular, and many in the trade considered them to be "one of the most effective pieces of selling equipment known to the science of retailing."[24] Anyone who has ever been lured over to a table in the local supermarket by the sight of cheeses or loaves of bread, all with their prices slashed, knows that this still holds true.

Owners also upgraded interior decor. The replacement of bare-wood floors with brightly colored linoleum tiles—a trend begun in combination-store days—continued, while fluorescent lights gradually edged out incandescent, giving stores the now-familiar bright white, rather than yellow, glow. The automobile of the supermarket—the shopping cart—began to replace the wicker basket, and the addition of drawbars to the checkout table allowed the cashier to pull the goods into view and more easily punch prices into the cash register.[25] The development of the supermarket interior was not completed, however, until the meat department, the last outpost where the clerk acted as intermediary, was converted to self-service. Introduced by A&P in 1939,[26] prepackaged meat did not become

Above:
Henke and Pillot; Houston; photograph
c. 1940. By the close of the 1930s, gon-
dola end displays, such as the cornucopia
of light bulbs here, had become standard
merchandising features of the supermar-
ket. (Progressive Grocer.)

Above, right:
Frozen-food display; Empire Market;
Troy, New York; photograph c. 1947.
By the late 1940s, frozen foods as well as
prepackaged meats had become a super-
market mainstay. Note the early two-tier
wire baskets and the use of photographs
(just above the freezer) to tempt shoppers.
(Progressive Grocer.)

commonplace until after World War II when both plastic wrap and refrigerated meat cases became widely available. Frozen foods, first introduced
in the 1930s as "frosted foods," were a supermarket staple by war's end.[27]

Along with these physical changes came dozens of innovations calculated for their psychological impact. Reflecting the emerging interest in
applying psychology to selling, food-industry trade journals brimmed
with information on how to motivate customers to buy as much as possible. *Progressive Grocer*, for example, discouraged its readers from erecting
towering pyramids of cans, which were once an industry mainstay, because they conveyed to the customer the message: "Don't touch or I'll
fall." Such examples of store-clerk art not only were generally frowned on
as a sales negative, but also suggested that employees were spending their
time unproductively.[28] Merchants were also advised by industry publications to put as much stock out as possible, because an abundance of products telegraphs that "I'm fresh and inexpensive—buy me while I last,"
while a skimpy assortment says "I'm all picked over."

During this period, almost every aspect of creating visual appeal was
evaluated for its effectiveness. Manufacturers even got into the act. Realizing that supermarket shelves represented millions of feet of free exhibition space for their products, they became increasingly concerned about
the way that consumers reacted to the sight of their merchandise. Companies redesigned their labels and changed their packaging for maximum
appeal.

After almost two decades of constant innovation in layout, fixture and
display design, and market psychology, along with the complete conversion to self-service, the interior program for the machine for selling had
basically been standardized by 1950. Markets were divided into a series of
aisles along which the customer drove a shopping cart, and these interior
highways were lined with products packaged and labeled to serve as miniature billboards to attract attention. Shoppers were usually unaware that
the sequence of visual events they experienced in a store was deliberately

choreographed. Merchants often placed the produce display, with its appetizing array of colors, contrasts, and textures, and general aura of freshness, first in the sequence. Then they customarily positioned the meat department along a side or rear wall, not only for easy access to the refrigeration and cutting room, but to act as a magnet to draw customers through the aisles. At the end of the tour, the shopper could count on finding ice cream or some other item that, while not a necessity, would be overwhelmingly tempting. The last stop was the checkout or tollgate. Here, racks of impulse items such as candy, razor blades, and cigarettes enticed the customer to part with some additional change.

Interestingly, by developing this format, food merchants had inadvertently created within the supermarket a microcosm of the new shopping areas that were rapidly spreading across postwar America—the suburban strips. The similarities between guiding a cart down the aisles of a nearby Acme or Grand Union and driving a car along the local Miracle Mile are striking. Like strips, supermarkets are traversed by highways. Each shopper maneuvers a vehicle down the interior streets, being careful not to collide with other traffic, while scanning the package labels that line the aisles like signs along the highway. Yet where the order in which signs appear along the roadside strip is often random (depending on when each wayside merchant purchased a piece of frontage land), the procession of visual events in the supermarket is preplanned and totally contrived. It is a masterwork of psychological zoning enacted in miniature, begun by pioneers such as Clarence Saunders, and still in practice to this very day.

During these same formative years, from 1935 to 1950, the exterior design of the supermarket, while less important than the interior program, underwent an interesting evolution as well. The chief function of the exterior was to serve as a stylish wrapper to attract attention, identify the business, and entice customers inside. During this period, the Streamline Moderne provided an up-to-date, inviting look for a majority of supermarket shop fronts. Walls covered with structural glass or porcelain-enameled metal, overhanging canopies with curved corners trimmed with fluted stainless steel, entranceways surrounded by glass block, fascias detailed with residual Art Deco zigzags or chevrons, and sign towers emblazoned with neon—all were hallmarks of the streamlined market.

Jack Cinnamon's Market; Highland Park, Michigan; rendering 1935. A modernistic supermarket exterior by Albert Kahn, Inc., the firm that had become famous for designing many of the automobile factories nearby, has its front built of stainless steel and black structural glass. The lower sign is made of black enameled letters backed with opalite glass and lit with incandescent lamps. The large sign is composed of stainless-steel letters outlined with neon tubes. (Albert Kahn Associates, Inc.)

Though streamlined markets were once de rigueur in supermarket design, relatively few survive today in anything near original condition. Visitors to Salt Lake City can catch a glimpse of the curving storefront of the Grand Temple View Market across from the Mormon Tabernacle, while drivers heading east into North Adams, Massachusetts, are greeted by a striking buff-colored, porcelain-enameled metal, streamlined facade bearing the name West End Market executed in baked-on red modernistic letters. While a number of other examples can be found, most food-store exteriors of this genre have been either remodeled or demolished.

In addition to the Streamline Moderne, other costumes dressed supers of the period as well. In the East and Midwest, it was not unusual to find half-timbered Tudor fronts or colonial markets crowned by a hipped roof and cupola, while Spanish designs with stucco walls and tile roofs were popular in the South and West. After World War II, Streamline Moderne and the period revivals generally fell from vogue. While some operators continued to cling to historical and regional references for packaging their markets—hipped-roof, red-brick buildings topped with a cupola were synonymous with A&P through the 1960s, for example—it was functional imagery, reflecting the growing influence of the Modern movement, that became the favored idiom for supermarkets in the postwar years.

Also during the 1940s and 1950s, the visual front—a large horizontal window extending across an entire facade—grew in popularity.[29] Still in use today, this innovation placed all that was going on inside the supermarket on outside display. Once, streamlined sign pylons, "colonial" cupolas, and Spanish-tile roofs were used to attract the notice of passersby. Now, with the switch to the visual front, the fluorescently lit spectacle of shoppers wielding carts and packers stuffing groceries into brown paper bags become the primary exterior lure (although in practice these activities were and still are often obscured by sale posters, stacks of cartons, and other attendant clutter). The remainder of the building was usually treated simply. Roofs were almost always flat, while walls, laid up in

Below, left:
Star Market; Watertown, Massachusetts; photograph 1939. (Progressive Grocer.)

Below, right:
Same Star Market shortly after closing; photograph 1981. Today hundreds of similar ghosts of supermarkets past can be found along the nation's taxpayer strips. (Author.)

National Food Stores supermarket, grand opening; Bay City, Michigan; photograph 1956. Plain brick walls, cantilevered or pipe-supported canopies, and expanses of glass forming a visual front typified supermarket exteriors throughout much of the 1950s. (Food Marketing Institute.)

brick or concrete block, or sheathed with enameled-metal panels—a carryover from the Streamline era—were generally unadorned. Entrance canopies were often unceremoniously supported by a series of columns made of lengths of plain cast-iron pipe.

It might appear at first glance that these features were so visually unassuming as to be of little commercial value in attracting customers. In actuality, architectural theatrics were not necessary in an era when the mere opening of a food store, as the following 1951 account testifies, had all the trappings of a gala Hollywood premiere:

Even blasé New Yorkers gawked at the razzle-dazzle last week when Food Fair Stores Inc. opened two spick & span new supermarkets. Skywriting planes soared overhead. Models paraded by in hats adorned with lobsters and sirloin steaks. . . . Mayor Impellitteri came to shop. Tex and Jinx McCrary put on a broadcast and television's Dagmar, surrounded by a crowd of 7,000, had her automobile license plate ripped off as a souvenir. Inside the air-conditioned stores, shoppers snatched at bargains (chicken at 39¢ a lb.), boggled at such curiosities as ostrich eggs at $15 apiece, llama steaks at $2.50 a lb.[30]

Searchlight beams radiated from street fronts, eager shoppers jostled one another at ballpoint pen giveaways, and children queued up in parking lots for a chance to board rocket-to-the-moon rides at ribbon-cutting ceremonies across the country. The machine for selling food had become a celebrated symbol of modernity. People were insane about supermarkets. From about ten thousand in 1946, the number of supers swelled to seventeen thousand nationwide by 1953,[31] and construction showed no signs of letting up. By the midpoint of the decade, supermarkets accounted for 60 percent of the nation's retail food trade.[32]

By this time, however, with so many supermarkets in operation, the novelty began wearing off. Because of the high degree of standardization that had developed within the industry, the interior of one market often looked much the same as the next. From awestruck tourists eagerly discovering pathways lined with food, shoppers were becoming commuters routinely traveling the now-familiar interior roads. The fact that a store

Farmers Discount Market; Fairfield, California; photograph c. 1972, Richard Longstreth. Supermarkets of the late 1950s and early 1960s were festooned with visual and verbal ("WOW") theatrics to attract customers. (Richard Longstreth.)

was bright, clean, and modern looking was no longer sufficient to guarantee trade.

B. Sumner Gruzen—long-time designer of supermarkets, including the early Big Bears—summarized the problem in 1955: "The personality of a market must compete constantly with the thousands of ingeniously packaged items which a customer can get in one store as well as in another."[33] Moreover, Main Street and the taxpayer strip had moved aside as the prime location for new markets, which now rose primarily along suburban commercial strips. As motorists sped along the local Miracle Mile, a food retailer was hard-pressed to avoid a contemporary maxim of highway architecture: get their attention with the latest eye-catching designs.

To combat the threat of sameness and make supermarkets more visible from speeding cars without tampering with the internal mechanism of the "machine for selling," many operators began to inject visual adrenaline into the outward appearance of their structures. Utilitarian exteriors gave way to dramatic roof shapes and gull-wing canopies, while gigantic pole-mounted signs shadowed over parking lots. Austere functionalism was out—Exaggerated Modern came into vogue.

A good example of the new look in markets was the prototype design for the Penn Fruit Company by Victor Gruen & Associates in 1956, which, through the use of a series of uninterrupted, soaring, laminated wooden arches, transformed the supermarket into a great concave form. The sign was integrated into the glass-infilled arched facade in such a way that building and sign coalesced into a distinctive trademark that could be reproduced in future units.[34] This period generated dozens of other striking designs as well, from the bold, horizontal canopies and towering canted sign pylons of the Super Dupers in the Northeast to the huge wise eyes of the enormous red owls that beamed protectively down on Red Owl Supermarkets in Minnesota.

THE SUPERMARKET: CHANGES IN FORMATS

By the opening of the 1960s, when the supermarket's share of the retail food trade had inched up to 70 percent,[35] competition among stores grew increasingly keen. More had to be done to remain competitive than constructing flamboyant exterior wrappers. The inside also needed some consideration. To address the problem, a major industry trade group, the Super Market Institute, commissioned the Raymond Loewy Corporation (headed by the great champion of 1930s streamlining) to study the future of the field. The result was a detailed report, released in 1960, entitled *Super Markets of the Sixties*.

Examining what consumers expected from a supermarket, the study found that, for many people, going food shopping was not merely a utilitarian chore—it was a form of recreation made possible by ever-increasing discretionary income. "The implication for the supermarket is fairly clear . . . to grow they must appeal to [the] . . . new rich mass market [that] will have an enormous option as to what to do with almost one half of their money."[36] The study also analyzed demographic changes—such as the expected shift to smaller households—and predicted the type of merchandise, such as "smaller portions of meat" and "smaller cans of groceries," that might be in demand in the future. The report then offered ways in which the industry could increase sales, not merely through attention-getting architecture, but by reworking and enlivening the interior shopping tour, which had undergone relatively little innovation since it had become more or less standardized by about 1950. In chapters with titles such as "The Department That Says Garden Fresh" or "Dollars from the Delicatessen," Loewy advised retailers to create a special atmosphere for each department and to expose customers to higher-profit items—from housewares to gourmet foods.

The conclusions of this trend-setting report and other similar studies had considerable impact on the industry, influencing the largest chains as well as the smaller independents. By the early 1970s, when many postwar babies had grown up into an affluent middle class, with especially quixotic tastes, supermarkets were ready for them, with delicatessens and new sections devoted to everything from exotic produce and natural foods to a vast array of foreign and domestic wines.

To increase sales further, market researchers also reactivated imagery from the past to "press the nostalgia button," in the words of one publication.[37] Names of venerable store departments such as "meat" and "produce" were upgraded to folksy selling phrases such as "O.K. Corral" and the "Garden Patch." Merchants stressed each individual department so as to invoke memories of the old-fashioned butcher shop or vegetable stand sans clerk. Ironically, the service store—once left behind for being out-of-date and inconvenient—was now being brought back to life as a selling symbol for modern supermarkets. The pendulum had swung back

Above:
Penn Fruit Company, 1956; Victor Gruen, architect; Camden, New Jersey; photograph c. 1956, Lawrence P. Williams. (Gruen Associates.)

Above, right:
Safeway supermarket, c. 1980; Laramie, Wyoming; photograph 1982. Here corbeled brick piers, a vestigial visual front (drastically reduced in area for energy conservation), and a wide wood fascia are used to make the visual statement: "We blend in with the environment." (Author.)

again—except the reincarnation was make-believe. Designers also made stores over according to themes—Wild West, Bavarian, colonial—in an attempt to reinvigorate the interior highways, and they learned what wayside pioneers had discovered along real highways in the 1920s: popular imagery sells.

As the 1960s progressed, exteriors of supermarkets also underwent considerable transformation. With the heightened public interest in protecting the environment and curbing what was perceived to be visual pollution, food retailers, along with other business owners, felt the pressure of negative popular opinion against the Exaggerated Modern of their newer stores. Mindful that epithets such as "garish" and "eyesore" hardly bespoke a bright future for flamboyant design, trade journals began to advocate the use of stone, wood, cedar shakes, and other hallmarks of the Environmental Look to give the outside of the supermarket a more earthy and permanent appearance. As a result, while stores became more visually aggressive on the inside, they became more self-consciously subdued on the outside, a trend the industry dubbed "blending." *Progressive Grocer* summed it up in 1969: "The blended store can be very deceptive. On the surface, the store creates little contrast with either the surrounding landscape or adjoining stores. Under this surface calm, however, beats the heart of an exciting, aggressive, well-merchandised store. It has to be this way, since the store's design is pointed toward making it an 'instant fixture' in the community."[38] This philosophy has continued to guide supermarket design up to the present day.

By the mid-1970s, the very foundations of the supermarket industry—cheap energy and a growing population that eats at home—started to be shaken. With the great jump in energy costs that followed the Arab oil embargo, operating budgets for heating, lighting, air conditioning, and cooling the hundreds of feet of refrigerated display cases soared. Expenses had to be cut somewhere. Owners looked toward computerized checkouts, for instance, to reduce their labor and inventory control costs. At

Edwards Food Warehouse (former Finast supermarket); Newton, Massachusetts; photograph 1981. The latter half of the 1970s saw the rebirth of the warehouse supermarket. (Author.)

the same time, the population began to level off, and building ever-increasing numbers of new markets could not be justified in a highly saturated marketplace. Moreover, the industry faced what it called "the eating-out challenge": restaurants, especially fast-food franchises, were taking away business.[39] So was a new generation of smaller food outlets—convenience stores. These condensed supermarkets, which are often combined with a gas station and whose main selling point is extended hours of service, have appeared by the thousands to spare anyone needing only a quart of milk from having to wander down yards of aisles.

These challenges have provoked a widespread controversy as to what form the supermarket should take—a controversy as yet unresolved. Some firms—especially those serving rural areas—still believe in the standard supermarket that carries a full line of food products and a limited variety of nonfoods, an updated version of the basic formula that had evolved by 1950. Others favor the construction of super stores that offer hundreds of different foods and nonfoods under one roof, thus reducing further the number of stores needed in a given market area.

But as the industry looks to the future, some operators are also beginning to resurrect the past with a new twist. In the depression era, old warehouses were converted into some of the nation's first supermarkets. Now, some old supermarkets are being converted back to warehouse stores that feature a limited assortment of merchandise displayed in its original cartons. To keep prices low, these enterprises encourage customers to bring their own bags and pack their own groceries.[40] Perhaps the day is not far off when shop-at-home systems using closed-circuit TV may render the supermarket extinct, but for the foreseeable future, the many offspring of Clarence Saunders and Michael Cullen are alive and well.

Miniature Golf Courses

MINIATURE GOLF courses have had a more dramatic and erratic history than most other types of roadside buildings. They burst upon the scene in the mid-1920s, had fully developed as a genre by 1929, mushroomed up in thousands of Main Street gap sites and vacant lots lining the taxpayer strip by 1930, rapidly declined in 1931, and had a reincarnation along the nation's Miracle Miles after World War II. Today these curious little landscapes peopled with tiny buildings, bizarre statuary, and Rube Goldbergian hazards still serve as oases of architectural whimsy along the great American roadside.

COTTONSEED HULLS, TOM THUMB, AND THE MINIATURE-GOLF CRAZE

At the turn of the twentieth century, there was only a scattering of dwarf-size golf courses in both Europe and the United States. A 200-by-270 foot, eighteen-hole course was reported, for example, to have been built in Germany about 1915, while on this side of the ocean, country inns occasionally provided front-lawn practice links so that guests could sharpen their game. During the 1920s, however, tiny practice courses ceased to be a random occurrence. The period following World War I saw a great surge in interest in golf as large numbers of Americans, from clerks to shop owners, in an attempt to boost their own status sought out the sport that had once been nearly the exclusive province of the upper social strata. Thousands of newly minted golfers were eager to find a way to practice putting on their lunch hour or on the way home from work, and they pressed everything from office floors to park lawns and parlor rugs into use as putting greens. Unfortunately, the resistance to a rolling golf ball presented by these ad-hoc playing surfaces did not approximate the manicured grass found on an actual golf course. A most unusual discovery radically altered this situation.

About 1922, Thomas Fairbairn, owner of a cotton plantation in Mexico, and two associates, Robert McCart and Albert Valdespino of El Paso, Texas—all apparently golfers who were themselves on the lookout for places to practice—found that cottonseed hulls, when trampled on the ground, made an excellent surface for putting golf balls. Seeing the commercial potential for this strange revelation, the trio applied for a patent for what they technically described as "a surfacing material for putting greens comprising comminuted flocculent material into a homogenous mass."[1] The patent was granted in 1925.

It was about this same time that two New Yorkers, John Ledbetter and Drake Delanoy, after building several indoor practice courses that were commercial failures due to unsatisfactory putting-green material, heard about the cottonseed-hull discovery and obtained permission to use the odd material on an indoor course they were constructing in downtown Manhattan. The new surfacing apparently worked well, the undertaking was reasonably successful, and the pair began building other tiny cottonseed-hull practice courses in vacant lots, on rooftops, and near tennis courts scattered about the metropolitan area.[2] While this venture marked the beginning of a new chapter in the history of miniature golf, it was through the efforts of a businessman and real-estate promoter from Tennessee, Garnet Carter, that the dwarf courses would soon be transformed from mere practice grounds into a wildly popular amusement and the object of a craze of gigantic proportions.

The story began in the mid-1920s when Carter built a housing development and hotel high atop Lookout Mountain, a large outcropping south-

east of Chattanooga. The hotel, called Fairyland, boasted "the largest ballroom in the South, homelike lounging rooms, spacious dining hall, delightful bedrooms, open fireplaces, [and] windows that frame thrilling views."[3] Additional amenities were located on the grounds of the hostelry. There was a swimming pool nestled in the rocks from which one had a spectacular view of the city off in the distance, a number of tennis courts, and a nationally famous golf links.

In 1927 Carter decided to add still another attraction: a miniature golf course, complete with trick hazards, surrounded by small statues of Little Red Riding Hood and other storybook figures. Now, he reasoned, visiting children would have a place to play golf. To his surprise, the course was soon taken over by adults, who both liked the fantasy setting and enjoyed the challenge of putting a ball through the miniaturized fairways, greens, obstacles, and hazards.[4] By adding the fantasy backdrop, Carter offered his patrons not just a golf game, as Delanoy and Ledbetter had, but a new form of amusement. He also realized that the idea was commercially marketable.

Not one to let an opportunity slide, Carter went into the miniature-golf-course business. He began by gaining permission to use the cotton-

Miniature golf course; Louisville, Kentucky; photograph c. 1931. Many miniature golf courses, such as this one, were squeezed into narrow city lots along Main Streets and taxpayer strips. (University of Louisville Photographic Archives.)

seed hulls; then he mixed the fluffy substance with green paint and boasted to potential investors that the miracle compound would "look like grass, feel like grass, play like grass, but wear indefinitely."[5]

Soon Carter began manufacturing courses for national distribution under the storybook name of Tom Thumb Golf. By the end of the decade, several factories were producing Tom Thumb courses under agreement with Carter, one of the largest being the National Pipe Products Corporation of Rochester, Pennsylvania, a firm that had manufactured gas-station fixtures and equipment. By 1930 this company employed more than two hundred craftsmen for the various phases of prefabrication, which ranged from bending metal pipe as edging for the greens (using equipment originally designed to make standards for filling-station signs) to hand decorating the little fountains, stairs, and other structures used as ornaments and obstacles.[6] Once completed, the various parts of the course were stock-piled, ready for delivery.

How were these components transformed into a Tom Thumb golf course? According to C. G. Mackintosh, construction engineer for the Tom Thumb factory in Rochester, the first step after site selection was to prepare a "special plan" designed to suit the individual lot, a plan that placed the playing features, lights, and fences in such a way that "if a ball gets off the fairway, it won't interfere with the play of others" and if hit too hard, "won't strike anyone else" (avoidance of accidents and potential lawsuits was a guiding principle of miniature-golf design).[7] As soon as the site was "cleared of rubbish and a good general grade . . . established," the greens and fairways were staked out. Then came the golf sets from the factory in about one thousand pieces weighing "something like ten thousand pounds. . . ."[8] About fifteen men worked on the job. Some installed the metal pipes that formed the edging for the greens and fairways, while others excavated "the ground to a depth of six inches or a foot below the level of the pipes" or "built up" the ground on "fairways which . . . [were] to have elevations."[9] A "filling crew" then tamped down a layer of rocks and cinders, inserted the cups, and "the cotton-seed-hull compound" was "spread . . . rolled and tamped" on top of the cinders.[10] Finally, the walks were built, and the hazards, buildings, and other features set in place. Mackintosh estimated that the average prefabricated course could be installed and open for business within six days.[11] The cost of a typical course of this type, minus the caddy house or office, was between one thousand and six thousand dollars, depending upon the size of the layout and the elaborateness of the obstacles and hazards.[12]

Carter marketed these courses aggressively in nationwide advertisements. His sales pitches had the dual purpose of enticing investors to buy a franchise and arousing the public's excitement in anticipation of Tom Thumb's arrival in their community. Excerpts from a Tom Thumb ad that appeared in the *Saturday Evening Post* in 1930 exhibited the bold confidence and boosterism with which the courses were hawked: "Thar's gold in them thar hills, stranger. . . . Millions are playing. . . . Big profits for you. . . . Hundreds of Tom Thumb courses are in operation. . . . Hundreds are being installed. . . . Watch for the one in your town. . . ."[13] In 1930, perhaps wisely sensing an imminent bottoming out at the very moment that miniature golf had reached its peak in popularity, Carter sold the Tom Thumb rights. By this time, he had been joined by hundreds of competitors, including a number of companies with similar prefabricating operations, along with thousands of individuals who designed, built, and operated their own courses. Nevertheless, Tom Thumb did represent an amazingly large percentage of the total market. Of the estimated twenty-five thousand courses[14] that had sprouted up nationwide by 1930, almost one fourth (more than six thousand) had rolled off the Tom Thumb assembly lines.[15]

In contrast to the secluded mountaintop where the game was perfected, these innumerable new courses, both Tom Thumb and otherwise, were predominantly located in urban areas, occupying rooftops, basements, and vacant lots along Main Street and the taxpayer strip. Most were of two general types: the putting green, a descendant of the practice links mentioned at the beginning of the chapter; and the fairyland, which evolved from the Lookout Mountain prototype. Putting-green courses featured miniature topographical undulations, sand traps, and other elements commonly found on regulation golf links that often required no small degree of golfing skill. The more popular courses, however, appear to have been of the fairyland type. The latter featured mechanical hazards placed in fanciful settings, with novelty rather than improving one's game of golf as their chief appeal.

The challenge in designing a fairyland course was to provide excitement while making the game relatively easy to play. Difficult hazards both discouraged customers and slowed down the game, causing a reduction in the number of players per hour and therefore a drop in revenues. Thus, each obstacle was designed to look insurmountable, while allowing even the most unskilled player to guide his ball past the gauntlet of distractions and achieve a score fairly close to par. By 1930 industry literature was filled with imaginative examples of hazards that combined ease of play with visual panache, such as the Water Wheel hazard, "easily . . . worked out by piping water and letting it flow onto a water wheel, which gradually turns, on which there are attached two cups or pans, which will hit the ball from one green level to a higher one," and the Whale, which "opens and closes its mouth, and . . . if you hit [it] . . . in the nose with your ball instead of in the mouth, it will spout water."[16] In fact a player

Illustration from How to Play Miniature Golf *by Morley B. Thompson, 1930. Shortly after the stock market crash, the national mania for playing the Rube Goldbergian hazards was seen as a hopeful sign by many contemporary observers that the jazz age might outlast the depression. A year later, however, the craze fizzled, and the economy worsened.*

roaming the lilliputian links at the close of the jazz age was often greeted by the same genre of attention-getting popular imagery (albeit in miniature) that motorists of the period were beginning to discover along the highway.

In addition to water wheels, whales, and fantasy motifs, course builders also exploited regional imagery. In South Pasadena, for example, a course named the Chiquita featured hazards reminiscent of the Old West, including "a massive old wagon wheel which stands upright in the earth so that the ball passes through the hub," and "the water-hole, a grim desert scene with bleached bones scattered about."[17] One New York City course even afforded players the opportunity to pretend they were on a transcontinental auto tour in miniature with each hole marked by a painted-canvas image of such regional tourist attractions as Niagara Falls, the Grand Canyon, or Hollywood.[18]

Besides being a fascinating new element on the American landscape, shortly after the stock market crash in 1929, miniature golf began to be viewed by many as an economic miracle in a time when the nation was first struggling to recover from the depression. In addition to providing employment, its popularity created a new market for clay, sand, asbestos, cork, felt, rubber, concrete, steel, and many other materials that generally were less in demand as a result of the economic crisis. This prompted many industrial trade journals and business publications to urge their readers to cash in on the new fad. *Steel* estimated that the nation's courses consumed more than twenty thousand tons of that metal for use in putters, pipe, holes, lighting standards, and office structures;[19] *Concrete* was ebullient because many miniature golf courses used concrete as the underlayment for greens, walks, and fairways;[20] while *Electrical World* eagerly eyed the business that nighttime playing created for electrical equipment manufacturers and contractors.[21] The reason for all this interest was aptly summed up by *Building Age* in 1930: "In a business condition as we are now experiencing, any new or unusual demand has a decided stimulation effect."[22]

This flurry of economic optimism while the nation was really slipping into a decade of adversity could not have occurred had the tiny golf courses not possessed some sort of magical mass appeal. Miniature golf gave the average American the opportunity to engage in mild competition while escaping into an environment reminiscent of a comic book, amusement park, animated cartoon, or Hollywood movie set. As the *Nation* observed in 1930: "When the pseudo-Klieg lights are playing full upon the humble householder from Hackensack, he may not only experience that comfortable country-club feeling superinduced by drooping plus fours and prehistoric posture; he may also be able to capture the illusion that he is John Barrymore at work."[23] The new amusement was further evidence of the growing trend toward democratization of what were once elite customs, pleasures, and pastimes. In the decade following World War I, private travel was made available to millions by the automobile, theater was mass marketed by radio and the movies, and manners were codified for the general public by Emily Post. Now, as Elmer Davis observed in *Harper's* in 1930, "Thanks to the miniature courses, every man can say that he plays golf . . . breaking in at last on that sport of the minor aristocracy—its appeal in a year of hard times was hard to resist."[24]

Not surprisingly, the question of why people were willing to pay to putt a ball around a vacant lot was the subject of much social commentary at the time. In the same *Harper's* article, entitled "Miniature Golf to the Rescue," Davis reported—only slightly tongue in cheek—that miniature golf had become a psychological palliative for a period of economically enforced leisure. He cited several reasons for the preeminence of the sport in 1930 over all other inexpensive amusements—reasons including "novelty," the fact that "men and women can both play," and that the game had "the advantage of the old nickle glass of beer; it is quick and cheap."[25] *Literary Digest* marveled how the activity appealed to people of such divergent social and religious backgrounds as "H.R.H. the Prince of Wales, and thirteen-year-old Sidney Schoenbrun, [the actual proud builder of a backyard course] of Flatbush"; it went on to point out that both "are brothers under the same skin," so to speak, due to their mutual love of miniature golf.[26] *Outlook and Independent* summed it all up: "In these days of Hoover prosperity, the Americans have found that playing the hazards is cheaper than playing the market."[27]

Aided no doubt by the barrage of favorable publicity, demand for the new amusement soared. By the end of 1930, millions of dollars had been invested in the nation's miniature golf courses, and many regions of the country were inundated with the lilliputian landscapes. The Los Angeles area, with its favorable climate, was one of the major centers of the new sport. Five hundred eighty-four construction permits for the miniature links were issued there in 1930 alone,[28] while a survey conducted by the *Boston Post* showed that the number of courses in New England tripled that same year.[29]

Amid this rapid growth, miniature golf took on the trappings of a mature industry while still in its infancy. Dozens of owners' associations started up, and a national trade journal, Los Angeles-based *Miniature Golf Management*, began publication; it featured everything from sources of equipment and new course designs to advice on how to placate municipal officials. Do-it-yourself magazines such as *Popular Mechanics* published plans for backyard miniature golf,[30] and backyard mechanics across the country tried their hand at making home-built courses from scraps of lumber, old tires, and other found materials. One family in Brooklyn (Sidney Schoenbrun's, in fact) built a four-hole course, Wee Willie, which its creators proudly proclaimed to be the smallest in New York—eight by twelve feet.[31] A theme song was even written for the trade titled "I'm Putt-Putting on Those Dinky Links All Day Long."[32]

However, all was not sanguine for the new industry in the heady year of 1930, for miniature golf was beginning to meet with considerable opposition. Parents grew concerned about their children's addiction to the game, while many residents of adjoining neighborhoods complained about noise, over-illumination, parking problems, and rowdiness. *American City Magazine* asked its readership, principally municipal officials, how they planned to develop lease fees for the use of public lands, license fees, zoning regulations, and restrictions on Sunday playing.[33] Efforts to construct a course in a residential district in Ontario, California, prompted a bitter "civic war," for the residents feared that the way would be opened for gas stations and other businesses to destroy "the most beautiful avenue in the world."[34] Meanwhile in New York, the state supreme court, in response to similar community opposition, ruled that miniature golf courses were not playgrounds or recreation centers and that the game played on them was not golf.[35] Industry euphemisms were cast aside—miniature golf was a business subject to zoning.

Even with this lowering cloud of legal limitations and community outcry, the industry began the 1931 season with heightened expectations. Even the *Boston Post* continued publishing Burt Hoxie's "Golf in Miniature Form" column—an oasis of cheerful news about course openings and schedules, engulfed by advertisements peddling everything from golf balls to caddy shacks.[36]

But despite this optimism, the miniature-golf boom did not economically or spiritually carry the nation past the crisis, as pundits had half-jokingly hoped.[37] The depression worsened, and people sought other forms of escape. As one operator lamented over the loss of an important segment of his course's clientele: "Kids are faddists. They're not crazy about golf like they were last year. The movies are putting on serials. Give the children their choice and they'd rather go to the serial than to the golf course. . . ."[38] Operators lowered prices, changed hazards, and even ordered attendants to play during slack times so the courses would look busy—but to no avail. On 6 September 1931, from the birthplace of the fad, the *Chattanooga Times* wondered, "Baby Golf Dies in the Cradle—Will It Ever Return?"

POSTWAR REINCARNATION

Although a number of the better-run courses survived after the boom went bust, the baby links did not stage a comeback until after World War II. In contrast to the early inner-city locations, postwar courses were usually constructed along suburban commercial strips and major tourist routes or near resort areas. They tended to be much larger operations, with refreshment stands and more elaborate hazards, and were often built as lures to attract motorists to other businesses such as motels, drive-in theaters, shopping centers, or golf driving ranges.

From a design standpoint, many of these courses followed in the tradition of Sidney Schoenbrun rather than Garnet Carter and were built from scratch by innovative handymen and contractors. Constructed of odds and ends, miniature links from this era often reflected a high degree of native genius, innovation, and handicraft. Putt-A-Round, in North Hampton, New Hampshire, built in 1956, is an excellent example of this genre.[39]

Motorists are first attracted to the course, located just south of Portsmouth on U.S. Route 1 next to the Sea Coast Drive-in Theater, by the

PUTT-A-ROUND GOLF COURSE, 1956;
NORTH HAMPTON, NEW HAMPSHIRE
(ALL PHOTOGRAPHS 1980):

Right:
General view, Putt-A-Round golf course.
(Author.)

Below, left:
Dutch Mill, Putt-A-Round golf course.
The windmill has dancing wooden shoes
activated by a washing-machine-agitator
mechanism. (Author.)

Below, right:
Jet, Putt-A-Round golf course. (Author.)

incongruous vision of a jet plane, a windmill, and a lighthouse sharing the same lot. A one-dollar admission is paid to a man in his late sixties standing at the window of a small boxlike office with wide, overhanging eaves. He, in turn, hands each player a well-sharpened pencil stub and a scorecard that lists the sequence of the visual events to come: "Over the Wave, Wheel of Fortune, Dutch Mill, Clean Sweep, The Loop, Blast Off!, Under the Bridge, Jeopardy, Double Trouble, No Tilting, Olde Grist Mill, Cookie the Bird, Toll House, The Jet, Hot Dice, Light House, The Well, and Mickey"—much in the way that town names on a road map evoke images of sights to come on a motor trip.

Each of these hazards is composed of fragments of cultural residue—old

appliances, boats, vehicles. The windmill is powered by a washing machine agitator-drive motor, while at the next hole, a mechanical clown (with a head fashioned from a nautical pulley block and a nose from a painted light bulb) passes a broom rhythmically over the fairway. Farther along, a miniature turnpike tollhouse flashes red-and-green stop-and-go lights at approaching balls, while a perforated metal cylinder capped by a bell-cast steel industrial lampshade forms the top of a miniature lighthouse. The game ends at the eighteenth hole, where players aim their putts at Mickey Mouse's mouth; from there the balls roll back to the office via an underground conduit.

While the hazards in this and other postwar handcrafted courses were still often based upon popular images such as the windmill, once commonly used in all roadside architecture, the actual designs and layouts were often the unique products of the builder's imagination, inspired by the inherent shapes and textures of the scrap parts from which they were made. In the case of Putt-A-Round, the man at the office, Ed Silva, turns out to be the designer, builder, and owner. When asked if the course was built from preexisting plans, he replied that the design was completely his own. In order to test the placement of lighting standards and ball trajectories, he built a working scale model and modified it by trial and error so that, in his words, "The finished course was guaranteed to work."[40] He deplores so-called experts who "use mathematics and make mistakes. . . . I do it the practical way!"[41] The course is his art, and its revenues seem to be only an added benefit.

This pride of authorship felt by Mr. Silva is not uncommon among a good number of other miniature-golf designers/operators as well.

Lighthouse, Putt-A-Round golf course. (Author.)

Putt-A-Round builder and owner Ed Silva and the clown from the obstacle called Clean Sweep. (Author.)

Suggested hazards for miniature golf courses as published by the National Golf Foundation, 1949. Many of these designs—such as the windmill and the loop-the-loop—had been perfected during the late 1920s and early 1930s and were again used in miniature golf courses after World War II. (National Golf Foundation.)

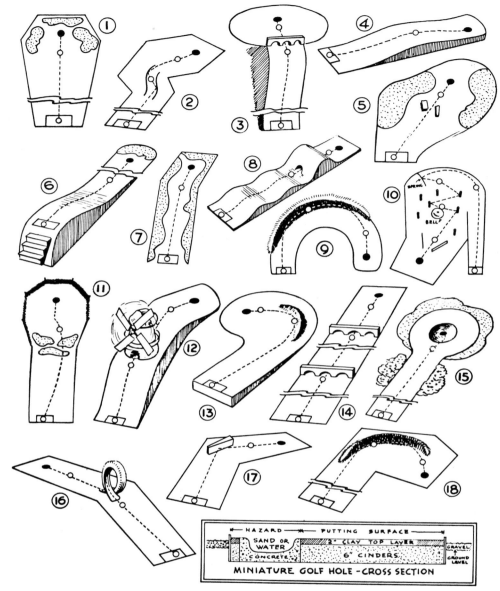

By the time they had built their courses, the sight of quaint little golf links did not seem to evoke the same passionate excitement as it had a generation earlier. Yet a windshield glimpse of people putting their way through a dwarf-size village still provoked a considerable degree of fascination. Because the reaction elicited by miniature golf in the roadside marketplace was now one of reliable curiosity instead of insane frenzy, postwar investors tended to build courses with the expectation of making a reasonable income rather than the hope of getting rich quick. As the National Golf Foundation pointed out in 1949, the game had become a "sound sports entertainment business; not the passing craze of the first boom-time. . . ."[42] Building and operating a miniature golf course also offered an additional reward—the opportunity to tinker around in one's

own outdoor landscaped hobby garden and to create roadside handicraft at a time when the strictures of Modernist architectural doctrine were beginning to sanitize wayside commercial design.

However, the spirit of Garnet Carter still lingers on. Although many handicrafted courses remain in business to this day, the trend since the mid-1950s has reverted back toward factory-built units reminiscent of the early Tom Thumb courses. These latter operations feature attractions ranging from traditional hazards such as windmills and loop-the-loops to giant fiberglass giraffes, elephants, gorillas, and dolphins.[43] Prefabricated fixtures have become so much a part of most recent miniature-golf-course designs that many owners of older home-built courses, in an attempt to update the image of their businesses, have been willing to pay as much as $995 for a nearly ten-foot-high rearing horse or $650 for a five-foot-high Fatso the Pig to set out in front of their establishments.[44]

A number of manufacturers of these instant attractions also offer a franchise package in which every last operational detail has been predetermined, from the best types of refreshments to sell to the preferred way to run a promotional tournament. Contrary, however, to the fast-food or motel industries, in which the best-surprise-is-no-surprise uniformity helps promote sales, in miniature golf, the constant changing of surprises helps sell the course. To accomplish this, one innovative franchiser, Lomma Enterprises, even has a "Swap-Shop" arrangement where an operator can exchange obstacles and hazards each year, assuring a fresh and inviting sequence of attractions.[45]

Above:
Green Valley Golf, c. 1976; Bakersfield, California; photograph 1982. Some of the more recent courses have the neat, slick, and tidy look of theme amusement parks rather than the ad hoc, handicrafted effect of earlier courses. (Author.)

Below:
Magic Carpet Golf, 1968; Tucson; photograph 1982. Miniature golf courses are veritable galleries of popular symbols. (Author.)

Right:
Factory-built miniature golf course, c. 1975; Scranton, Pennsylvania; photograph c. 1979. Today portable miniature golf courses are being installed in everything from shopping malls to fitness centers at roadside hotels. (Lomma Enterprises, Inc.)

Below:
Magic Carpet Golf, 1968; Tucson; photograph 1982. Development pressures (in this case, in the form of residential expansion) often pose the same threat to miniature golf as they do to regulation golf links, drive-in theaters, and other low-density land uses at the urban fringe. (Author.)

While miniature golf has never again achieved the same level of public adulation that it did in its halcyon days at the beginning of the depression, the pint-size links still have a considerable following. Rising land values near urban centers—a factor that has led to the gradual disappearance of other wayside entertainments such as the drive-in theater—have claimed many older miniature golf courses as well. However, new links have sprung up not only in less-valuable locations, but in new places, such as the recreation halls of roadside "sports hotels" such as Holiday Inn's so-called Holidomes. Thus this most curious form of amusement does not seem to be in any immediate danger of extinction. As for the great-granddaddy of these reincarnations of Tom Thumb, high on Lookout Mountain, under the tall trees meandering through the rocks, one can barely make out the grades of the fairways of Carter's original course, which was finally demolished in 1958, four years after his death.

Site of Garnet Carter's first miniature golf course; Lookout Mountain near Chattanooga, Tennessee; photograph 1981. Traces of the fairways are still detectable around the large rock outcropping here. The site is now partially occupied by a basketball court. (Author.)

Drive-in Theaters

WHILE MOST roadside building types evolved gradually, the drive-in was deliberately invented. It took shape from a single prototype and—except for some technological improvements and minor variations in plan, construction, and decoration—has remained basically unchanged in form and function for half a century.

THE INVENTION

A do-it-yourself dream that blossomed into a multimillion-dollar industry, the drive-in was conceived by Richard M. Hollingshead, Jr., son of a New Jersey manufacturer. In the early 1930s, Hollingshead began experimenting with showing movies out-of-doors. By setting up a projector on his automobile hood and aiming it at his garage, he ingeniously combined two of the things that people were most reluctant to give up during the depression: cars and movies.[1] Seeing the commercial potential of his discovery, he further perfected the idea and was granted a patent for the invention in 1933.[2]

The patent covered all the basic elements still found in today's outdoor movie theaters: a location in a field "preferably by a highway," a screen facing the field and shielded by a large wind-resistant "screen house" (later called a screen tower), a series of inclined ramps radiating out in a semicircle around the screen, and a projection booth located at a suitable distance from the screen.

Hollingshead also outlined operational and technical details. After paying admission at a gateway, customers would drive to the first ramp with an unobstructed view of the screen. Sound would come from speakers mounted near the screen or located at various positions about the field, while the movie would be projected through a special funnel-shaped guard, which had air fanned through it constantly to keep the projection lens free from a buildup of insects.[3]

To put the patent into action, Hollingshead teamed up with his cousin Willis Warren Smith, who owned a chain of parking lots and thus had considerable experience in acquiring open fields that would eventually be blanketed with cars. They selected a site fronting Admiral Wilson Boulevard, a busy thoroughfare with a traffic volume of 125,000 cars a day, to be the home of the world's first alfresco cinema palace.[4] Besides its proximity to industrial Camden, the location had an added advantage—the potential to draw thousands of motor-borne theatergoers from nearby Philadelphia, where there was a ban on Sunday movies at that time.

The installation had a thirty-by-sixty-foot screen located twelve feet above the ground, in front of which curved seven rows of car ramps with a total capacity of four hundred cars. The sound system was developed by Camden-based RCA Victor and consisted of a cluster of speakers mounted on the screen tower. The whole complex cost about twenty-five thousand dollars to build, admission was twenty-five cents per car, plus twenty-five cents per person, up to a maximum of one dollar.[5]

The theater's opening on 6 June 1933 prompted a mixed response. *Architectural Forum* called it "an idea with a *Popular Science* smack to it."[6] *Popular Science* liked the way it turned one's car into a "private theater box."[7] And *Literary Digest* questioned "whether or not the public will be willing to exchange the intimacy of an indoor theater for the convenience of an outdoor one."[8]

Hollingshead formed a company, Park-In Theaters, that sold the right to use the drive-in concept to other investors for an initial fee of one thousand dollars plus 5 percent of gross receipts.[9] Under this arrangement, a second theater was built on Pico Boulevard in Los Angeles in

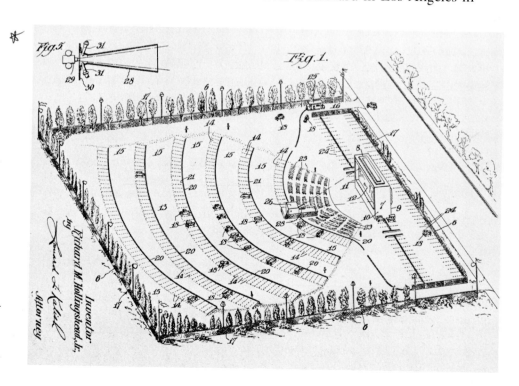

"Perspective View of an Outdoor Theater"; U.S. patent number 1,909,537; Richard M. Hollingshead, Jr.; filed 6 August 1932; patented 16 May 1933. A car entered the driveway (#16), passed through a "collection booth" (#25), drove to an empty "stallway" (#18) on one of the radiating ramps (#14), to watch a movie on a screen framed by the "screen house" (#7) and projected from a "projection booth" (#26). Figure 5 (top left) is the funnel-shaped guard to keep the lens free of insect buildups. The trees at the perimeter shielded the theater from outside view.

1934. A few years after its opening, an admiring writer in *Collier's* described this new place for Angelenos to act out their ever-growing passion for motorized living:

Out on Pico Boulevard we located drive-in service as it neared its peak. We drove in through a tollgate, a girl seated in a booth took money for tickets, and we entered the Drive-in Theater. An usher, bearing the badge of his office—a flashlight—jumped on the running board and guided the car to a space marked out with white chalk lines. We leaned back and watched the picture shown on the open-air screen. The usher lingered on to tell us:

"We can take around five hundred cars. . . . We run two shows a night. When it rains we shut down. Our big business is during the summer. The way we keep from disturbing people is by dividing the space in sections and taking the cars to one section at a time. Yes, we charge more than most of the neighborhood houses, but people seem willing to pay."[10]

Following the success of the Camden and Pico Boulevard theaters, the concept spread. More outdoor cinemas opened in the next few years, including those at Providence and Lynn, Massachusetts, in 1936, and Miami in 1937. However, by 1941 the number had risen to only about fifty units nationwide.[11]

Besides the general economic climate, what accounted for the slow initial growth? For one thing, it took a number of years to overcome opposition from indoor-theater owners. Threatened at first by the competition, these "hardtop" theater operators mounted a continuing public-relations campaign against the outdoor cinemas to scare away potential investors. Legal problems also helped retard development. Some owners, instead of buying a license from Park-In, chose to bypass the fee and simply build their own versions of the "ozoners," as they were called in the trade. A long court battle ensued, which dragged on for almost twenty years, and was never fully settled.[12]

This confusion over patent rights served at first to dampen investor enthusiasm, but as the conflict wore on, operators either paid their fee or just found a field, put up a screen, and took their chances. Also, by the

Below, left:
World's first drive-in theater, opened 6 June 1933; Camden, New Jersey; photograph c. 1933. (Theatre Collection, Free Library of Philadelphia.)

Below:
"California's First" drive-in theater, opening day in 1934; Pico Boulevard, Los Angeles. Screen tower, backboard, conventional billboard, and illuminated sign topped by a miniature streamlined auto all made a continuous sales pitch to passing motorists. (The Huntington Library).

"California's First"; Pico Boulevard, Los Angeles. Cars lining up for the opening. Note open-front supermarket, top left. (The Huntington Library.)

late 1930s, many hardtop theater operators began to disregard their own propaganda and invest in their own "eyesores" and "neckers' hangouts," as they had once referred to drive-ins. The number of drive-ins began to increase.

Other obstacles to early expansion stemmed from technical problems inherent in the original design. Perfecting the sound system, for example, was a great challenge. Because early drive-ins had the speakers located on the screen tower, the surrounding neighborhood often heard the sound-track along with the audience. Also, because sound travels more slowly than light, lip synchronization was a problem, especially for viewers in the back rows. To solve this dilemma, theater operators experimented with speakers placed between the cars, either in recesses dug into the ground and then covered by metal grates or on posts; but these systems required the driver to keep the window open for full volume, and the holes became filled with dirt and were hard to maintain. Ultimately a solution was reached by 1941—the in-car speaker with individual volume control.[13]

Picture difficulties accompanied the sound problems. Drive-in owners faced the same annoying problem that plagues anyone trying to set up a home slide show—when the projector is tilted up and the screen is vertical, the image becomes distorted. In order to eliminate this keystoning effect, by the 1940s screens began to be angled slightly downward.[14]

As might be expected, traffic presented problems. Inside the theater, ramp-design needed modification. The ramps in the original patent sloped in the rear but dropped off abruptly in front, forcing drivers to back up when exiting. This not only complicated circulation but created a safety hazard. The solution, also generally adopted in the 1940s, was a drive-over ramp, inclined in front as well as back to enable cars to exit forward.[15] *drive out/in* Also, drive-ins originally came under fire from highway authorities because the line of cars waiting to enter often backed up into the street, creating severe traffic tie-ups. As a result, shortly after the drive-over ramp appeared, so did long entrance roads that acted as vehicle-holding areas.[16]

Other changes helped to make a night at the drive-in more appealing. Owners added restrooms and snack bars, paved vehicle ways to cut down on dust, and sprayed insecticides around the perimeter of the premises to reduce the drive-in's greatest drawback—attacks by squadrons of hungry mosquitoes.

Cover, *Drive-In Theater Study, 1949.* Backed-up traffic was one of the problems that plagued early drive-ins and aroused the concern of highway officials. Consequently, owners modified designs to include larger holding areas for ticket lines. (*American Association of State Highway Officials.*)

THE POSTWAR DRIVE-IN BOOM

Thus, with most of these obstacles overcome and improvements in place, the concept of the drive-in theater basically was perfected about the same time the postwar boom got under way; whereas just a handful of the theaters had existed in 1946, more than 1,700 screen towers loomed over the roadside landscape by 1950.[17]

Why did millions of Americans by the late 1940s decide to take to the highway, pay a toll, and park in a darkened field to peer through their windshield at a movie? Observers in the theater industry offered multiple explanations. Most stressed the obvious appeal of the drive-in for families with young children—an abundant market after the war. By letting the *family at weekend* children fall asleep on the backseat, parents could spend an evening together without having to find a baby-sitter. Invalids and the handicapped could go to the movies without having to be transported up flights of steps and down the long corridors and narrow seat rows of a conventional theater. Viewers could munch on snacks, chatter to each other, and wander to restroom or concession stand without annoying other patrons. Moreover, there was no need to dress up. The same appealing come-as-you-are informality that attracted people to motels and drive-in restaurants lured them to drive-in theaters.[18]

Many of these observations were borne out by industry surveys. A study conducted by *Theatre Catalog* in Minneapolis in 1950 reported that

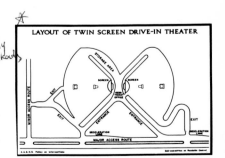

Twin screen layout, 1949. Multiple-screen drive-ins became popular in high-volume trade areas in the postwar period. (*American Association of State Highway Officials.*)

more than half of the patrons polled had children with them and that almost a third said that they attended only drive-ins.[19] This latter statistic supported the claim by the drive-in industry that drive-ins had the potential for reaching a so-called virgin market, a whole new audience who did not normally go to hardtop movie houses.

Drive-in owners experimented with many attractions in an effort to draw in this expanded market. Kiddie playgrounds, picnic benches, and swimming pools materialized in front of the screen towers and elsewhere on the theater grounds. One especially popular attention getter was the monkey village, a miniature zoo for monkeys plunked down in the theater complex. The 1950 *Theatre Catalog* devoted an entire page to such "villages," cautioning owners to "take good care of the lively animals," to "keep their houses continuously clean," and "to always bear in mind that visitors to the villages often became theater patrons."[20] The Miniature Train Company of Rensselaer, Indiana, claimed in trade-journal ads that its G-12 Streamliner "could be set up and operated anywhere by one man" and had the potential to increase the box-office take by one-third.[21] At the Cactus Drive In in Albuquerque, babies' bottles were warmed for free. Some drive-ins provided kennels, and a Memphis operator went so far as to install booths where customers could drop off the family wash, which would be cleaned, dried, and folded by the end of the show.[22]

To win over those customers who did not bring the kids, other attractions included shuffleboard courts, horseshoe pitching pits, even nightclubs built into the screen tower. However, many teenagers and adults had their own special reason for flocking to the drive-ins—a reason seldom acknowledged by the industry but much touted in the popular press—the chance to take a date to a dark and comfortable sanctuary, one that offered privacy without the social stigma of a lovers' lane, a perfect

Campus Drive-in, opened 1948; San Diego; photograph 1982. The unusual and evocative nighttime scene of hundreds of cars centered around a luminescent altar changes to an empty field of poles in daylight. (Author.)

spot for imitating the romance on the screen. *Literary Digest*, which in 1933 had wondered whether the public would exchange the "intimacy" of the indoor movie palace for the "convenience" of the drive-in, had missed an essential point. Drive-ins would become wildly popular because they provided a place for moviegoers to engage in activities other than watching the show. As the Pico usher interviewed by *Collier's* in 1938 mused: "You see, an auto's a lot more comfortable than a theater seat . . . we get an awful lot of couples. They like the privacy."[23]

Some drive-in owners were able to offer first-run movies, especially the larger theater chains such as Walter Reade or Loew's, which had added drive-ins to their already sizable collections of conventional movie houses. Most smaller operators, however, with less clout in the world of film distribution, often had to wait until a movie was shown in the local hardtop before it could be obtained for display outdoors. Instead of the latest movie, they offered their customers the opportunity to enjoy a novel experience: passing through a tollgate, gliding with headlights out through a dark maze of automobiles, mingling with other people at intermission, and then stealing back to one's own rubber-tired enclave, while seeing a second-run film.

From a design standpoint, the "interior" of the drive-in needed little embellishment; it sold itself. By daylight a field bristling with poles, lorded over by a big white square, the drive-in under the cover of darkness is transformed into an eerie and ghostly scene: hundreds of cars huddled around a huge luminescent screen glowing with gigantic moving images.

The exterior of the drive-in, however, presented a different problem. While the inside was hidden from view except in the evening, the outside was on twenty-four-hour display, and its appearance determined the public's first impression of the theater. Therefore, exterior surfaces were the logical place for the owner to invest in visual showmanship.

Not surprisingly, drive-in designers borrowed some of the dazzle of the downtown cinemas to make their roadside statement. However, for sources for their designs they usually passed over the fabled movie houses of the 1920s, often referred to by theater historians as the golden age of motion-picture-palace architecture. During this decade, audiences across the country were regaled with theaters ranging in style "from bewilderingly eclectic to near-perfect replicas of the finest royal palaces of Europe and the Orient [to] imitation wonders of the world from Mayan tombs to Babylonian hanging gardens. . . ."[24]

Yet baubles by the thousands added up to a considerable outlay. As the depression deepened in the early 1930s, cinema attendance declined and owners trimmed theater construction budgets accordingly. Designers faced the challenge of somehow perpetuating the sense of spectacle and visual excitement to which theatergoers had become accustomed without having the financial resources to create an elaborately detailed period setting. Consequently, by the late 1930s,[25] a whole new and equally interesting genre of movie theaters had emerged (one that eventually suggested solutions for the problem of what to do with the drive-in's roadside face).

Kent theater, built late nineteenth century, modernized 1948; East Greenwich, Rhode Island; photograph 1971, Richard Longstreth. The Hollywood Moderne styling typical of hardtop cinemas just before and after the war strongly influenced the design of drive-in theaters. (Richard Longstreth.)

White wall surfaces sculpted in Art Deco angles and streamlined curves and bathed in multicolored lights took the place of the elaborate exterior detailing of the previous era, while interiors began to exhibit innovative materials such as glistening mother-of-pearl Formica and sheets of etched translucent plastic. Many designers appeared to be enthusiastic about this new phase of theater architecture. For example, S. Charles Lee, a noted West Coast theater architect, ebulliently stated in 1941 that "the exterior of the theater of tomorrow will probably be more fantastic than the theater of yesterday. Lights will play an important part in the decoration and the staid old architecture designed to last 100 years will be abandoned in favor of a more spectacular display that will be reshaped about every 15 years."[26] By the end of the decade, dozens of downtown theaters across the country, from the Inwood in Dallas and the Esquire in Chicago to the modernized Wyo in Sheridan, Wyoming, sported a new look in cinema design that might be labeled Hollywood Moderne.

By the time the nation entered World War II, higher incomes and an increased need for psychological escape helped fill the movie houses again. After the Japanese surrender, however, the boom in theater attendance began to evaporate, and hardtop theater construction slowed to a trickle. Just the opposite was true with drive-in theaters. By this time, they were going up by the hundreds.

During this period of rapid expansion, some drive-in theater operators simply had a series of ramps bulldozed up, a screen tower slapped together out of telephone poles and plywood, and a projection house laid up in cinderblocks. Then they bought some speakers and a projector and opened for business. Others commissioned seasoned theater architects, such as Rapp and Rapp and S. Charles Lee himself, to design their drive-ins.[27] Still others hired the same sign companies responsible for the luminous displays on downtown and neighborhood movie houses to create roadside "eye appeal."

Many of the same techniques that imbued the local movie house with visual panache on a low budget were used in decorating the more elaborate of the ozoners. For example, by the late 1940s, facades of conventional movie theaters were being designed to function as giant illuminated advertisements extending sufficiently skyward to be seen from speeding cars as well as from the Main Street sidewalk. Similarly, the back of the drive-in screen tower, if visible from the highway, offered unlimited possibilities for catching the attention of motorists whizzing past. To increase its sales value to the theater owner, the tower was often accentuated with streamlined buttresses, stepped wing walls, and other eye-catching devices. Screen tower back panels were often enlivened with flamboyant displays featuring mimetic or regional images. The Rodeo Theater (1949) in Tucson, for example, boasted a cowgirl twirling a neon lasso; the Tropicaire in Miami (1949) had a giant planter filled with flood-lit live palm trees built on the tower; while San Diego's Campus Drive-in (1948) featured a gigantic cheerleader, still extant, brilliantly outlined in a neon kaleidoscope of colors. A wide range of exterior extravaganzas adorned other theaters. The Gratiot Drive-in (a one-thousand-car theater built at

Sidney Lust's Drive-in Theatre; c. 1948; George M. Peterson, architect; Beltsville, Maryland; photograph 1949. An excellent example of an early postwar drive-in, Sidney Lust's was built at a cost of $180,000 to accommodate one thousand cars. Sidney Lust's was located on the Route 1 approach strip at the urban fringe of metropolitan Washington, D.C. (National Archives.)

Same view of Sydney Lust's Drive-in Theatre; photograph 1971, Richard Longstreth. Pylons had been added to both sides of the screen tower when the screen was widened for Cinemascope in the 1950s. (Richard Longstreth.)

the outskirts of Detroit about 1948) sported an alluring visual tour de force. *Theatre Catalog* described the rear of its 115-foot-high screen tower shortly after opening day: "[It has] a triple cascade motif over which 1700 gallons of water are pumped each minute. The cascades are lighted from beneath in multi-colored patterns for a very pleasing and decorative effect. The iridescence of the tower has become the trademark of the theatre as it is now being used in the theatre's advertising."[28]

In Cowpens, South Carolina, the owners of the Cherry Hill Drive-in were concerned about providing full-time security for their theater, so they built their twelve-room home beneath the slanted supports of the screen tower. They then capitalized on this odd juxtaposition of uses by covering the front facade of the house with pillars and a roof; the result was a bizarre but certainly unforgettable hybrid composition: a plantation house with a screen tower growing out of its top.[29]

Besides the screen tower exterior, the second most important device for calling attention to the drive-in was the attraction board usually located near the edge of the highway. These double-sided signs, designed to catch the traffic from both directions, bore the illuminated name of the theater, a translucent message panel giving the name of the current show, and key selling phrases such as "Technicolor," "pony rides," "free diaper service," or other enticements. A smaller version of the image on the back of the screen tower was sometimes repeated on the board to attract still greater attention. Some theater designers went a step further and attached the attraction board to the screen tower, thereby giving the illusion of a conventional theater. In either case, by evoking the image of a theater marquee, the attraction board bestowed upon the drive-in the visual power of that universal symbol that automatically signals "movies."

*Screen tower of Gratiot Drive-in, c.
1948; Ted Rogvoy, architect; Roseville,
Michigan; photograph c. 1949.
Hundreds of Detroiters drove miles along
the Gratiot Avenue taxpayer strip to the
outer reaches of the metropolitan area
just to marvel at the astonishing sight of
a waterfall cascading down the back of a
giant movie screen. Today the waterfall
no longer flows, but the pumping equipment is still intact. (Community
Theatres.)*

In 1950 the government finally approved depreciation schedules specific
to the industry, making ozoners an even more attractive investment. Previously, drive-in equipment, which deteriorated rapidly from being outside, was depreciated at the same rate as its sheltered counterparts in the
conventional theater. After this boost to the drive-in boom, expansion was
slowed momentarily in 1951 when nonessential construction was banned
during the Korean conflict.[30] But a year later, this prohibition was lifted,
and the boom reignited. During the same decade, Cinemascope came into
vogue and operators began to install much wider screens. Often this was
accomplished in existing drive-ins by tacking on supports to either side of
the older screen towers and then nailing an expansive new screen across
the front of the old one. Today many original screens from the 1940s and
early 1950s can be found perfectly preserved, buried under the furring
strips and asbestos mill board used in the conversions.

Interior of Gratiot Drive-in, showing original screen; photograph c. 1949. (Community Theatres.)

The drive-in's growing popularity, and the changeover to Cinemascope, also had a marked effect on new theater design in the mid-1950s. Since by now the public was well conditioned to attending drive-ins, and because the switch to Cinemascope was expensive, owners were less inclined to spend money on architectural detailing and advertising spectacles. Operators relied increasingly on prefabricated screen towers, which had a visual persona similar to the back of a roadside billboard. Although

Side elevation of Gratiot Drive-in, screen tower; photograph 1982. A visual textbook on the history of drive-in theater screens, left to right, includes the original screen tower, c. 1948; Cinemascope screen, c. 1950s; and a prefabricated screen, 1962. The fourth screen, set perpendicular at right, was also prefabricated; it was installed recently, when the theater was divided into several smaller cinemas. (Author.)

Above:
Bellwood Drive-in Theatre, c. 1948;
Michael DeAngelis, architect; Richmond,
Virginia; photograph 1971, Richard
Longstreth. But for the screen tower, the
attraction board was the most important
device for luring motorists into the the-
ater. (Richard Longstreth.)

Above, right:
Fast Food, c. 1960; Route 9, near Glens
Falls, New York; photograph 1981. So
powerful was the attractive force of the
image of the drive-in theater screen tower
that it was exploited by the builders of
this fast-food stand. (Author.)

some custom-built, highly decorated theaters were still constructed, many less-than-inspiring operations built of prefabricated components relied on the deep-rooted popularity of the drive-in, coupled with the information on the attraction board, to lure customers in.

THE DECLINE

After reaching a peak in popularity in 1958, drive-in theaters have since entered a period of gradual decline. Competition from television is often cited as the cause for the ozoners' slow disappearance, but statistics do not totally support this claim. Between 1954 and 1963, banner years for the television invasion into the nation's living rooms, the number of conventional movie theaters decreased by 38 percent. Drive-ins, on the other hand, reached their climax in 1958, and only decreased in number by 12.5 percent by 1963.[31] Thus television initially hurt downtown and neighborhood movie houses far more than outdoor theaters. However, in the 1970s, when a home without a television was as rare as a suburban family without a car, shopping-center cinemas multiplied along the nation's Miracle Miles, causing the number of hardtop theater screens to rebound nearly to their 1954 level, while the number of ozoners continued to decline.

What, then, has caused the drive-in to take a place on the endangered-species list? Certainly the novelty of using the car as an outdoor theater box had begun to dull by the mid-1960s. This gave rise to a spate of new gimmicks, as owners attempted to resuscitate the nation's love affair with open-air movie viewing. In Albuquerque a drive-in called the Autoscope was built in 1963 (only to close a few years later) in which movies were projected via mirrors to a battery of three-by-five-foot television-like screens, one located in front of each car.[32] Back East in Brattleboro, Vermont, an enterprising operator built a motel within full view of his drive-

Drive-in theater, c. 1970; Madera, California; photograph 1982. Recent drive-in construction has been pared down to the bare essentials. (Author.)

Cactus Drive In Theatre; Albuquerque; photograph 1982. Opened in 1947, this theater was demolished the year after the photograph was taken. (Author.)

in theater. Each room was outfitted with a speaker, offering customers the option of driving in or "lying in."[33]

However, even more fundamental problems vexed the industry. For instance drive-ins have always been plagued with inherent physical limitations. In most parts of the country, running a drive-in is a seasonal business. Efforts to keep theaters open in inclement weather—including using

Citrus Heights Drive-in, aerial view; U.S. Route 40 near Sacramento, California; photograph c. 1960. U.S. Route 40 in back of the screen is now Interstate 80; old U.S. Route 40 can be seen in the lower right-hand corner. Already being encroached upon by urban expansion here, the theater was eventually sold for development. (Steve Levin.)

in-car heaters, rain shields, even roofs (so that they became like hardtop theaters with autos for theater seats)—could not alter the adverse impact of this fundamental operating restriction.

Then there is the problem of decaying physical plants. By the 1970s, many drive-ins were twenty years old, or older. Often constructed hastily in the first place, a good number were simply wearing out from deferred maintenance, constant exposure to the weather, and vandalism. Also, the nation's declining birthrate meant fewer children, previously a cherished drive-in mainstay, so many theaters switched over to X-rated films.

However, probably the most important single factor in the downfall of the drive-ins is that the spreading cities absorbed what were once the older approach strips of the 1930s, 1940s, and 1950s. Land became increasingly valuable, and zoning laws gradually caught up with the drive-in—often making it more difficult to obtain permission to build new theaters, while successful theaters were frequently hard pressed to find room for expansion. Even if a drive-in managed to remain reasonably profitable, its value as a theater was often outweighed by the site's potential for more intensive development.

As a result, the drive-in has joined other traditional large recreational land uses at the city's edge—the small private airport, golf course, amusement park—as a prime candidate for subdivisions. Where once hundreds of cars could be seen by night eerily encircled about a glowing image, there are now office buildings, condominiums, and shopping malls. In areas where patronage has declined and land values have not risen, many drive-ins have simply been abandoned, leaving the ghostly hulk of a screen tower as a symbol of mid-twentieth-century America's passion for the automobile.

Attraction board, Salisbury Drive-in; Salisbury Beach, Massachusetts; photograph 1980. (Author.)

Motels

*E*ACH EVENING thousands of travelers perform a familiar roadside ritual—looking for a place to spend the night. For those preferring the predictable, a free phone call is all that is needed to make sure that an air-conditioned, plush-carpeted, brand-name highway hotel room, identical to the one stayed in the night before, awaits at the destination. For the more adventurous, a huge assortment of other sanctuaries-for-hire lie along the highway—from motel rooms with boomerang-shaped furniture and televisions in space-age cabinets to tourist cabins replete with knotty-pine homeyness—where motorists might find either a pleasant bargain or occasionally spend the night in a sagging bed covered in cigarette-burned blankets, awakened by the roar of an ailing air conditioner. Nevertheless, each wayside hostelry, whether standardized or full of surprises, is a clue to the evolution of an essential yet fascinating species of <u>twentieth-century commercial architecture.</u>

FROM FREE CAMP TO PAY CAMP

Obviously most busy highways did not always lead past a lineup of Holiday Inns, Motel 6s, and Kozy Kabins. In fact at the beginning of the century, pioneering auto tourists had few places along the open road where they could rent a room after a long day's drive. Occasionally they came across wayside inns, relics of coaching days that survived the railroad; but for the most part, motor travelers wishing to spend the night nestled in the sheets of an actual bed had little recourse other than ending the day in a community large enough to support a hotel.

<u>The downtown hotel, with its easy access to the railroad station, had long been indispensable to train travelers.</u> For tired, dust-covered motorists in need of a few hours' sleep before setting out on the road the next morning, however, parading through dingy commercial-house lobbies was not always a pleasant prospect. There they could expect to encounter the

Orndorff Hotel; Tucson; photograph c. 1910. After a long day's drive, early auto tourists could stay either at a down-town hotel, as would travelers arriving by train, or simply camp by the side of the road for free. Eager to attract motor-ists, the owners of this older hostelry placed a sign out front (far left) declar-ing: "We will house your auto for one dollar a day." (Arizona Historical Society.)

Below, left:
Tin can tourist camp; Florida; postcard view c. 1920. (Lars H. Rolfsen).

Below, right:
Camp Nebraska entrance gate; central portion, 1925; office wings, c. 1928; Nebraska Avenue, Tampa, Florida; pho-tograph 1984. This rare example of an early auto-tourist camp began as an au-toist's campsite about 1918 and was con-verted to a cabin camp (some of the early cabins are still standing) in the mid-1920s. Today Camp Nebraska is a park-ing ground for recreational vehicles. (Author.)

unsavory gaze of cigar-chewing salesmen or, in hotels with higher preten-sions, the scrutiny of their manners, clothing, and baggage.

Consequently, a growing number of autoists began to exercise the new freedom to stop the car and get out any place along the route that had been lacking in railroad travel. They brought camping gear, found an attractive spot along the roadside at day's end, pitched a tent, lit a fire, and then slept in their own makeshift camp.[1]

This spontaneous and ad hoc solution for securing a free night's rest along the wayside generally worked smoothly until after World War I, when what had been a trickle of tourists grew into a deluge. Landowners began to object to the litter; pollution; destruction of crops, fences, and foliage; and invasion of privacy that inevitably resulted from the unregu-lated use of the roadside for free accommodation. Soon barbed wire and "no trespassing" signs greeted campers at favorite overnight spots.

A TIN CAN TOURIST CAMP, FLORIDA.

Fortunately for motor campers, local business interests usually took the opposite view. They reasoned that if swarms of auto tourists could be persuaded to stay nearby, then campers would be likely to eat in local restaurants and shop in the stores along Main Street. Before long, dozens of communities started building municipal tourist camps where visitors could set up house. Often situated in city parks or vacant land near downtown business districts, these new installations offered campsites, parking, and sanitary facilities—usually at no cost to the guests. As *Harper's* recounted a decade later, in 1933: "By day dusty sedans, piled high with pots and pans and tired children and khaki bedding rolls, moved over the roads; at nightfall . . . they tented on trampled grass, where naked municipal spigots rose from the ground and yesterday's newspapers rustled in the wind, where the travelers themselves, sitting on running boards, swapped road lore and boasted of their mileage."[2]

The camps became exceedingly popular, for tourists now had the security and reassurance of a comfortable destination where they could gas up the car or browse at local stores, all for the same price as sleeping in an open field. The camps also became the object of considerable local pride. For years railroad stations had served as the principal gateways for communities. Now, along with the depot, free tourist camps formed a traveler's first impression of a town—an impression that would spread rapidly by word of mouth along the auto-camping circuit.

American Tourist Camp; Henderson, North Carolina; photograph c. 1930. Once municipal camps began imposing fees, private campgrounds proliferated along highways coast to coast, offering guests inexpensive tent sites or the comfort of cabins. This particular establishment rented camp space for $.30 and cabins from $1.25 to $2.50 a night. (Library of Congress.)

Competition heated up between neighboring towns as each strived to build the most popular motor camp. Communities added scores of extra conveniences—including picnic tables, fireplaces, flush toilets, showers, sheltered eating and recreation areas, even electrical hookups—and then proclaimed these inducements on signs placed along roads leading into town. By 1922 the U.S. Chamber of Commerce estimated that more than one thousand of these town commons for transient travelers had been built from coast to coast.[3]

Despite initial enthusiasm from both tourists and community boosters, the heyday of free municipal auto camps was suprisingly short lived. By mid-decade, with thousands of low-priced cars on the market, everyone from office clerks to factory workers was now able to pack the family in a flivver and take to the open road. Ever on the lookout for ways to see the most on a meager budget, hoards of these <u>new tourists</u> descended on the municipal campgrounds with their free accommodations. At the same time, affluent and middle-class motor travelers—those guests that towns had sought to attract in the first place—<u>began to forsake the public lodging grounds</u>, for after a long day's drive, they were never sure with whom they might be spending the night. Municipal officials also became concerned over who might roll into town and set up house on any given evening.

<u>Many of these fears and apprehensions were grounded solely in class prejudices,</u> and the majority of camp guests were still by and large responsible and law abiding. Nevertheless the auto tourists were not without an unsavory element, <u>an underclass of motorized transients vividly depicted by Frank Brimmer,</u> author of books on auto camping, in *The Magazine of Business* in 1927: "These 'white gypsies,' foraging farmers' crops, stealing like real gypsies, have placed an odium upon many otherwise wholesome camps. The out-of-work workers, the gasoline bums, the pay-as-you-go fellows, the hard-luck kids, and a small but troublesome proportion of downright criminals, all but ruined some fine camps."[4]

Town fathers explored ways to discourage those they deemed undesirable from using their camps. Some tried requiring visitor registration on the theory that campers with something to hide would go elsewhere. However, the most often used remedy for weeding out undesired guests, as well as helping fund upkeep of facilities, was to charge a fee.

The decision to make tourists rent their campsites had more far-reaching consequences than originally intended. Ironically, by conditioning travelers to expect to pay for a place to pitch their tent, municipal-camp operators provided incentive for private competition, eventually causing their own downfall. Highway-side homeowners began converting spare bedrooms into guest rooms, while farmers and landowners seized the chance to set up their own campgrounds and cash <u>in on the many motorists only slightly more enthusiastic about stealing through someone's living room in a "tourist home" than parading about the lobby of a hotel. Soon fields across the continent bloomed with a new cash crop—the tourists, cars, campfires, and tents of thousands of new private campgrounds.</u>

By the late 1920s, even some of the most successful municipal tourist

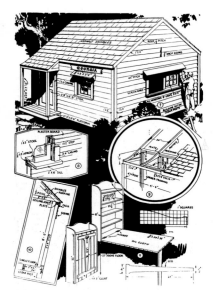

How to build "Tourist Cabins That Get the Business," Popular Mechanics, July 1935. Armed with do-it-yourself plans and a modest sum of money, any reasonably skilled handyman could whip up a brood of cabins and start his own motor court. Note the homebuilt oilcloth-covered fold-out table, a good example of the way courters furnished first-generation cabins on a tight budget.

THE NEW TYPE OF RESIDENTIAL AREA.

camps, such as Overland Park in Denver, felt the effects of the new competition. Opened in 1915, this park sprawled over 160 acres and had facilities for up to two thousand auto campers. After a steady increase in
patronage through the early 1920s, the park's guest count began to plum-
met, even though tourism continued to rise in the state during the same
period. Frank Brimmer cited the opening nearby of more than fifty pri-
vately owned camps as the reason for the decline.[5]

Some of these new private camps were substantial business ventures;
Camp Grande in El Paso offered tourists campsites at fifty cents a day
and rental tents already pitched for one dollar. Campers could park their
cars and set up their tents under a long log shed called "rustic row" for a
dollar fifty. The camp also boasted a grocery, laundry, bakery, barber-
shop, gasoline station, and telegraph and post office. In 1926 alone, Camp
Grande served 172,000 campers arriving in forty-three thousand automobiles.[6] Most private tourist camps, however, began on a much humbler
scale.

As more and more campgrounds dotted the roadside landscape, competition within the fledgling industry grew even more heated, and operators
were forever on the lookout for ways to snare passing tourists. Discovering that travelers were willing to pay additional money for more perma-

*Vermonter cabins; vicinity of Benning-
ton, Vermont; photograph c. 1947, Robert L. Weichert. In the open countryside,
where broad road frontage was affordable, courters arranged their villages of
cabins to attract the most attention possible when seen from a passing car. In this
case, guests could sprawl in their lawn
chairs and gaze at a free, and soon to be
virtually extinct, attraction—the sight of
a farmer plowing by horse. (Weichert-
Isselhardt Collection.)*

nent yet completely private accommodations, owners began providing cabins for rent as an alternative to tent sites.

First-generation campground cabins were usually rudimentary affairs—wooden enclosures with screened openings, often without furniture. Campers usually supplied their own bedding. A description of the tourist cabins built in Tallahassee in 1925 by self-styled "tin can tourist" Gilbert Chandler shows what was conjured up on a low budget with a high degree of improvisation: "The cabins and rooms were ceiled inside with ordinary pink building paper and painted outside with yellow ochre. . . . The cabins were then furnished with home-made tables and benches and were wired for electricity. We did not have to furnish beds and stoves as tourists who stopped at the camps carried these articles with them. Our place was considered a very modern tourist camp in those boom days of Florida."[7] Guests generally appreciated the convenience of cabins, despite their home-crafted appearance, over the annoyance of tents. Cabins did not have to be lugged around in the car and pitched each night. They were more watertight, resistant to wind and storms, and slightly more like a hotel room, yet they offered the privacy and inexpensiveness of a tent.

Site, background
prolific

THE MOTOR COURT

Given the popularity of the cabins and the fact that more rent could be charged and for more seasons of the year, by the late 1920s many operators stopped providing tent sites altogether and began offering motorists accommodations housed exclusively in cabins. A new term suddenly found its way into the lexicon of wayside commerce—"cabin camp."

This term, however, proved to be relatively short lived. By the early

English Village East; Indian Head, New Hampshire; postcard c. 1940. The quaint cottage was one of the most commonly exploited images for motor-court cabins. The owners of this well-kept lineup of what they advertised as "Deluxe English Village Bungalows" in the White Mountains, wooed potential guests with individual flower gardens and the promise of a cozy night by the fire. (Miriam Trementozzi.)

1930s, with the transition from tent camp to cabin camp virtually completed, the term "camp," which was still associated in the public's mind with run-down lots full of auto gypsies, was generally dropped in favor of the word "court." This term better defined the little hamlets of cabins, and it connoted enclosure and safety—a respectable enclave. A wide array of prefixes for "court" began appearing on signboards across the country, giving rise to such names as cabin court, cottage court, tourist court, and apartment court. And owners became known in the trade as "courters."

Along with the rhetorical transformation from camp to court came many physical changes. Moving away from the haphazard assemblages of tents and cabins, court layouts now tended to result more from thoughtful planning. To attract the most attention possible, courters arranged their cabins far enough back from the road so as to appear private and quiet, yet close enough to be as visible as possible from the highway. On rural plots with broad road frontage, cabins were often stretched out in long U-shaped, crescent-shaped, or in-line rows parallel to the road, to have maximum visual impact when noticed from the window of a speeding car.

In more populated areas with higher land values, courters had to settle for sites with narrower road frontages. There, more land efficient, in-line rows perpendicular to the road, and tighter versions of the U- and L-shaped plans, came into favor. In either case, placement of internal roads and parking places demanded almost as much thought as did the location of the cabins. An obvious pathway leading from highway to office to cabin-side parking place was widely regarded as an essential visual cue for guiding motorists into the court.

Along with layout, exterior imagery became an extremely important factor in enticing guests. Courters had their establishments clothed in

Mission Courts Hotel, c. 1935; between Dallas and Fort Worth; photograph 1942. This court, replete with Mission Revival costumery calculated to evoke an image of old Texas, caught the interest of Farm Security Administration photographer Arthur Rothstein a month after the bombing of Pearl Harbor. The U-shaped continuous guest-room structure forming a courtyard with an office (here disguised as a mission in miniature) strategically located at the entrance, became a popular motor-court layout for small sites with narrow road frontages during the interwar years. (Library of Congress.)

many of the same sales costumes other roadside businesses at the time found fashionable, with domestic architecture being the most common source of exterior imagery. In contrast to the scattering of tentlike enclosures of the cabin camps, motor courts began to take on the look of tidy villages of miniature cottages, often decorated with low-cost embellishments from wooden-picket gable sunbursts to shutters and window boxes, and surrounded by landscaped grounds sprinkled with trellises, plantings, and lawn furniture.[8] To further drive home the image of safe, comfortable informality, owners often christened their courts with names such as U Like Um Cabins, Kozy Kourt, and Para Dice.

Regionally evocative sales costumes also grew in popularity. Dozens of courts were crafted to look like tepees, missions, adobe huts, or log cabins. Names such as Wigwam or Alamo, coupled with regionally stereotypical plantings—palm trees in the South, cacti in the West—helped to assure that each illusion-by-the-roadside conformed to the travel-poster image of a particular locale. Mission Village Auto Court, begun in 1929 to cater to the thousands of tourists traveling each day between Los Angeles and the Pacific beaches, is an excellent case in point. Founded by author and producer Robert E. Callahan, the village consisted not only of seventy-two "pueblos and cottages typical of the old days" but also a substantial sideshow, the Historic '49 Hangtown Museum, which, as *Tourist Court Journal* reported in 1938, contained "an antique bar, 12,000 horse shoes, Indian relics, old wagon wheels and historic remembrances" assembled to give guests a flavor of "Old California" while "only twenty minutes from downtown Los Angeles."[9] Still other court owners disregarded cozy cottages and regional stereotypes in favor of a kaleidoscope of themes designed purely to attract attention: miniature windmills, dwarf-size villages, and a host of other fantasy motifs.

Court owners frequently lavished the most visual attention on the focal point of the cabin ensemble, a building, larger than all the rest, containing an office and the owner's living quarters. Usually located near the road in front of the cabins to serve as gateway between highway and lodging, this structure was commonly designed to emphatically communi-

Windmill Motor Court, 1928; Shelburne, Vermont; photograph c. 1935, L. L. McAllister. Casting the motor-court office in the image of a windmill poised in front of an arc of tidy cabins was a well-used exterior sales trick. (University of Vermont Special Collections.)

cate a court's particular selling theme—hence the biggest tepee in the camp, the windmill in the windmill motor court. Sometimes the muffled form of an old house could be detected underneath the sales gimmicks, revealing to the keen-eyed passerby that today's cabin village was often yesterday's farmstead.

Once lured onto the premises and officially registered at the office, each motorist-turned-guest was now ready to unlock the most important selling point of every court—the cabin interior, the feature that would determine the long-term reputation of the business. By the early 1930s, the amenities contained within the four walls of the motor-court cabin represented a considerable advance in comfort over the bare-bones appointments of the cabin camp of a few years before. Crude bunks and Spartan furnishings gave way to more commodious accommodations. Real beds, dressers, desks, rugs, lamps, pictures—even if castaways from the owner's house or purchased secondhand—helped make cabins feel less like camp and more like a guest's own bedroom. Even as early as 1927, for example, visitors to Harry L. Wood's trendsetting El Colorado motor tourist camp, built in 1927 in Manitou Springs, Colorado, to catch the lucrative Pikes Peak tourist trade, discovered "a comfortable living-room well furnished . . . ceilings . . . beamed with lodge-pole pine . . . a kitchenette with an electric stove and an attractive corner which serves as a dining-room . . . electric lights, shower and toilet [and a] sanitary garbage can . . . sunk into the ground just outside the rear door."[10] Thousands of other motor courts regaled their guests with comparable appointments, and by the mid-1930s the transition from a place to camp out to home-away-from-home was virtually complete.

By 1933 the thirty thousand "tourist cottage and camp establishments" then estimated by the American Automobile Association to line the nation's highways represented a stirring new presence along the open road. In fact as the decade approached its midpoint, the site of these "curious little broods of frame and log and adobe shacks with their Mother Goose and their Chic Sale[11] architecture"[12] (as one observer in *Fortune* called them) drew a good measure of national attention. In 1933 John J.

*Branding Iron Motel; Laramie, Wyo-
ming; photograph c. 1975, Richard
Longstreth. By the late 1930s, the curvilinear motifs of the Streamline Moderne
had been added to the visual vocabulary
of the motor court. (Richard Longstreth.)*

McCarthy and Robert Littell, writing for *Harper's*, even went so far as to
make a most prophetic prediction, not to come true for another half a
century, that the motor court was a form of highway folk craft worthy of
serious study: "Before it is too late, someone with a camera and a passion
for Americana should motor about the country collecting material for a
monograph on the architecture of the tourist camps, courts, cottages of
the early 1930's."[13]

Along with the quaint architecture, all this new construction and the
apparent economic success it represented during the depression intrigued
many contempory observers. Unlike miniature golf, which fizzled soon
after a meteoric beginning, the motor-court industry appeared to be an

*Guest accommodations, Colonial Hotel
Courts; New Orleans; postcard c. 1940.
Motor-court appointments, by the dawn
of World War II, had changed dramatically from the homemade furnishings of
only a few years earlier. While this court
was advertised under the powerfully selling watchword "colonial," each room—
with its streamlined metal furniture, bed
with Simmons Innerspring Mattresses,
casement windows, venetian blinds, telephone, steam heat, and air-condition-
ing—was quintessentially modern.
(Kathlyn Hatch.)*

economic phenomenon that could thrive in hard times, bolstered by the millions who discovered that riding the highways provided low-cost diversion. The Federal Housing Administration also aided the business by liberalizing its regulations in the mid-1930s to permit the financing of cottages under two thousand dollars with no down payment.[14] *Harper's* summed it up in 1933 by declaring the "Three Hundred Thousand Shacks" lining the nation's roadsides a new American industry—"one of the few features of the American landscape that the depression is causing to grow by leaps and bounds."[15]

While roadside lodging appeared more immune from economic hardship than many other sectors of the economy, the industry was still susceptible to the general spirit of the times with the pressure to cast aside older visual metaphors in favor of Moderne and Modern imagery. As with other types of wayside enterprise, this shift was no accident; nor did it come about merely by osmosis. Motor-court owners were barraged with the same campaign to modernize that was launched for other budding wayside businesses from auto showrooms and gas stations to supermarkets.

One source of this chorus of advice to modernize the motor court was the architectural profession. As the depression deepened, architectural magazines began exhorting their often unemployed constituency not to overlook motor courts when they foraged for new commissions. As early as 1933, *Architectural Record*, for example, declared that "the construction of 'shacks' for autoists has been the single growing and highly active division of the building industry during the depression years."[16] In 1935 the same publication featured modern designs for "Tourist Cabins" in a portfolio of special building types.[17]

While some architects succeeded in gaining commissions in an industry dominated by homegrown and contractor design, an even more effective medium for directly encouraging masses of courters to think modern was publications such as the *Tourist Court Journal*. From its inaugural in 1937, this new trade organ featured scores of articles advising court owners to modernize their establishments. The journal's consulting architect, E. H. Lightfoot, for example, regularly reminded readers to shun windmills and miniature missions in favor of a more modern aesthetic: "Regardless of where a court is erected it should be built of stucco with a sand finish, using modern architecture with its attractive simplicity and simple lines, and be painted pure white."[18] Its pages also overflowed with other scraps of advice, including testimonials by courters on the virtues of updating their operations, with titles such as "The Motor Court Moderne."[19]

Before long the effects of this campaign to modernize the motor court began to appear along the highway. Although courters continued to build villages of quaint cabins in large numbers until the early 1950s, domestic, regional, and fantastic imagery gradually gave way to motifs of somewhat higher-style origin. By the late 1930s, the Streamline Moderne with its curvilinear windows and rounded corners, and the International Style—unornamented flat-roofed cubes with corner windows—began to appear in the design of motor courts around the country.

During this same period, motor-court interiors underwent a similar transformation, encouraged to no small degree by depression-weary manufacturers who discovered that each of the thousands of cabins lining the American roadside was a potential showcase for their wares. Makers of beds, blankets, chairs and bathtubs wooed court owners with advertising and discounts so their items might be put on display and tried out by thousands of overnight guests. At the same time, the more enterprising court owners, eager to maintain a competitive edge, cooperated by snapping up large quantities of everything from innerspring mattresses and coin-operated radios to deluxe bathrooms with sunken tubs and hot and cold running water. As *Business Week* marveled in 1940:

To producers of building construction materials, linen, plumbing fixtures, furniture, and electrical equipment, the auto courts represent a new and steadily growing market. Their total investment in furniture runs to about $50,000,000 and in plumbing and bath fixtures about $37,000,000. They use 560,000 beds and mattresses (403,200 of them innerspring), 245,000 gas stoves, and over 100,000 fans. So attractive are sales opportunities that such big suppliers as Simmons Co. (mattresses) are creating special divisions to service the auto courts.[20]

While the Chicago, New York, and other World's Fairs are often recognized as the most effective marketplaces of modernism of the 1930s, the power of the motor-court room in transmitting the message "buy modern" during the same period should not be underestimated. After spending the night in one of these tiny, roadside exhibition centers, experiencing in the present what their own houses could be like in the future, a number of guests undoubtedly replaced their own old metal bedsprings with innerspring mattresses, and their claw-foot bathtubs with sleek sunk-in models—to the benefit of manufacturers and court owners alike. Only a few years before, motor courts had edged out cabin camps by providing all the comforts of home. Now "more than the comforts of home" became an industry slogan.

Consumers amply rewarded this investment and constant improvement. By the end of the decade, the motor court had done more than supplant cornfield campgrounds—the maturing industry was beginning to pry an increasing amount of business away from the very institution that since the advent of the railroad had had an undisputed grip on the lodging industry—the hotel. In 1937 the results of an American Automobile Association survey showed that 61 percent of the traveling public used hotels, 12.5 percent stopped at motor courts, while 22.5 percent stayed at tourist homes. By 1939 the courts' share of the market had jumped to 26 percent, while the hotels' declined to 46 percent.[21]

Industry publications cited a number of recurring reasons why an ever-increasing number of travelers preferred motor courts. Travel-weary guests could register and retreat to their cabin without being observed by other guests in the lobby, elevators, or corridors; and the car was parked just a few steps from the cabin. No regiment of tip-hungry help needed reckoning with. The motor-court cabins afforded cross ventilation, while most hotel rooms had only a single window. Well-sited motels were generally quiet, while dense traffic noise penetrated city hotels by day, and often rowdy conventioners disturbed guests at night. Also, many people feared hotel fires; courts with their individual cabins provided for a quicker escape. Finally, the courts were generally cheaper. As one salesman from Rocky Ford, Colorado, summed it up: "The motor court of today has everything a good hotel has, with free garage, no tipping—also more privacy."[22]

Underlying these practical considerations was the more subtle, psychological appeal of the motor court. The little cabins offered individual housing in a minisuburban setting—enabling depression-era city dwellers to rent a freestanding, grass-surrounded dream cottage for a night or two. Once more the car, that most cherished possession, could come along too. Decentralized, modern, and outside the confines of the traditional city, in many ways the new lodging places may well have heightened in millions of Americans the desire to live in little houses set back from the road on a broad lawn—a dream that turned to reality in postwar suburban America.

Faced with the motor court's growing popularity, old-guard hotel owners met the roadside newcomers threatening their livelihood much like service-store owners attacked supermarkets, and theater operators did drive-ins. They lobbied for legal restrictions to hobble the upstart industry and helped put forth, at any convenient opportunity, the image that motor courts were illegitimate businesses that existed for one-room-for-an-hour love-nest income rather than respectable places to bring the family. They also made vain attempts to incorporate motor-court features into their operations—such as providing guest parking in nearby garages and then having large signs reading "motor hotel" mounted on their roofs.

Despite these efforts, although the largest big-city convention hotels continued to thrive, the motor-court boom helped to drive hundreds of smaller, older (and shabbier) hotels to ruin. As early as 1933, *Harper's* was already predicting: "The Commercial Houses, the Railroad Hotels down by the switching yards, where lonely drummers chew cigars in fetid lobbies, are so infinitely more dreary than even the second-rate tourist cabins that no motorist who has learned the simplicity and cheapness of Camp Joy or U Wanna Kum Back will even go near such hotels as these again."[23]

FROM MOTOR COURT TO MOTEL

The outbreak of World War II suddenly dampened the motor-court takeover, although only temporarily. With gasoline rationed and automobile production curtailed, millions returned to riding trains and rapid transit. Hotels, with their centralized locations convenient to public transportation, swarmed with businessmen and military personnel. Many motor courts did not generally fare as well. Along with a good number of service stations and roadside restaurants such as Howard Johnson's, some courts in isolated locations closed their doors during the war years. A few more-fortunate establishments, especially those near defense plants and

Above:
A&E Motel; Lexington Park, Maryland; photograph 1980. (Author.)

Above, right:
A&E Motel; Beltsville, Maryland; photograph 1981. By the postwar years, concrete block and brick became as common as clapboard and stucco; utilitarian and functional imagery began edging out the quaint and the streamlined; long, attached buildings triumphed over individual cabins; and the term "motor court" lost favor to the name "motel." (Author.)

military installations, swelled with dependent families and defense workers. But when the war was over, the roadside lodging industry quickly revived, and the gradual gains that had been made by motor courts in luring business from hotels before the conflict, now turned into a rout.

Along with continued success came many changes in the maturing industry. During the postwar period, for example, the word "court" rapidly lost favor to the term "motel." Credit for the invention of "motel"—a contraction of "motorist hostel" or "motor hotel"—is generally given to West Coast architect Arthur S. Heineman, designer of an establishment called the "Milestone Motels," which opened in San Luis Obispo, California, in 1925.[24] After the war, the industry rallied around the more-modern-sounding term, which had been used occasionally during the motor-court era of the 1930s, and the word, emblazoned in neon, became an increasingly common sight along the roadside by the late 1940s.

During the postwar years, motor courts changed in appearance as well as in name. Individual cabins, each with its own plumbing and furnace, slipped from fashion as single buildings comprising a string of rooms, less costly to construct, gained in favor. These long, low structures, like the individual cabins that had preceded them, were often laid out parallel to the highway in straight lines, V shapes, or crescents to attract maximum attention. On sites with narrow road frontages, owners had to settle for less-visible structures arranged perpendicular to the road and rely on bold, bright, inviting signs to lead customers in.

During the same period, architectural costumery changed along with layout. Charming cottages and little tepees began to fall from vogue, as did the sleek, curving forms of the Streamline Moderne. Instead more and more new postwar motels, in response to building-material shortages and the growing influence of Modern architectural prescriptions, exhibited the same bare-bones, stripped-down utilitarian functionalism that influenced the design of other roadside businesses. After enduring years of pent-up demands during depression and war, people no more needed architectural theatrics to lure them to motels than they did to lure them into gas stations or supermarkets. An illuminated sign with the word "motel," coupled with some neon lighting along the eaves of the building, was usually enough to keep business flowing in.

The extent to which a dash of electronic wizardry ordered up from a local sign company could transform even the plainest motels into dazzling nighttime roadside spectacles was vividly depicted by journalist Bernard DeVoto in 1953: "Neon tubes stripe the front . . . outline its eaves and gables, and frequently frame the windows as well. Columns of neon, six to twenty-four inches through, three to ten feet high, stand before the suburb's proudest establishments. Some are floodlighted in addition and none is too humble to possess a flashing sign in blue, orange, crimson and green. The tourist closes the Venetian blinds, turns out the lights . . . and may still read the Gideon Bible without eyestrain."[25] As competition increased and the novelty wore thin by the mid-1950s, many motel de- signers followed the trend toward Exaggerated Modern, and the long buildings filled with little rooms began to display soaring roofs and other ~~special individual balcony.~~ space-age theatrics.

In contrast to the preference for low-budget external showmanship, motel builders continued to spend considerable sums of money furnishing the rooms. Unless guests had a comfortable stay, repeat business was un- likely, and a motel could quickly gain a bad reputation. In 1949 *Hotel Management*, which by then had branched into writing for the motel trade, advised its readers on what a typical guest room should contain to stay competitive:

Innerspring mattresses and box springs,—woolen blankets; Heavy Chenille bed ~~boxing idea co-operative.~~ spreads; Percale sheets.—Dresser with large mirror; Writing desk (all furniture is of oak).—Two large easy chairs; One or two straight back chairs.—Luggage rack.—One or more smoking stands and at least three ash trays.—Large floor lamp, bed lamp, desk lamp and ceiling light (all with 100-watt bulbs, including bath).—Wall to wall carpeting.—Rubber mat outside door.—12 by 16-inch origi- nal water color picture; Several prints—some in groups—giving the room a homey lived-in look.—Cross ventilation—two large windows.—Venetian blinds and either sheer curtains or colorful draperies.—Window air conditioners; Ceil- ing fans; gas heaters.—Coin-operated radio on night stand.—Closets and draw- ers lined with quilted satin paper.—Closets have many coat hangers and a laun- dry bag.

Writing desk contains 10 sheets of writing paper; 7 envelopes; scratch pad; several post cards; blotter; business cards; sewing kit with buttons, thread and needle, pins, rubber bands, paper clips.—Telegram blanks; laundry and dry cleaning list; sample coffee shop menu; calendar and house directory. Bathrooms have: Tile shower; Plastic shower curtain; Bath mat; Facial tissue in chrome con- tainer; Two 12-oz. drinking glasses; Three bars of soap; Four face towels, four bath towels, two wash cloths.[26]

The overall formula, both exterior and interior, seemed to work well. In the decade from 1946 to 1956, the number of motels swelled to approxi- mately sixty thousand nationwide.[27]

Despite this phenomenal growth, by the early 1950s a number of prob- lems plagued the motel industry. First, many older motor courts, once praised for their charm, homeyness, and quaint differences, had now become cause for complaint. As Claire Hoffman, director of the Shell Travel Bureau, reported in *Tourist Court Journal* after completing a motel-inspection tour from New York to Texas in 1947, many motels along the way had unpainted cabins, untidy grounds, and offices so dirty they "looked like run-down soda pop shacks."[28]

Along with deteriorating motor courts, the basic mom-and-pop partnerships—the heart of the roadside lodging business since the days of the tent and cabin camps—also showed signs of running down. Tending a motel was much like overseeing a family farm, with operators virtually trapped by the routine of a twenty-four-hour, seven-day-a-week business. Most of these "business hermits," as motel consultant C. Vernon Kane called the family motel teams, lacked the financial resources and the management skills for improvements in what was now a highly competitive market.[29]

Probably the greatest threat to the industry, however, was the specter of being bypassed. Motel owners about to be commercially marooned by road realignments or, even worse, new limited-access superhighways had relatively few options. If their motel was still visible and accessible from the new road, they could take a number of actions to avert disaster. In a 1950 *Tourist Court Journal* article entitled "When the Highway Leaves You," industry observer Earnest W. Fair described the creative countermeasures taken by a Utah courter who found himself in a similar situation: "He built [on the new highway] a new tourist court with great accent on a flashy front and with the frontal appearance of a large establishment. That brought motorists to a stop. When the new tourist court was filled, it was easy to send them to [the old court, which he now dubbed] his "annex" because it was close by and because once the traveler had come to a stop he loathes to start up and go hunting for accommodations again."[30]

For motels completely cut off, fewer alternatives existed. An owner could unload the property on an unsuspecting buyer or develop a new use for the premises such as low-cost housing for transients. For some, especially in isolated areas, the only choice was abandonment. As a result, to this day ghost motor courts, with their eerie gatherings of tumbledown cabins, are still a relatively common vision through the windshield.

FROM MOTEL TO HIGHWAY HOTEL

Though aging physical plants, unsophisticated management, and bypasses hampered the motel industry, its concept still held enormous commercial potential. By the 1950s, the roadside-lodging field was ripe for an invasion by corporate chains. As one analyst summed it up in *Fortune* in 1959: "The motel was like the stationery-store business. You had these thousands and thousands of little courts run by middle-aged, semi-retired couples. They had the world by the tail—a market yelling for improvements—and they couldn't handle it. Then, almost overnight, the big money began to flood in from everywhere—and I mean from everywhere."[31]

Motel corporations formed by these new investors generally took one of three forms—referral, franchise, or company-owned chains. The first type had its origins in the late 1930s when, as a logical outgrowth of state and regional tourist-court associations and motor-court recommendation services such as the AAA, groups of motor courts began banding together under common family names and logos, publishing their own membership directories, and setting up common minimum standards. Similar to the voluntary chains in the supermarket trade, these new operations came to be known as referral chains.

Best Western, its illuminated golden crown sign still a familiar sight along the roadside, is a good example of a well-known referral chain. Founded by California motel owner M. K. Guertin in 1946, with only fifty membership motels, the company rapidly expanded in the 1950s; by 1980 it had swelled to more than 2,700 affiliates worldwide.[32]

Next there were the franchises. Under the franchise system, a local investor put up the capital needed to erect a motel according to the design, accommodation, service, and maintenance standards of the corporation granting the franchise. In return the owner gained rights to use the franchise logo and benefited from massive advertising and a national reservations system.

The granddaddy of franchised chain motels is Holiday Inn. Years after it had become a success story, founder Kemmons Wilson described what had motivated the birth of his company: "In 1951 my wife Dorothy and I loaded our five children into our station wagon and started on a vacation to Washington, D.C., from our home in Memphis. It didn't take long to find that motels had cramped, uncomfortable rooms—and they charged extra for children."[33]

Seeing the need for a chain of comfortably appointed, consistently run, and reasonably priced motor inns, Wilson joined forces with prefabricated-home builder Wallace E. Johnson, who already had a reputation as the "Henry Ford of the home building industry."[34] Together they built the first Holiday Inn, consisting of three single-story buildings arranged around a swimming pool, on the outskirts of Memphis in 1952. From here they went on to interest scores of local investors around the country, and Holiday Inn rapidly grew to become one of the largest franchised motel chains in the nation.

A year later, roadside-restaurant magnate Howard Johnson followed suit, and his company began selling franchises for motor inns along with his family restaurants. The company's entrance into the field was prompted by local investors who built motels next to Howard Johnson's restaurants and then reaped profits from the visual association and fortunate proximity without any financial reward to the chain.[35]

Direct ownership—all motels within a chain being owned totally by one company—was proposed as early as 1931, when National Auto Haven of Chicago announced plans to build more than one hundred 21-bedroom wayside motor inns, "early American in architecture and furnishings but modern in services offered," in the Midwest.[36] This and most other similar plans failed, in part because of the prevailing opinion

The first Holiday Inn Hotel Courts (note the curious transitional suffix), 1952; Sumner Avenue, Memphis; photograph 1952. Except for the now-familiar and soon-to-be-extinct "Great Sign" (right), the complex, with its office-restaurant surrounded by long, unadorned single-story lodging structures, resembles other conventional motels of the period. (Holiday Inns, Inc.)

within the industry that motor courts needed the personalized, full-time attention of a husband-and-wife team. The idea of direct ownership returned, however, by the mid-1950s, as hotel corporations such as Sheraton, seeing the success of the franchises and referral chains, entered the motel business.[37] Some corporations had enough capital to own each of their roadside ventures entirely, while others franchised out part of their operation. As they gained in financial strength, some franchises, such as Holiday Inn, even began developing their own company-owned properties.

Under these various systems of ownership, chains rapidly assembled the financial, management, engineering, design, and marketing expertise to revolutionize the industry and overcome many of the problems that dogged the smaller husband-and-wife operations. With greater financial resources at their disposal, they could afford trained professional management and could compete favorably with the oil companies and emerging fast-food chains for choice locations around interstate highway interchanges. Being bypassed had been the nemesis of the family-run motels. For the chains, new roads spelled opportunity.

To expand their systems quickly and cheaply, many chains adopted center-core construction, a low-cost World War II building technique, with one or more stories of rooms arranged back to back along a utility core and the bathrooms of every four units grouped at the intersecting corners.[38] All doors and windows faced outside, and circumferential walkways served the rooms. (Thousands of center-core motels are still in existence.) By the late 1950s, on sites that demanded more intensive development, companies turned to mid-rise construction, with enclosed central corridors, and elevators. Regardless of the type of construction, owners generally decorated the buildings with a mild appliqué of the commercial

The original Holiday Inn building still stands on Sumner Avenue in Memphis; photograph 1981. No longer owned by Holiday Inns, it is now the Royal Oaks Motel and Hunan Restaurant. (Author.)

imagery currently in vogue. (Howard Johnson's was a notable exception—the chain housed its motel offices under bright orange roofs capped with ray-gunlike cupolas to capitalize on the symbolic value of its familiar roadside restaurants.)

Exceptions notwithstanding, exterior design was no longer as important as in the days of the early motor courts, because motels could not be sprawled along the road for maximum visibility on expensive interchange sites with narrow road frontages. This did not present a serious problem, however, since Wilson, Johnson, and their fellow entrepreneurs had transformed chain motels into branded products, where the name was the guarantee, and the contents were totally predictable. Giant highway signs such as the famous pulsating, multicolored neon Holiday Inn masterpiece known as the "Great Sign" (this classic mid-twentieth-century highway icon is now being replaced by a black High-Tech Look successor) became the primary exterior sales instruments. As with canned goods on a supermarket shelf, the label became more important than the actual container. The mere sight of a company's sign along the highway was all that was needed to instantly remind motorists of the motel chain's most important selling feature—the standardized guest room—the same way the Jolly Green Giant of the supermarket shelf conjures up the image of a can full of peas. Only instead of little green orbs floating in a metal cylinder, the image is of two full-size double beds, a night table, comfortable chairs, a combination bureau/desk, telephone, color television, and a full bathroom with toilet, sink, tub, and shower fitted into a long rectangular room (the standard chain-motel accommodations by the late 1950s).[39]

Companies also added other selling features to supplement this basic formula, including hotellike lobbies (designed so that guests, if they wished, could still pass from the registration desk to the room relatively

Howard Johnson's restaurant and adjacent Skyline Motor Court; Waynesboro, Virginia; photograph 1950. The fact that many sharp investors, such as the owner of this newly opened Skyline Motor Court, built their motels next to a busy Howard Johnson's, prompted the chain to enter the roadside-lodging business in order to reap any additional profits themselves. (National Archives.)

court { external privacy .

unobserved, thus preserving a cherished motel tradition), restaurants, display rooms, meeting rooms, indoor swimming pools, and saunas. As a result of this hybridization of features, by the late 1950s the distinction between motels and hotels became increasingly blurred. In fact, as the interstate-highway network penetrated the inner cities, many chains built downtown motels, with adjacent parking garages, that functioned much like the older Main Street railroad hotels—only now the bulk of patrons came by car rather than train. As early as 1957, C. Vernon Kane prophetically stated in *Architectural Forum* that already "a motel, in the final analysis, is a motel simply because it is called by that name,"[40] and even that distinction did not last for long.

the site again,

Just as the term "motor court" came into fashion to rhetorically elevate the cabin villages over the tent and cabin camps, only to be supplanted by the word "motel" to distinguish the sleek, one-building operations from their rustic ancestors, the word "hotel" has now made a comeback. Companies have dropped the term "motel" in favor of a spectrum of revised rubrics from "motor inn" and "motor lodge" to "highway hotel" or simply "hotel." Once motorists shunned hotels to camp out in open fields. Now they stay in hotels by the highway.

While chain-owned highway hotels now dominate the roadside-lodging industry, motorists on a tighter budget can still find less-expensive alternatives. Just as buy-it-out-of-the-box, pack-it-yourself supermarkets and self-service discount gasoline stations have challenged the big chain supermarkets and major oil companies, a new genre of highway hostelries has sprung up across the country as an alternative to the Hiltons and Ramada Inns. With names such as Econo Lodge and Days Inn, these no-frills, chain-owned budget motels offer highway travelers Spartan yet comfortable rooms usually at a lower price than the leading highway hotel chains.

Low-cost-housing builders Bill Becker and Paul A. Green are two of the leading pioneers of the bargain-basement chain motel. In 1962 they opened their first budget hostelry in Santa Barbara, Calilfornia, and christened it Motel 6. Soon the pair built similar units, all with one overriding characteristic—a single room in any Motel 6 could be rented for the same price, six dollars a night.

Not surprisingly the upstart chain received a similar reception to that accorded George Urich when he opened the first discount pump-it-yourself gas station in Los Angeles in 1947. According to *Dun's Review*, the chain often found "power lines cut, signs spattered with paint and windows smashed in" shortly after opening in a new community—cheerful greetings most likely arranged by nearby motel operators.[41]

Charterhouse Motor Hotel, shortly after completion in 1958; Alexandria, Virginia; photograph 1958. By the late 1950s, the chain-operated motor hotel with multistory construction and a lobby, surrounded by ample free parking, began to pry business away from the older family-owned motor courts and motels. In this particular example, the rakish canopy and vaulted entrance portico capture the same sense of motion and excitment as the cars of the period. (Imperial 400 National Inc.)

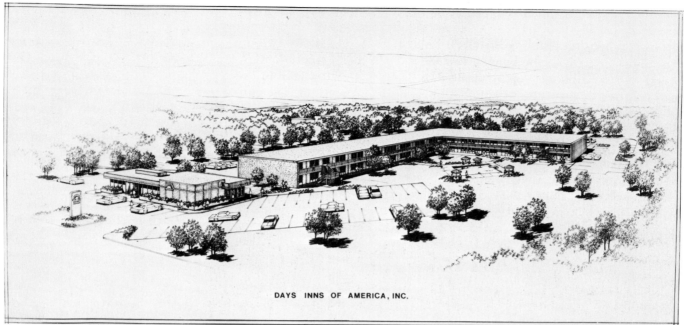

DAYS INNS OF AMERICA, INC.

Days Inn; drawing 1979. This proposed complex for one of the many budget motel chains to spring up in recent years features center-core construction with exterior stairs and balconies and is sheathed with diagonal flush boards and cedar shakes to give it the Environmental Look. (American Hotel and Motel Association.)

Today it is possible to travel from coast to coast and, except for some gaps in the Northeast, rent a carpeted single room with comfortable bed, one chair, a round imitation-wood-grained table, and a spotless bathroom, all for the still amazingly low cost (as of this writing) of only $16.95 for one person, $20.95 for two, or $25.95 for four plus a crib ($.90 extra for a key to the black-and-white television hanging on the wall)—less than half the average cost of a room at one of the leading highway hotels. But for

Holiday Inn sign; Worcester, Massachusetts; photograph 1982. Urban-renewal clearance programs, coupled with the extension of the interstate-highway network through downtown areas, have made inner cities choice locations for highway hotels. Note the juxtaposition of traditional urban land use and roadside commercial land use shown here. The densely packed row of nineteenth-century commercial blocks occupies about the same amount of land as does the Holiday Inn sign. (Author.)

*Motel; Van Buren Street, Phoenix; pho-
tograph 1982. Today the fate of many
older motels and motor courts is far from
certain. (Author.)*

these prices, especially in the summer, unless guests arrive early or re-
serve and pay for their room ahead of time (Motel 6 has resisted the
added expense of a computerized reservation system), they are likely to be
greeted by a red neon "sorry" above the office door.

The sight of this perfunctory message, however, need not send travelers on a tight budget into a state of panic. Nearly the entire history of
roadside lodging can usually be found just a few miles down the highway.
Thousands of long, rakish, neon-ringed family-run motels survive, and
one can still come across an occasional motor court with its little brood of
cabins waiting to be rented for the night. A good number of communities
even still maintain municipal campgrounds, although these are now often
crammed with recreation vehicles rather than the tents of half a century
before.

Restaurants

O<small>F ALL</small> the structures, signs, and symbols that stream before the automobile windshield in late-twentieth-century America, none appears to have a more deeply rooted track to the inner psyche than the familiar shapes, colors, and graphics of roadside restaurants. Orange roofs, golden arches, and plastic visages of a colonel in his white summer suit all trigger an instant mental review of familiar menus—from fried clams and hamburgers to cardboard-boxed chicken—while the sleek lines of streamlined diners spark an image of bacon, eggs, and home fries. How did such highly intelligible connections between architectural costumery and wayside gastronomy come about?

QUICK DINING AND THE EATING-OUT BOOM

The evolution of the thousands of quick-service restaurants that line today's highways actually began years before the inauguration of the auto age, in the second half of the nineteenth century. During this time, national customs of dining away from home were already on the way to a considerable revolution. The old tradition of leisurely dining, involving a substantial spread of several courses served by an attentive waiter, still prevailed, but in a growing number of circumstances old customs were gradually being supplemented by quick, informal dining, with fast service from more-limited menus. The eat-and-run cuisine of the Civil War encampment, the legendary chuck wagon of the Old West, the station-restaurant where meals were hastily consumed during railroad stops, and the railroad dining car where food was prepared in postage-stamp-size kitchens all helped to introduce Americans to fast cooking and fast eating in this period of westward settlement and rapid industrial growth.

Industrial workers—short on time but possessing sufficient pocket change for a lunch or supper break—especially became habitués of places offering a fast repast. In factory towns, or wherever shifts of laborers

Refreshments stand; New York, New York; photograph c. 1870. This ghostly glimpse of one of McDonald's distant ancestors reveals how some enterprising individual tacked an addition onto the front of a small, ramshackle house, braced up an attention-getting sign scaled for a Main Street storefront, and began hawking soda, root beer, pies, and cakes to pedestrians entering Central Park. At the time this photograph was taken, the stretch of Fifth Avenue where this stand was located was still urban fringe peopled with squatters' shacks, scavenger pigs, and roaming farm animals. Within a few years, the frontier of urban development shifted northward, and mansions replaced the shacks. (The New-York Historical Society, New York, New York.)

congregated day or night, a new breed of eatery opened its doors to catch the crowd. Very modest in appearance, of a single story, these establishments took up residence on side streets near factory gates and on the main thoroughfares to work. Called a variety of names from beaneries, greasy spoons, and stool lunches to other even less flattering sobriquets, they provided an alternative to the lunch pail.

By century's end, with the rapid expansion of commercial cities, white-collar workers also began to partake of the fast lunch. The hectic tempo of the typical downtown office worker's day—travel in on the trolley, join the stream on the sidewalks to work, rush out at noon, return to work, go home on the trolley—set a pace that made them natural customers for fast-lunch spots. Not surprisingly, a number of restaurant species evolved to cater to this new trade.

Cafeterias designed specifically for the luncher on a timetable allowed customers to move along a line while selecting from a display of daily items, then pay for a tray's worth, and carry it to a table.[1] Delicatessens provided sandwiches for office lunches as well as cold cuts and groceries for home consumption. Additionally, dozens of retailers, from pharmacies to variety stores such as Woolworth's, installed lunch counters over which a combination cook-and-server supplied food to customers sitting on a long row of stools. Other merchants rented empty stores, installed a

Cartoon, Life, *19 September 1907. As the custom of eating on the run spread from blue-collar workers to the white-collar industries, the "quick lunch room," depicted in this cartoon as a skull nestled in the dark metropolitan canyons, was sometimes seen as symbolic of the evils of early twentieth-century urban expansion.*

Beanery; Susquehanna, Pennsylvania; photograph c. 1900. Such workingmen's lunch spots became common factory-gate landmarks by the turn of the century. This beanery was located across from the huge locomotive repair shops of the Erie Railroad. (Historic American Engineering Record.)

counter along one wall and some tables along the others, and soon the luncheonette was born.[2]

Not all these new opportunities for eating away from home evolved to serve busy workers, however. Recreational eating was on the rise as well. Probably the best evidence of this is the meteoric success of a Civil War–era invention, the soda fountain. By the turn of the twentieth century, Americans had developed such a passion for ice-cream sodas, sundaes, and fizzy soft drinks that thousands of drug and candy stores across the nation installed soda fountains while a new institution began to make its debut—the ice-cream parlor.[3] Along with soda fountains, stands selling everything from hamburgers and popcorn to pies, cakes, soda water, and candy and ice cream sprang up along amusement-park midways and county fairs, astride beachfront boardwalks and at entrances to city parks, all to satisfy leisure-time hunger.

By the decade after World War I, the nation had entered a full-fledged eating-out boom, with the estimated number of restaurants jumping 40 percent between 1910 and 1927.[4] In New York City alone, the number of eating establishments more than doubled—from seventy-five hundred in 1915 to a spectacular seventeen thousand only ten years later—compared with a corresponding 13 percent increase in population.[5] This particular census did not even take into account delicatessens or candy stores that also sold food.

Obviously, an important change in social behavior was in evidence, one that contemporary observers attributed to the greater number of men and women working away from home, the decline in the use and availability of domestic help to prepare meals, and Prohibition, which eliminated legal barroom competition in the years between 1919 and 1933.[6] Technological development also bolstered the trend toward eating out. Advances in packing, storing, refrigerating, shipping, and preparing food made the business of cooking and selling meals to large numbers of people easier.

At this juncture, the restaurant population explosion was joined and aided by another boom—the tremendous rise in production and availability of the automobile. A symbiosis developed between two emerging forces—the urge to ride in the car and the urge to eat out. In this relationship, the restaurant could both serve the hungry motorist and provide an opportunity to make a trip in the car more pleasant. The car, in turn, made it all the easier for people to go out to eat as a form of recreation. And to the hopeful wayside entrepreneur, it offered the freedom of situating a restaurant along the margins of any well-traveled road where land could be acquired inexpensively—and where local health, zoning, and other regulations would permit.

The rise of restaurants dedicated to the auto trade also coincided with another important development—the image of an eating place was rapidly becoming as influential in drawing customers as was the food it offered. By the 1920s, due to intense competition, good cooking alone no longer guaranteed success in the restaurant business. As industry analyst Raymond S. Tompkins concluded, in *The American Mercury* in 1931, now every restaurant owner "needs . . . a four-year course in advertising, accountancy, architecture, and psychology."[7]

Nowhere would such skills become more important than along the highway, where the successful food merchant needed to make sure that a restaurant's exterior would send a message readily understood by the class of patron he was aiming for: be it a family with finicky taste, a salesman in a hurry, workers on the way home, or teenagers out for a joyride. By intuition, trial and error, and in some cases careful calculation, operators began to differentiate among customers and develop specific types of restaurants for specific types of patrons.

Soon the roadside-restaurant family tree divided into scores of inter-twining branches. Highway cafés, custard stands, barbecue stalls, coffee shops—the list is long, the distinctions often blurry. Three of the most prominent categories will be treated in some detail in the remainder of this chapter—family restaurants, food stands, and diners.

FAMILY RESTAURANTS

Before the 1920s, most anyone traveling long distances by automobile had relatively few places, save for an occasional wayside inn or resort hotel, to purchase a meal along the open highway. This posed a special problem for families, who had either to bear the expense of dining at those city lunchrooms and restaurants along the way (often located in the better hotels) considered clean and respectable enough for women and children or, as many preferred, to bring their own food and picnic by the side of the road. Obviously there was a definite need for wayside eateries that would be more convenient than either the downtown restaurant or the picnic, with a respectable ambience that would discourage inappropriate behavior and undesirable clientele.

TEAROOMS

Many motorists found a solution to this quandary in an institution called the tearoom, which commanded great popularity nationwide in the inter-war years. Tearooms were an excellent example of the ascendancy of image over menu that was starting to transform the restaurant industry. The very name "tearoom" conjured up a safe, discreet, prohibitionist image—the polar opposite of "saloon"—aimed especially at the woman in the car. Tearooms were often located in buildings with historical associations, such as old houses, inns, barns, or gristmills. Not only were these structures often inexpensive to buy or rent, but they also lured those urban refugees driving around the countryside seeking quaint villages and rural hamlets. Savvy tearoom owners capitalized on this appeal of respectability coupled with a yearning for the historic and nostalgic. Their bill of fare was simple: serving "afternoon tea, ice cream, cold drinks . . . a regular luncheon or supper, and on Sundays a regular dinner."[8] It was atmosphere they offered, often reinforced by quaint names such as Silver Spring, Pine Cone, Wishing Well, Tintern Tea Garden, or Copper Kettle.

Tearooms opened up along major tourist routes to resorts in New England, the Poconos, the Smoky Mountains, and along the old National Road, among others. So popular had the genre become by the early 1920s that tearoom operators supported their own publication: *Tea Room and Gift Shop*. The majority of operators were women; not energetic farm wives earning extra income in an extension of the family kitchen, but independent-minded entrepreneurs of some sophistication and often of the same social class as their patrons. For them the tearoom was an opportunity to combine their skills in cooking, decorating, and hostessing with practice in running a business and making money.

*The Rose Garden Tea Room; Vero Beach,
Florida; postcard c. 1925. Often located
in remodeled mills, in colonial-period
houses, or in new structures designed to
evoke an aura of quaint, rural informality (such as this one), roadside tearooms
flourished in the early interwar years, offering motoring families a wholesome and
respectable place to eat. (Author's collection.)*

THE ROSE GARDEN TEA ROOM, VERO BEACH, FLORIDA

The story of the Bottle Hill Tea Shop in Madison, New Jersey, published in the special *Tea Room Booklet* in *The Women's Home Companion* of
1922, typifies the published accounts of tearoom success. Founded by a
"group of Wellesley women,"[9] in a landmark Revolutionary War–era inn,
the Bottle Hill was transformed into a thriving restaurant specializing in
waffles, chicken, shortbread, and tea with cinnamon toast. Bottle Hill also
sold tasteful gifts and offered so-called colonial decor.

It was dusty and dingy from lack of use and care, but a month's patient and
energetic work transformed it. . . . Our visions of a glowing fire on old andirons
drawing customers on a rainy day faded, however, when we found that it would
cost nearly three hundred dollars to put the chimney in a safe condition. But a
college woman never gives up. A really old open Franklin stove, thirty dollars
worth of stove pipe, and the vision of glowing fire became a reality. . . . The
room was then ready for its furnishings . . . quaint old, hooked rugs, a comfortable wing chair . . . a corner cupboard filled with interesting bits of china and
old pewter.[10]

Despite the enthusiasm and zeal of their feminine proprietors, tearooms
were not without problems. The fact was that most tearoom owners were
amateurs. Helen Woods, an independent tearoom consultant who claimed
to have advised more than sixteen hundred would-be restaurateurs in all
facets of the business, concluded that a quaint name, an old building, and
acceptable food were not necessarily the keys to instant financial success.
In her opinion, experience in running a household did not automatically
make a woman an accomplished tearoom operator; instead, to be successful, proprietors needed some previous business experience, even if only in
office work, and many had no such background. Woods and others in the
trade also urged a broader appeal for the tearoom in order to include the
man of the family, "the one who pays the fat check . . . when a man
[who] is hungry after a long motor ride comes to a place called, for example, 'The Canary Bird Tea Room,' he is pretty likely to step on the gas

and drive on. . . . ."[11] She suggested renaming the tearoom "a motor inn" and urged her clients to forgo some of the quaintness and gentility and serve what might tempt a man to stop for a meal with his family: "good home-cooked food."[12]

Woods anticipated the shape of roadside restaurants to come. Tearooms, hampered by intense competition and amateur management, began to fade from the roadside (today it is still possible to happen upon an occasional roadside restaurant that originated as a tea house). But in the late 1920s, demand was still growing for attractive restaurants that were full of evocative imagery, yet run as reliable businesses, with clean facilities and a bill of fare that would please the entire family.

By demonstrating that a market existed for moderately priced roadside eateries, considered acceptable for family dining and packaged in quaint surroundings, tearoom operators had unknowingly tested the market for a new genre of way stations. As both Raymond Tompkins and Helen Woods had predicted, great opportunities now existed for the entrepreneur who could apply the right mix of business skills and image to a motor-age inn.

Probably the most successful businessman to discover the winning combination was one Howard D. Johnson. This roadside commercial pioneer's efforts became virtually synonymous with the development of a whole new genre of eatery—the family restaurant chain.

THE FAMILY RESTAURANT CHAIN

That most famous of roadside institutions, Howard Johnson's, had its beginnings in 1925 when, after the failure of his father's cigar business, twenty-eight-year-old Howard decided to make his living as a variety-store proprietor, taking over a financially ailing combination drugstore, newsstand, and soda fountain in a taxpayer block in Wollaston, a section of Quincy, Massachusetts. Deeply in debt, Johnson needed a better-than-average trade in order to survive, and as a ploy to bring in customers, he undertook still another business on the side—manufacturing ice cream with a butterfat content far exceeding the product's legal minimum.[13] His guess that a richer ice cream would appeal to the Prohibition-induced sweet tooth of his neighbors in Wollaston proved right. As his next step, Johnson set up a stand at a nearby beach and, to his amazement, sold more that sixty thousand dollars in ice cream in one summer. He soon opened up other seaside stands in the area and in 1929, at the invitation of the Granite Bank, opened up a restaurant in the ground floor of their new building in Quincy Square, a venture that lost more than one hundred thousand dollars before it began to make any money. In debt, Johnson looked for some gap in the restaurant trade that was not being filled, much as he had done with ice cream just a few years before.

He discovered the market he was looking for while driving from Boston to the communities along the Massachusetts shore. Here out on the highways, there were thousands of potential customers. Soon after, Johnson opened his first roadside restaurant along one of Boston's arterial high-

Howard D. Johnson, photograph c. 1947. A master synthesizer and marketer, Johnson combined the hot dog stand, tearoom, and soda fountain under one bright orange roof and became master of a roadside family-restaurant empire. (Howard Johnson's.)

THE DUTCHLAND AT
Route 1 and Fillmore Ave.
Elizabeth, N. J.

Let's Go to Dutchland!

ARCHITECTURAL EVOLUTION OF
HOWARD JOHNSON'S:

Above:

Dutchland Farms; Elizabeth, New Jersey; postcard c. 1935. The architecture of this early chain of roadside restaurants influenced the design of Howard Johnson's. (John Baeder.)

Above, right:

Howard Johnson's; Middleboro, Massachusetts; photograph c. 1937. This early Howard Johnson's was actually located in a converted Dutchland Farms. (Howard Johnson's.)

Right:

Howard Johnson's; Reading, Pennsylvania; photograph c. 1947. By the late 1930s, the company had adopted a general exterior selling theme similar to Dutchland's, sans windmills, consisting of an overscale Neocolonial house with entrance portico, multipaned shuttered windows, and dormers. Strictly ornamental, the latter features were often outfitted with curtains and a lamp to serve as a beacon of homeyness to weary nighttime travelers. The building was capped by a massive gable roof sheathed with orange enameled metal tiles and then a cupola and trademark weather vane with a silhouette of Simple Simon and the Pieman. (Howard Johnson's.)

ways, and by the mid-1930s, he owned a string of wayside eating places up and down the Massachusetts coast.

In 1935 Johnson decided that he could expand his operation far more rapidly by permitting individual investors—he called them agents rather than franchisees—to build their own Howard Johnson's according to the general specifications and standards of the parent company. In addition to providing the agents with his organization's expertise in restaurant management, Johnson sold them food products from his ice-cream factories and commissaries as a way to ensure uniformity in the meals they served. He kept an ever-watchful eye on them as well, assessing how well they kept his standards, which were crucial to the success of the chain.

By 1940 Howard Johnson had built himself an empire of roadside restaurants, with more than 125 units (only about a third of them company owned) stretching from Maine to Florida doing a gross annual business of fourteen million dollars a year. He had recently succeeded in securing an exclusive contract for the rights to open restaurants along the new Pennsylvania Turnpike. And he could add to his list of accomplishments what

Left:
Howard Johnson's; Dedham, Massachusetts; rendering 1947, Charles Goodale. Although all franchises were readily recognizable as Howard Johnson's, no two restaurants were exactly the same in size, layout, or detailing. Teams of architects—under the guidance of the company's supervising architect, Joseph A. Cicco—customized each unit to fit its site, the anticipated traffic volume, and the whims of individual franchisees. This particular restaurant is a hybrid of Neocolonial and Moderne. (Howard Johnson's.)

may well have been the largest roadside restaurant at the time, a six-hundred-thousand-dollar extravaganza on Queens Boulevard in New York City designed to serve the thousands of visitors on their way to the New York World's Fair. He was also becoming a celebrity, the subject of numerous feature articles in such publications as *Fortune* and *Business Week,* each of which in some way paid homage to the self-made young hero of the auto age who had managed to make a fortune several times over in the midst of the depression.[14]

Johnson's success derived from an uncanny ability to recombine current ideas into a new synthesis that unerringly appealed to a middle-class family on the road.[15] Ice cream, for instance, was an extremely common treat, but Johnson's restaurants offered an unusual selection of flavors embellished with a touch of showmanship—he served it in a distinctive cone-

Above:
Howard Johnson's; proposed shop front; Atlantic City, New Jersey; c. 1946. The company's architects even transplanted the orange roof, dormers, and cupola formula (here jutting out over a visual front and supported by a raking streamline pylon) from the roadside to Main Street. (Howard Johnson's.)

Left:
Howard Johnson's; Hicksville, New York; photograph c. 1960. By the mid-1950s, the company began switching over to a modernized design, with many of the homey touches sanitized out. This version consists of a visual front, a lower-profile hipped roof still clad in orange tiles, and a stylized, finned cupola. (Howard Johnson's.)

shaped scoop that formed a rim of extra ice cream at the bottom, suggesting to the customer that he was getting an exceptionally large portion. Similarly, he added a wedge-shaped bun in a colorful cardboard trough to the familiar hot dog, making the Johnson version of this very ordinary snack a bit different—and therefore special.

Rather than pioneer, the Howard Johnson's chain borrowed its format from other successful restaurant types. In fact under every orange roof were two formats, each with its own distinctive atmosphere. One section consisted of a dining area with a homey tearoom ambience where wholesome-looking waitresses dressed in prim uniforms provided service. Another area of the restaurant had a counter rimmed with stools where customers could order hot dogs, ice cream, and other simple, fast fare. By merging the respectability and full-meal service of the tearoom with the casual, quick-bite convenience of the soda fountain, luncheonette, and hot dog stand, Howard Johnson addressed most everyone's needs in a single stop.

In the same way, he followed the lead of others for the architecture of his restaurants, but he added his own twist. He married the unusual bright orange roof with the familiar—a colonial motif. Growing up in the Boston area, Johnson no doubt observed the fascination that the area's great preserves of eighteenth- and early-nineteeth-century buildings held for its thousands of tourists. He also saw the powerful symbolism of the colonial house successfully harnessed, not only by local tearoom operators, but also by the builders who were making this style a common idiom of the middle-class suburb during the interwar years. The colonial look—familiar yet formal—provided an apt image for Johnson's glorified tearoom/hot dog stands. He was hardly the first to use it; the Dutchland Farms chain, for example, had a similar design for their roadside restaurants in the early 1930s. In fact, about 1935, the same time Howard Johnson opened what the company claims to be the first of his now-familiar orange-roofed roadside restaurants, in Dorchester, Massachusetts, he also opened up another wayside eatery in a converted Dutchland Farms in Middleboro, Massachusetts.[16] This fact further supports the widely held contention that Dutchland directly influenced the architecture of Howard Johnson's.

In pristine white clapboards, each Howard Johnson's restaurant loomed at highway's edge like a very tiny colonial mansion, its spreading hipped roof of jarring brilliant orange topped by a prim white cupola. Here and there were turquoise accents—an illuminated ladder sign in the shape of a broken pediment stood out front, with Simple Simon and the Pieman, designed for Johnson by freelance artist Joseph Alcott and logo of the chain since the early 1930s, on display above. The entire ensemble functioned as a beacon of traditional values, yet at the same time managed enough flash to catch the attention of the passing motorist. It was a very successful conception.

Through its buildings, the chain also tried to convey warmth and welcome to the traveling families it sought as trade. In some units, a set of homey lamps glowed cheerfully in otherwise nonfunctional dormer windows; and in many, this domestic theme continued on the inside with knotty-pine paneling and even a set of ruffled curtains. So immersed was Johnson himself in his corporate imagery that he lived in a house with an ambience very similar to that of his restaurants.

A sharp eye will discern that, aside from the general parameters of the design, the exteriors of any two Howard Johnson's restaurants from this early period are rarely alike. The reason is twofold. First, from very early on, the parent company retained a staff of house architects to develop prototypes, design the company-owned units, and assist in the design of agent-owned franchises. As part of their job, the staff changed and updated the designs from time to time. Secondly, agents could select a variety of individual details as long as the basic formula of white clapboards, orange tile roof, and cupola remained inviolate. Thus modernistic doorways, International Style ribbon windows, and a mélange of other details were often amalgamated into the designs—without altering the overall symbolic clarity that instantly communicated "Howard Johnson's."

During World War II, the ban on nonessential driving had the same disastrous effects on roadside family restaurants as it did on gas stations and other highway businesses. Many units were temporarily closed and boarded up. Johnson, however, kept his company afloat during the war years by putting his know-how into managing cafeterias in defense plants and military installations.[17]

In the years immediately following the war, rival companies in the family-restaurant market began to pose a threat to his preeminently successful formula. Among these were the giant Hot Shoppes organization, which evolved out of an A&W stand that J. Willard Marriott opened in 1928, and the Blake brothers' Friendly family-restaurant chain begun in New England in 1935. None of the rivals, however, could match the number of restaurants at Johnson's command or his personal fame and influence. By the late fifties, some five hundred "HoJo's" served customers nationwide, including those operated in conjunction with the company's new chain of motels. Strict standards of uniformity worked well for Johnson, who personally policed his chain with surprise inspection visits, assuring that fried clams ordered by customers in Florida met the same standards as the fried clams served by his restaurants in Maine.

With its postwar expansion, the company finally modified its colonial design by incorporating Modern elements, including a few of the trappings of technological mannerism inherent in the Exaggerated Modern style, which made its appearance in the 1950s. Although some of the company's agents still insisted on the traditional colonial look for their franchises, in the majority of the newer units, all-glass visual fronts replaced clapboards and old-fashioned multipaned windows. In keeping with the new look, the HoJo's orange roof spread down over the building in a lower, ranch-house-style pitch, and the cupola became a fantastic mutation of its former colonial self, abstracted into a turquoise pyramid rising from a stack of ray-gunlike fins. The effect of the new design, although it represented a marked departure in image for Howard Johnson's, was only mildly futuristic compared with the jutting and soaring

The Bucket, c. 1935; Eagle Rock, California; photograph 1980. This stuccoed likeness of a lunch pail, complete with a lid and handle brackets, is a survivor from the heyday of the mimetic roadside food stand. (Author.)

forms of the roadside's more typical examples of the Exaggerated Modern. Its lines were boxy, clean, and crisp—befitting a multimillion-dollar corporation investing in the high-priced real estate of the frontage strip and interchange cluster. For its context, the new look was decidedly conservative.

Howard Johnson's Exaggerated Modern image prevailed into the 1970s, when both the technological mannerism introduced in the 1950s and its colonial predecessors succumbed to an earth-toning program. The company gradually switched over to the Environmental Look by replacing the white, orange, and turquoise color scheme with shades of brown and tan, shearing off cupolas, and closing in the old visual fronts with solid expanses of beige-colored walls. Changes took place inside as well. Salad bars joined the old standbys—ice cream, fried clams, hot dogs—on the menu. Many HoJo's units added the saloon to the cluster of restaurant types under one roof by acquiring liquor licenses. Others redecorated with hanging plants, stained glass, and oak finishes for an interior look reminiscent of the Ground Rounds, the company's newer youth-oriented chain. Out front the aging neon Simple Simon signs disappeared one by one, as Johnson's pioneering synthesis of eye-catching exterior selling motifs was gradually dismembered. (Howard Johnson himself died in 1972.)

FOOD STANDS

Paralleling the growth of the roadside family restaurant came the development of another important category of wayside eatery—the roadside food stand, which began as a modest (even at times primitive) spot for highway travelers to pause for a brief meal and eventually blossomed into a multibillion-dollar corporate extravaganza: the fast-food restaurant. Along the highway, after World War I, a motley assortment of hopeful victuallers, from retired factory workers to farmers' wives, quick to see that, next to gasoline, food was the commodity most demanded by the multitudes taking to the road, began setting up business in an assortment of shacks and shanties bedecked with giant hand-painted signs to sell everything from hot dogs and boiled eggs to, as *Fortune* observed in the early 1930s, "regional specials . . . shore dinners in Maine, crab gumbo in Mississippi, fried-chicken dinners in Maryland."[18]

HOT-DOG KENNELS TO HAMBURGER CHAINS

Some of the fare served in this first crop of roadside eateries was undoubtedly of acceptable, perhaps even exceptional, quality—but not all. Free of the scrutiny of health inspectors and mindful of the transience of the typical "eat and run," one-time customer, owners of roadside stands were often tempted to offer substandard cuisine and poor sanitation. From the mid-1920s into the late 1930s, articles appeared in the popular press cautioning the public about the perils of supping at the proverbial "Ptomaine Joe's Place":

At the last roadside hot-dog stand you patronized how clean or otherwise were the dishes, the knives, the forks, the spoons, the glasses? How clean do you surmise, were the utensils in which the food had been cooked?

Was there an opalescent skin of soap or grease on top of the water in your glass? Did you have an urge to give your coffee spoon a going-over with your sleeve, handkerchief or napkin while the lady or gentleman behind the counter wasn't looking?

Did you by chance pick up a stomach-ache or a case of trench mouth at the place?[19]

Food-stand design was as variable, and controversial, as the quality of the food. Some operators adopted the Coney Island approach to roadside marketing by casting their stands into bizarre shapes that often mimed the name or function of the restaurant. Thus, ice-cream stands took the form of giant ice-cream freezers and milk cans, while refreshments at the Toad Inn (1931) in Santa Monica, California, passed through a window cut between the front legs of a giant toad. Others followed the lead of the tearooms (as Howard Johnson later did) and adopted the quaint little house format. This latter approach was most acceptable to elite tastemakers in the waning years of the City Beautiful movement just before the depression. In 1928 Mrs. John D. Rockefeller and the American Civic

Roadside stand; U.S. 80 between Dallas and Fort Worth; photograph 1942, Arthur Rothstein. The cacophony created by the commercial messages festooning individually owned roadside food stands became the butt of much contemporary aesthetic criticism. (Library of Congress.)

Association even cosponsored a competition, billed as "a far-reaching effort to clean up the miscellaneous hodgepodge of unsightly 'hot dog' stands and the accompanying riffraff of roadside markets. . . ." Entrants' designs were judged by qualities such as "sheer charm" and "picturesqueness."[20]

Despite such efforts, the majority of early food stands more closely conformed to what was just described as the cause rather than the remedy. Often disparagingly referred to as "hot-dog kennels" (whatever the menu), many roadside meal stops constantly endured a barrage of criticism for their unprepossessing, ramshackle appearance.

Meanwhile, in sharp contrast to the gastronomic and aesthetic anarchy associated at the time with dining quickly along the highway, a novel type of urban food stand was evolving in the nation's cities that would ultimately set new standards for speedy roadside dining. Only a few years before, factory workers had harbored the same uncertainty toward greasy spoons and stool lunches that motorists now felt about the hot-dog kennel. Along Main Street and the taxpayer strip, as well as near the factory gate, a ripe market had developed for eateries that served low-cost meals of predictable quality, in clean surroundings.

Enter Edgar W. Ingram and Walter L. Anderson. The pair, an ex-insurance executive and a short-order cook respectively, teamed up in 1921 to open a small eating house. The resulting enterprise met with such extraordinary success that within a few years it blossomed into an entire restaurant system that is still in operation to this day.[21]

The success of the venture resulted from a two-part formula: decent, cheap food, and evocative and memorable architecture. First the team sought out a focus for the menu—a food item with popular appeal that could be cooked quickly and by someone with minimal training so as to allow for sale at a low price. The hamburger met all these conditions.

ARCHITECTURAL EVOLUTION OF WHITE CASTLE:

Below, left:
First White Castle, opened March 1921; Wichita, Kansas; photograph 1929. Built of rock-faced concrete block, a material that gained in popularity in the early years of the century for the building of low-cost walls that had the look of stone, this tiny cubicle could be distinguished from hundreds of volumetrically similar lunch stands of the period by its castlelike crenelated parapet and tower. (White Castle.)

Below, right:
White Castle; Broadway, New York, New York; photograph 1930. In 1926 the company began building larger, white glazed-brick restaurants, with more massive corner towers, stained-glass transoms, corbeled instead of crenelated parapets, and lights for nighttime illumination. The gleaming white boxes were designed to attract attention no matter where they were situated; this one was nestled between a parking lot and the rear of an apartment building. (White Castle.)

And Anderson, who had opened up his first lunch wagon in a remodeled streetcar in 1916, had had a great deal of experience with hamburgers. He knew that, at the time, many people distrusted the typical short-order hamburger because they suspected its thick meat patty had been padded with gristle and bad or old beef. Many quick-lunch restaurant customers also found the usual cold bun unappetizing. So Anderson, attempting to eliminate suspicion as well as warm things up, would place a patty of meat on the griddle, flatten it with a spatula, mash some shredded onions into it, and place both halves of the bun over it.

Now, in developing their budding hamburger restaurant chain, the two entrepreneurs capitalized on Anderson's discovery by standardizing his technique, using only good beef in uniform-size patties, cooking them on griddles for prescribed cooking times. Hence, from unit to unit, they managed to offer a tasty, inexpensive product of consistent quality.

The next obstacle to be overcome was the negative public perception that all hamburger stands were greasy spoons. Fortunately Ingram had as great a talent for manufacturing images as Anderson had in preparing meals. It was Ingram who ingeniously coined the name for the system— "White Castle," because, in his words, "'White' signifies purity and 'Castle' represents strength, permanence and stability."[22] For decades to follow, the name was synonymous with hamburgers. It also helped cast the image of the structures for selling the burgers: small, rectangular buildings made of rock-faced concrete blocks, complete with crenelated parapet and corner tower. The tiny, castlelike design adapted easily to a variety of sites, cost relatively little to build, and served as an instant advertisement and drawing card for the chain.

Though furnished with the long counter and stool arrangement common in beaneries and lunch wagons, the inside of the castles nevertheless reinforced the overall image of wholesomeness and cleanliness implied by the chain's name and architecture. Tile, and later porcelain-enameled and stainless steel, covered as many surfaces as possible. These materials looked so appealing when sparkling clean, and made even the slightest

Below, left:
White Castle; Hempstead Turnpike, Queens, New York; photograph 1936. As the chain expanded to locations farther out along the taxpayer strip to serve residents of the interwar suburbs, the company introduced easy-to-assemble, prefabricated, porcelain-enameled steel units in 1932. They were complete with buttresses, crenellations, battlements, and stained glass, as well as gleaming enamel, tile, and stainless-steel interiors. (White Castle.)

Below:
White Castle, opened 1981; Columbus, Ohio; photograph 1981. The newest generation of castles—while still clad with porcelain-enameled steel panels—have battlements sheathed with Environmental Look, stained-wood siding. (White Castle.)

stain or smudge so obvious, that employees, like sailors polishing the bright work on a ship, must have felt impelled to keep the surfaces shiny.

By combining a limited menu focused on one mass-produced item cooked to uniform standards, an attention-getting building, and an interior indicating a high level of sanitation, the founders of the White Castle System developed a retail format that revolutionized the short-order trade. Within a few years, dozens of similar hamburger chains, such as the Little Tavern in the Washington, D.C., area, Krystal in the mid-South, and national arch rival White Tower, opened for the growing market of the quick-lunch trade.

Ingram and Anderson and their competitors had demonstrated that the chain concept—long applied to grocery and variety stores—could be successfully adapted to the food-stand branch of the restaurant industry. These forerunners of today's fast-food emporia served as important object lessons in standardization (of exterior image, interior decor, and menu) and influenced the shape of roadside food stands in years to come.

DRIVE-IN RESTAURANTS

Another important milepost in the evolution of the fast-food restaurant was the development of the drive-in. The idea of eating out in one's vehicle is not purely a product of the auto age. By the turn of the century, Fortune's Drug Store in downtown Memphis, for example, was one of many urban pharmacies and soda fountains to have a crew of waiters serving soda-fountain items to customers waiting in their buggies.[23] Naturally this novel arrangement also proved to be ideal for feeding motorists.

While it is difficult to positively pinpoint the first food-stand operation to use the automobile as a rubber-tired stand-in for the dining room, restaurant industry publications frequently confer the distinction on the Pig Stand Company of Dallas, Texas.[24] On an investment of seven hundred dollars, the original Pig Stand opened in September 1921 on the Dallas–Fort Worth highway; a second was constructed shortly after. The units resembled the conventional walk-up refreshment stands that could already be found in any amusement park—a boxcarlike building with large rectangular food-service windows cut in the long side facing the sidewalk, and signs and soft-drink advertisements mounted on the roof. All this, but with an unexpected twist: curb service. Customers would pull up along the curb and read their order from a menu mounted on the wall to a waiter who would then bring the food out to the curb and pass it on a tray through the car window. Soon Pig Stands dotted the South and California.

In 1924 another company joined the Pig Stands—A&W. Founded in 1919 by Roy W. Allen, the company expanded the concept of curb service by building on bigger lots with room for customers to drive off the street and park on the premises, and they introduced "tray girls," who proved to be one of the drive-ins' main attractions. A&W was also a pioneer in food-stand franchising, allowing local investors to sell its products and duplicate its architectural and graphic trademarks. The franchise system was already in use in a number of industries—from auto sales to gasoline retailing. Because it decreased the amount of capital needed from the central company, franchising allowed for far more rapid growth of chains than company ownership (as practiced by firms such as White Castle).

Soon thousands of individual wayside restaurateurs (especially in warmer climates) introduced the new drive-in curb service to their operations. Chains such as White Castle followed suit as well in an attempt to vie for the motorists' dollars.

Apparently the public needed no prodding to accept the drive-in restaurant as part of the repertoire of dining along the roadside. This was especially true in the country's most auto-oriented city, Los Angeles, which became a mecca, as one observer described in *Collier's* in 1938, for "catering to lazy people."[25]

Archeologists digging in the buried ruins of Hollywood, in the year 5000 A.D., are going to be hard put to explain the strange temples erected by the forgotten cinema tribes, dedicated to the worship of the Great God Hamburger. Probably it is the only spot on earth where a lunch counter eclipses the city hall. . . . The English language, unfortunately, lacks the power to tell exactly what a curb-service stand designer does when he puts his soul in his work but the results can be seen on the boulevards about Los Angeles in the shape of modest structures representing investments of up to one hundred thousand dollars, spent mostly for neon lights, colored glass and chromium plating.[26]

Along with altering accepted patterns of wayside eating, drive-ins also affected the design of roadside food stands. While theoretically food could be carried from kitchen to car from most any building, the programmatic

Drugstore; Savannah, Georgia; photograph c. 1930. The concept of curb service—drawing a wagon or car up to the curb in front of a business and being waited on—originated on Main Street rather than along the roadside strip, contrary to popular legend. In this case, soda-fountain treats would have been carried out to the curb by a clerk. (Georgia Historical Society.)

Thirst Station by day and by night; Savannah, Georgia; photographs c. 1930. The next phase in the evolution of the drive-in restaurant was to set a building back from the curb to allow for off-street parking and eating. This particular example is patterned closely after house-with-canopy gas stations of the period, but with counter, grill, fountain, and stools instead of gas pumps. A sun-bonneted carhop can be seen serving a customer in the black sedan in the daytime scene. (Georgia Historical Society.)

imperatives of curb-service architecture—to attract and then accommodate as many cars as possible in varying climates for the lowest possible investment—led to the development of a distinctive drive-in-restaurant building type consisting of a rectangular or circular building capped by a giant sign or illuminated pylon, around which customers parked their cars like spokes radiating from the hub of a wheel. Loballo's in Dallas was typical; it was

a flat top, one story, concrete and steel structure forty feet in diameter with a 14-foot overhang that runs completely around the structure. Both interior and exterior walls are of tile, while the floor is terrazzo and the ceiling stucco. The windows are long and wide, giving the occupants of parked cars access to a view of the activities going on inside. It is air conditioned and 2700 feet of neon tubing provide a unique lighting effect that can be seen equally well by motorists and those who arrive in the city by air.[27]

During the war years, the rationing of gasoline, rubber, critical metals, and many types of foodstuffs caused numerous roadside stands and drive-ins to cut back on their operations or to close. Then the industry emerged from its war-spun cocoon into an era that craved and coddled its automobiles as never before. The drive-in entered its golden age. By 1964, more than 35,000 eateries in the United States called themselves drive-ins, with California leading the nation with 2,145 and Texas a close second with 1,845.[28]

Probably the most noticeable architectural improvement in the postwar drive-in was the addition of shelters for cars, in the form of deeply cantilevered main roofs, and especially separate, freestanding structures like those used to shield attendants at the new self-service gas stations. More than mere shelters, these canopies were designed to serve as powerful lures for passing traffic. As Lane's Aluminum Industries, a leading prefabricator, proclaimed in one of their advertisements prepared for drive-in operators: "In fishing . . . the right bait is all important . . . and if you're trying to catch more customers it's even more important. That's why you'll look to Lane for exciting, eye-appealing canopies."[29]

Fortified with raking roofs and dazzling signs, drive-ins from the early

1950s to the mid-1960s bristled with Exaggerated Modern motifs, sweeping in arcs and Vs, jutting at contorted angles, and pulsating with light. In many cases, the buildings even conveyed the same rhythm as the cars buzzing along the highways in front of them or the music blaring out of the cars' radios. In 1964 the *Drive-In Operators Handbook* deftly came up with a most fitting phrase to describe this powerful synthesis of building, car, and culture: "the rock n' roll style."[30]

Yet within this glittering spectacle there was a human centerpiece. Decked in a special uniform and in some cases even gliding from kitchen to car on a pair of roller skates, the young tray girl (now called a carhop) was as much of a drawing card as the bizarre architecture. She was beyond a doubt the queen of the drive-in—its functional and spiritual heart. The cute teenage waitresses also became one of the drive-in owners' most vexing problems. Not only did carhops add to labor costs, their presence converted the drive-in into a high-school hangout. Revving engines, squealing wheels, and profane exclamations discouraged the family trade, while the strident blare of auto horns demanding service and saluting friends raised the ire of neighbors in nearby residential areas.

Some operators explored electronic and semiautomatic alternatives to the carhop—from automated serving devices, which shunted trays from kitchen to car, to specially designed radios.[31] The former, however, required a large initial outlay to install and then involved maintenance expenses as well. Speaker systems were more successful and particularly well liked because they helped eliminate horn honking when a customer was ready to have a tray retrieved.

Despite these efforts to reduce costs, increase turnover, and eliminate noise, by the early 1960s the reputation of the drive-in was becoming tarnished. In Detroit, for example, a planning-commission study prepared in 1963 cited a long list of problems commonly associated with drive-in operations, including litter; noise from voices, radios, and cars; excessive lighting; youthful rowdiness and socializing; drinking; violence; and a general negative effect on adjacent property values.[32] Cities across the country from Perth Amboy, New Jersey, to Vallejo, California, began to consider—and in many cases pass—anti-drive-in laws mandating fencing along property perimeters to reduce noise and excessive light, hours of allowable operation, and standards for litter control and trash removal.

The drive-in business was also plagued with other difficulties that no amount of technological theatrics, or even laws, could solve. Like their cousins the drive-in theaters, drive-in restaurants ran into seasonal problems. Companies began to manufacture in-car heaters, but neither a heater nor the more typical canopy could make the automobile an attractive place to eat during a Midwestern blizzard.

Seasonal restrictions, coupled with the rising specter of legal restrictions, made the drive-in an increasingly unattractive proposition. By the close of the 1970s, only a handful of chains—including a few of the early drive-in pioneers such as A&W, Steak 'n Shake, and Big Boy—provided curb service at their units. The drive-in stage in the development of food stands had run its course.

Carpenter's; Los Angeles; photograph c. 1932. An early Los Angeles drive-in in action. By the late 1930s, Los Angeles had become the eat-in-your-car restaurant capital of America. (The Huntington Library.)

FAST-FOOD STANDS

The most recent step in the evolution of eating fast along the highway is the development of the modern self-service food factories known today as fast-food restaurants (the term, in general currency by the 1970s, refers to limited-menu self-service restaurants where mass-produced food is served up virtually moments after the customers order).[33] To begin it is helpful to turn the clock back to about 1939, when two ex–New Englanders, Maurice and Richard McDonald, opened a drive-in restaurant in San Bernardino, California.[34] As was typical of many drive-ins at the time, McDonald's had become a mecca for teenagers. Nevertheless, with the relatively slow turnover inherent in curb service, the brothers could not reach a high enough customer-per-hour count to make the kinds of profits they wanted.[35]

Following in the tradition of Michael Cullen and George Urich, they recognized the national merchandising trend toward self-service in grocery stores and filling stations and decided to find out if the public, now well conditioned by drive-ins to eating dinner in cars without benefit of napery, china, or the formal rituals of mealtime manners, "was ready for a self-service drive-in."[36] So, in 1948, the McDonalds dismissed the carhops and—taking things a step further—pared down both service and menu to the absolute minimum. With that, their restaurant became a key prototype for the dozens of self-service fast-food companies to emerge over the next four decades.[37]

By 1952 the brothers were producing an estimated one million of their fifteen-cent hamburgers and twenty-cent malts and shakes and 160 tons of ten-cent portions of french fries a year in their 192-square-foot food factory.[38] Improvements in assembly line techniques, and rigid standardization—concepts pioneered by early urban hamburger chains such as White Castle—permitted this staggering output. Paper cups were filled with milk-shake mix in advance and stockpiled in a freezer so that they could instantly be placed on the mixing machines, while fries were mass produced in batteries of deep-fry vats and then placed under infrared lamps to be kept warm.[39] A hamburger, beverage, and fries could be served in about twenty seconds—hot food at lightning speed for a low price, as promised. By the early 1950s, the brothers, realizing they had developed a highly marketable restaurant format, took the cue from A&W, Howard Johnson's, and other roadside-restaurant franchises; soon a small number of other McDonald's opened up in Arizona and California.[40]

Enter Ray Kroc, a former Lily Cup salesman who at the time was engaged in peddling milk-shake machines to restaurants, drive-ins, and soft-serve stands on the national circuit. Accustomed to selling one or two machines at a time to a given restaurant, Kroc became curious about the McDonalds, who required a huge battery of the shake mixers. Visiting San Bernardino in 1954, he became fascinated with the operation; seeing a vision of thousands of McDonald's lining the highways of the continent, Kroc convinced the brothers to allow him to franchise their concept nationwide.[41]

One important understanding of the agreement was that all franchises sold by Kroc would duplicate the standard building design, which the brothers had commissioned in 1952 from architect Stanley Meston. Aided by his staff architect Charles W. Fish, and in close collaboration with the brothers, Meston had developed what would become one of the midtwentieth century's most familiar architectural icons—the now-famous structure with overhanging slanted roof, visual front, wall panels decorated in red-and-white striped tile, and the flanking golden arches. This eye-catching design, with some slight modifications, became the basis for Kroc's first franchise unit in Des Plaines, Illinois, in 1955, and for other McDonald's franchises that, guided by Kroc's energy and entrepreneurship, numbered two hundred by 1960.

The McDonalds' concept, sold by Ray Kroc, caught on quickly. By the mid-1950s, restaurant trade journals began to thicken with advertisements soliciting potential franchisees for a wide assortment of fast-food ventures. Among the companies seeking investors was Burger King, a Florida eighteen-cent hamburger chain founded in 1953 by Matthew Burns and Keith Cramer. Burger King grew to forty-one units by 1955 and eventually be-

ARCHITECTURAL EVOLUTION OF
MCDONALD'S:

Below, top:
Advertisement soliciting prospective franchisees, September 1952. This rectangular structure with walk-up self-service windows, topped by a round cantilevered overhang, closely resembles the first self-service McDonald's. The design reveals its drive-in restaurant ancestry. (McDonald's Corporation.)

Below, bottom left:
Rendering, dating from 29 December 1952, by Charles W. Fish, of the now-legendary golden arches design; Stanley Clark Meston, architect. (Charles W. Fish.)

Below, bottom right:
First McDonald's of the Ray Kroc era, 1955; Des Plaines, Illinois; photograph 1981. The structure, which originally conformed closely to the red-and-white-tiled Fish/Meston prototype, had been altered by the time of this photograph, but subsequently the company restored it as a McDonald's museum. (Author.)

came McDonald's chief rival. Still another chain, developed around the persona of a flamboyant restaurateur and self-proclaimed Kentucky colonel, Harlan Sanders, was Kentucky Fried Chicken. Founded by Sanders in 1955 when a highway bypass around his original roadside restaurant caused a precipitous decline in trade, KFC grew to be one of the giants of the fast-food trade. By 1960 thousands of other limited-menu, self-service roadside franchises serving everything from tacos to doughnuts to pizza had become familiar fixtures along the Miracle Mile.

Commercial success for a good many of these ventures was immediate and sustained. From the customer's standpoint, the service was extremely fast, tipping was not required, the premises were generally clean, and the food was predictable. After all, fast-food entrepreneurs adhered to the same formula that governed the chain motel: the best surprise was no surprise. As far as the owners were concerned, the format solved the many problems posed by the drive-in. Self-service and mass production reduced labor costs and allowed for staffing by relatively unskilled teenagers paid at minimum wage, provided a turnover rate many times that of curb service, and attracted suburban families while generally escaping the teenage hangout problem that vexed the drive-ins. McDonald's Kroc, for example (who ultimately bought out the McDonald brothers in 1961), established a policy early on that prohibited vending machines, pay telephones, jukeboxes, and other amenities that encouraged loitering. So as the drive-in restaurant declined in the mid-sixties, fast food thrived, and many a former drive-in operator went on to purchase a Dunkin' Donuts, Wendy's, Pizza Hut, or some other franchise.

One problem seemed to carry over from the drive-in's heyday: the opinion that restaurants of this type detracted from "the neighborhood." By the early 1960s, the epithet "eyesore" was being applied with increasing vehemence to the highway strip. Along with gas stations, fast-food restaurants, as one of the rapidly multiplying roadside services, bore a large measure of the criticism. Before long many of the larger chains responded to the cry for reform and began to alter the image of their food

stands. McDonald's, for example, in 1968 began replacing its original red-and-white slant-roof structures flanked by golden arches with brick-veneered buildings capped by mansard roofs. The arches were relegated to a wall appliqué or to the sign.[42] Over the next decade, other chains, from Burger King to Dunkin' Donuts, converted to the Environmental Look as well.

Shifts in format coincided with changes in exterior costumery. As the novelty of eating in the car wore thin, structures were built larger to accommodate indoor seating.[43] "Drive-thrus" were also added for eat-in-the-car diehards and the take-home trade. Companies expanded their menus. New and more-expensive fare—from fish fillets and apple pie to quarter-pounders—joined the bargain burger. By the 1970s, industry giants such as McDonald's and Burger King, anxious to boost profits by staying open longer hours, had added items such as eggs, pancakes, and orange juice to their menu and effectively burst into the breakfast trade along the Miracle Mile. With wider menus and indoor dining, the distinction between the food stand and the family restaurant was becoming increasingly blurred.

With the Arab oil embargo of 1973, the dawn-to-midnight fast-food restaurant—long a mainstay of the suburban strip—began to sprout up in the nation's cities. The canny companies carefully hedged their bets while expanding their market at the same time. The rationale was simple. If oil shortages continued to depress profits in their roadside outlets, they could still rely on customers arriving by foot, bus, or subway.

Transplanting roadside quick eats to Main Street did exact its penalties. Placing stock architecture and plasticized interiors beside or within urban blocks that were just being recognized for their architectural and historic import aroused much public ire. After a number of skirmishes, many chains again adapted to still another change in values. Soon metropolitan

McDonald's, 1977; Saddle River, New Jersey; photograph 1985. This is a typical contemporary roadside McDonald's, with mansard roof. (Author.)

burger factories sported imitation stained-glass windows and Tiffany lamps, murals with historic photographs, and wood and brass accents. Outside, discreet name plates and diminutively scaled Kentucky colonels, golden arches, and other trademarks became common, in an attempt to show respect for historic exteriors. It was not long before fast-food restaurants cast in the Old Building Look made an appearance along the roadside strip as well. The marketing of history as a backdrop for roadside eating, first pioneered by the industrious women of the tearoom and then commercially codified by Howard Johnson, had finally overtaken the corporate scion of the old "hot-dog kennel."

DINERS

No discussion of the evolution of wayside eateries could end without mention of a separate but parallel development to the food stand—the diner. The history of the diner extends at least as far back as 1872, when Walter Scott of Providence, Rhode Island, decided to open a beanery on wheels and began serving workers sandwiches, boiled eggs, pies, and coffee from a horse-drawn express truck.[44] The idea of an urban chuck wagon caught on rapidly and underwent many improvements and modifications as it spread to other cities. In Worcester, Massachusetts, by the late 1880s, Samuel M. Jones had started manufacturing wagons large enough for customers to eat inside. Innovator Charles Palmer modified Jones's designs and took out a patent in 1891; he then set up a lunch-wagon factory. Thomas H. Buckley opened up a competing manufactory in 1892, and as the old century came to a close, a new industry was born.[45]

By the early 1900s, the little rectangular four-wheeled wagons—their sides punctuated by several windows and a center door, and the whole adorned with painted scrollwork, geometric patterns, and landscape scenes so they looked like a cross between an omnibus and a circus wagon—became a familiar sight in cities across the Northeast and even as far away as Denver.[46] Business was often so good that owners found they no longer needed to roam the streets in search of trade. Many rented an odd piece of land, set in place their specially manufactured lunch wagons (retired horse-drawn street-railway cars were often pressed into service as a makeshift substitute), and built a wooden shroud around the wheels to give a more permanent look. Soon the little carts, dwarfed by the neighboring commercial buildings with their glass store fronts and bracketed cornices, became a new, and somewhat incongruous, addition to Main Street.

Soon a spate of other lunch-car manufacturing companies came into being, including Tierney (1905), Worcester Lunch Car (1906), and Jerry O'Mahony (1913),[47] and by the 1920s the nation was experiencing a full-fledged dining-car (or "diner" as they were called by this time) boom. Now with wagons remaining in one place for a long time instead of maneuvering through traffic each day, larger and more commodious designs were possible. Although longer and somewhat wider, this new generation of lunch cars, with their ribbon of tiny windows and monitor or barrel roofs, still bore some resemblance to their lunch-cart and horsecar ancestors, only the new units were now semipermanent structures. First shipped by rail, then tugged along by horses or motortruck, the diners rolled on vestigial wheels down narrow streets, beneath underpasses and overhead wires, to finally be settled onto some sliver of land called home.

Inside, the new diners exhibited the carefully arranged, compartmentalized compactness of ships' galleys and railroad dining cars. As one observer noted in *Literary Digest* in 1932, the typical lunch-car interior

[is] as utilitarian as a machinist's bench. It shimmers with burnished nickel, quarter-sawed oak, black marbleite, and colored tile. Lined up against the wall, within short reach of the . . . counterman, is the entire operating equipment of the diner: stoves, warming-pans, coffee urns, refrigerator section, storage bins, silver, dishes, and so on. On the other side of the marble counter that divides the car lengthwise are from twelve to twenty-four stools, and back of them, in the newer models, a row of tables for two or four. The diner is ventilated by blower fans which expel the fumes of frying steak and onions that formerly caused the eyes as well as the mouth of the lunch-wagon patron to water. . . . The humble dog-wagon with its sandwich-pie-coffee menu, gradually had been transformed. The lunch wagon is not a wagon at all, but a pretentious, semipermanent, *bijou* restaurant, designed by engineers familiar with Pullman-car and ship architecture.[48]

What was the appeal of operating, or for that matter eating in, a restaurant that looked like (or in some cases actually was) a trolley car beached on Main Street, by the railway station or factory gate, or along the taxpayer strip? For the owner, the diner was a way of converting a few hundred dollars in savings—many diner companies allowed their products

Palace Night Lunch; Connecticut (town unknown); photograph 1906. By the turn of the century, boxlike lunch wagons—such as this more or less permanently parked one, its wheels masked by a board valance—had become a familiar sight not only near factory gates but also along the Main Streets of New England. (John Baeder.)

to be purchased on the installment plan like appliances, furniture, and automobiles—into an instant business. Most diners of the period came fully equipped. All the thinking and planning was done at the factory. Even the most novice operator could be in business within a day or two after the manufacturer's field crews rolled a crisp, sparkling, factory-fresh dining car onto its new site. The new owner was free to worry about food rather than the look and layout of the premises.

Along with relatively low cost and instant gratification, diners offered a readily recognizable image. Despite the many competing manufacturers, by the mid-1920s diners had become rather standardized in appearance. Whether made by Worcester, O'Mahony, or some other manufacturer, a new diner by one maker looked much the same as one by another. Diners sighted by a traveler in a strange neighborhood or city had the potential of triggering the same goodwill associated with a favorite car back home. Thus each diner purchased was like a membership card in a de facto chain. The owner had the benefits of symbolic recognition that a White Castle or Howard Johnson's might inspire without having to sacrifice autonomy to any central control.

Finally, if business prospered, the old car could always be turned in, like an automobile, in exchange for the newest model. One German immigrant blacksmith-turned-cook, Fritz Plassmeyer, bought his first diner in Trenton, New Jersey, in 1928 for $2,500 and subsequently purchased a larger diner every time his business expanded; by 1948 he was the proud owner of a deluxe model worth $150,000—six different diners on the same site in thirty years, an average of one every six years.[49] Owners of conventional buildings had to remodel periodically; diner owners simply traded up.

During Prohibition years and the concurrent eating-out boom, diner patronage skyrocketed. No longer seen as only a workingman's hideout, diners sported menus expanded to include breakfast, lunch, dinner, and late-night snacks served by waitresses at tables and booths as well as at the counter; they now appealed to a much broader clientele. As *Literary Digest* pointed out, by the early 1930s the diner had become one of "the most democratic of all eating places [as illustrated by] the roll-call of patrons: actors, milkmen, chauffeurs, debutantes, *nymphes du pave*, young men-about-town, teamsters, students, streetcar motormen, messenger boys, policemen, white wings, business men—all these and more rub elbows at the counter."[50] This switch from portable workingman's beanery to prefabricated restaurant with broad appeal was further underscored by the fact that by 1938, as estimated by the *Christian Science Monitor*, "25 per cent of the patrons of the better wagons [were] women and children."[51]

The cozy little cars also provided an alternative to both the limited fare of the hot dog or hamburger stand and the full-menu Main Street restaurant. Eating at the diner was also cheap. The cachet of good inexpensive food served up quickly in a novel setting carried over into the depression years. By the early 1930s, an estimated four thousand portable lunchrooms were scattered about the country, the greatest number concentrated in the East, with one hundred to two hundred new cars streaming out of the nation's diner factories each year.[52]

This boom amid the bust made diners, along with motor courts and other wayside enterprises, an object of fascination, a safe investment, a seemingly recession-proof business. While major industries lagged, the lunch-car business expanded at a rapid clip with the national dining-car population climbing by the end of the decade to about six thousand units, with an average take of from about four hundred dollars to as much as two thousand dollars weekly.[53] New units ranged in price from fifteen thousand dollars to more than fifty thousand dollars.[54]

The decade following World War II saw the decline of many nineteenth-century institutions, as everything from trolley cars to downtown hotels succumbed to the onslaught of car and highway. Yet the diner, which could just as easily be plunked a few parking-space widths back from the curb of the highway strip as sandwiched between buildings along Main Street, not only survived in the postwar years but prospered. Nevertheless the need to attract the attention of motorists and truck drivers in the modern-is-better postwar period prompted diner manufacturers to produce cars with more exterior and interior pizzazz.

To keep up with the times, old standbys such as Jerry O'Mahony, along with newer diner makers such as Paramount, Fodero, Kullman, and Mountain View, broke with long-standing traditions. Monitor and barrel roofs gave way to flat roofs. A more prominent exterior parapet allowed for higher ceilings on the interior. Sides glimmered in fluted stainless steel like the latest railroad coaches and long-distance motor buses. And big exterior windows replaced the little double-hung streetcarlike windows,

Prospect Diner; Hartford, Connecticut; photograph c. 1929. This crisp-looking new diner with monitor roof, built by the Dining Car Division of the J. G. Brill Company of Philadelphia, is typical of the larger wood-and-steel dining cars numerous companies were producing hundreds of by the 1920s. A poured-concrete foundation, brick steps, freshly seeded lawns, overflowing flowerboxes, shrubbery, and an electrolier suitable for illuminating any respectable City Beautiful scheme are all orchestrated to dispel the slightly unsavory reputation of some of the earliest wagons and trolley lunches. (Author's collection.)

bestowing upon the diner the advantages of the visual front—then strongly touted for almost all modern sales structures.

In 1948 *Saturday Evening Post* writer Blake Ehrlich skillfully celebrated in words the attractive power of these "glittering chrome-and-neon inns that cost as much as $150,000"[55] as viewed by a postwar motorist:

A diner flaunting its chromium curves on the edge of a traffic circle caught the rays of the afternoon sun and flung them full into the driver's face. We swung off the road and stopped, then reeled across the gravel to the diner. [Inside]. . . neon, freon, glass brick, slick brick and plastic. There was nothing carlike about it. It consisted mainly of a huge room which seated more than 120 customers, and was almost as wide as it was long. [Now shipped in sections and joined on site, postwar diners could expand beyond railroad-car widths.] It was solidly put together with hard surfaces for resistance to dirt. From composition floor to fluorescent lights, the place was spotless and almost odorless. It was as compact as a submarine, but a submarine designed by a nightclub decorator. A built in vestibule eliminated the windy drafts afflicting old-style diners. Almost lost on the far side of the structure, and fronted by streamlined stools, was the expected counter, also built in. Behind it gleamed an array of short-order devices, built in. In fact, everything was built in but the customers.[56]

While still "as utilitarian as a machinist's bench" in function, this next

Inside the Prospect Diner; Hartford, Connecticut; photograph c. 1929. Interior arrangements consisting of a front row of tables, then an aisle, stools, counter, and back bar of easy-to-clean stainless steel, had become general industry standards by the 1920s. Note the luggage rack and window latches—trolley and railroad coach components adapted to the diner. (Author's collection.)

generation of dining cars was packaged to sell. As one industry observer remarked in the trade journal *Diner* in 1949, the modern diner "is a thing of streamlined beauty glistening with shining backbar appliances, luxurious in interior funishings . . . appealing to all levels, male and female, rich and poor."[57]

After a decade of relative prosperity, beginning in the mid-1950s diners gradually began losing ground to drive-ins and emerging fast-food chains. To counter this economic encroachment, those diner makers that survived first decorated their streamlined designs with soaring canopies and other Exaggerated Modern trappings, then abandoned the vehicular look altogether. The most successful operators—often entrepreneurial Greek and Italian families, restaurateurs at heart who had outgrown the old diners and wished to cater as much to suburban families as to truck drivers— needed more room for larger tables and full-size kitchens to accommodate expanded menus. They also preferred buildings that, instead of looking like jazzed-up railroad coaches, seemed a more appropriate setting for a family's meal out.[58]

Manufacturers obliged by tooling up to produce still another generation of diners—large sprawling single-story rectangular structures festooned with everything from classical columns and plastic mansards to wrought-iron trellisses and imitation stone cladding. Representing an investment often approaching a million dollars—for structures, site work, and fixtures—these great-great-grandchildren of Palmer's little lunch cart are more like roadside family restaurants. They bear a genetic resemblance to their wheel-mounted ancestors only in that they are premanufactured and then joined in pieces at the site and in most cases are still called "diners."

Undercarriage of Kitchenette Diner; Cambridge, Massachusetts; photograph 1978, Eve Yorke. After more than forty years in the same location, the Kitchenette (a Worcester lunch car) was moved—first by horses as a publicity stunt, then ultimately by flatbed truck— to a new spot in nearby Allston. The car's original four-wheeled undercarriage was found intact when the diner was extracted from its old site. (Eve Yorke.)

Streamline Moderne diner in scrap yard of the Musi Dining Car Company; Avenel, New Jersey; watercolor 1975, John Baeder. (John Baeder.)

Modern Diner, 1940; Pawtucket, Rhode Island; photograph 1975, Richard Longstreth. One of the few surviving Sterling Streamliners, this diner's canted prow and flow-line trim create such a sense of motion that it looks like a train barreling out of a tunnel. This kinetic creation was the work of the J. B. Judkins Company of Merrimac, Massachusetts, a venerable builder of coaches, founded in 1866. Judkins converted over to custom auto-body production in the early twentieth century. When the auto work soured during the depression, the company turned its energies to building diners in the period just before World War II. (Richard Longstreth.)

What of all the hundreds of older diners that were traded off as their owners traded up? Some have gone the way of old streetcars and automobiles and have wound up in the scrap yard. Hundreds of others are still in use, although their number is gradually dwindling. Most are still run by committed operators, often families, who maintain their dining cars with the same buff-and-polish fervor one might use on a classic automo-

Miss Worcester Diner, 1948; Worcester, Massachusetts; photograph 1981. By the late 1940s, the products of the Worcester Lunch Car company—like the diner here, located across the street from the company's manufacturing plant—appeared retardataire when compared with the streamlined diners of the period. (Author.)

Randolph Diner, 1969; Randolph, New Jersey; photograph 1985. Most diners built in recent years—such as this arcaded example by Kullman, which was trucked to the site in sections and then joined—bear little resemblance to their lunch-car ancestors. (Author.)

bile. A number of old diners have even been resurrected and refurbished.

Diners constitute one of those rare institutions to have survived long enough to be rediscovered by another generation in virtually unaltered form. The little dining cars have been the subject of a rash of recent newspaper stories, magazine articles, books, and lectures. They have also become the passion of photo-realist painters such as John Baeder who are drawn to the highway landscape of today as Edward Hopper and his contemporaries were inspired by the decaying industrial cities of the depression era. This outpouring of interest in diners is quite understand-

Oasis Diner, 1980; Boulder, Colorado; photograph 1981. More "Art Deco" than Art Deco, this completely new diner reveals how the current diner revival, following in the path of most architectural revivals, reinterprets old forms through mannerism and exaggeration. (Author.)

able. Most older examples of the diminutive lunch cars bear a close resemblance to railroad coaches and trolley cars—objects that have long been imbued with a powerful national mystique.

Should the resolve to study and selectively preserve the nation's cultural legacy (which has recently reached beyond the residue of elite culture to include industrial districts, agricultural complexes, urban neighborhoods, Main Streets, and an occasional diner) be extended to the broader spectrum of roadside architecture?

Epilogue

FOR FUTURE GENERATIONS to be able to watch selected replays of today's movie through the windshield and gain an accurate picture of everyday life in twentieth-century America, the selective conservation of the roadside commercial legacy cannot be left to chance. The structures, signs, and symbols that make up the movie's cast are, in fact, highly vulnerable artifacts.

The preservation of the structures that form the roadside commercial landscape is a far more formidable task than the preservation of most other building types. Take the issue of exterior change, for example. When a roadside building is outfitted for a new use, its owners are usually eager to recloak the structure with a fresh image. After all, the need for an up-to-date sales costume to appeal to motorists is one of the programmatic imperatives of architecture for speed-reading. As a result, while the exteriors of most other kinds of structures remain recognizable throughout successive changes in function, the appearance of a roadside commercial building is much more likely to be ephemeral.

Photographic and written documentation is often touted as an acceptable alternative to actual physical preservation. However, this strategy is rooted in a mistaken assumption that the nation's archives are brimming over with valuable information on the commercial car culture. Perhaps because this phenomenon is considered so commonplace, it has been inadvertently overlooked by many custodians of historical collections. So, while archives are often crammed full of pictures of local Main Streets, for example, few have photographs of life along the nearby Miracle Miles. Movies, video tapes, oral histories, and other useful forms of documentation on the subject are almost nonexistent.

What about the archives of major corporate chains? Some, such as Texaco and Sears, Roebuck, have excellent files on the architectural legacy of their companies. Most, however, have saved little written or pictorial evidence of their own history. State historic preservation agencies, with their federally funded historic resources inventories, would appear to be another valuable source for documentation. Yet only a handful of states have thus far extended their efforts to include the architecture of the roadside.

Meanwhile, a growing number of roadside commercial structures have actually been the objects of preservation efforts. In Tampa local preservationists have been working to conserve a late Streamline Moderne Publix supermarket (1954). Near Natchez, Mississippi, Mammy's Cupboard (1939)—a filling station in the shape of a giant black woman—was spared from being leveled by a highway construction project through the efforts of the Society for Commercial Archeology, an organization founded in 1976 for the purpose of encouraging the preservation of roadside commercial architecture. Recently, after resisting most local attempts to save the rapidly dwindling number of their early red-and-white hamburger stands, the McDonald's Corporation restored Ray Kroc's first franchise unit (1955) in Des Plaines, Illinois, for use as a company museum. Howard Johnson's, White Castle, Texaco, and other stewards of roadside commercial landmarks would do well to follow suit.

Such individual efforts, no matter how commendable, are only a small beginning in the attempt to conserve evidence of the twentieth-century commercial roadside. While each individual building's design expresses the excitement of its period of ascendancy on the Miracle Mile—in flashing razzle-dazzle, or curving lines of flow, or quaint domesticity—as a solitary example, it presents only a static instant in the phenomenon of driving down the road. Experienced during a trip behind the wheel, roadside buildings become a series of commercial messages that blink on and off in sequence. However, they lose this kinetic dimension when they are treated as individual icons and are isolated from the chaos of the highway strip, and removed from the enframement of the windshield.

A clearer picture of the twentieth-century commercial roadside could be revealed to those living in the future if we maintained a number of types of strips in toto. But most historic preservation techniques currently used for preserving groupings of buildings—from so-called "living history" museums to historic districts—are designed to interpret the past for an audience of pedestrians and may not be entirely appropriate for conserving today's heritage of mobility. Most likely, solutions will be discovered by combining existing techniques with new approaches not yet found in the lexicon of historic preservation.

"End of the Road House, or Reel'n in the Dotted Line," 1976; section looking west. Here architectural visionary Daniel V. Scully, intrigued with the idea of bringing the experience of driving down the road indoors, has created a design for a house in which each room would be a stop along an interior highway (which ultimately coils into itself). As the twenty-first century approaches, a number of American architects are attempting to develop a symbolic vocabulary expressing the nation's nearly one-hundred-year-old addiction to the automobile, the highway, and personal mobility. (Daniel V. Scully.)

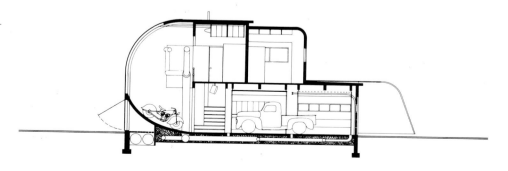

McDonald's; Portland, Oregon; photograph 1984. One of the growing number of instances where a major roadside chain is opting for historic preservation over demolition, this old red-and-white McDonald's hamburger stand, built in 1962, was restored for use as a children's party center in 1981. As part of the project, the company built one of its new, mansard-roofed restaurants a short distance away. (Author.)

Why think of retaining even a glimpse of those gauntlets of hucksterism that crisscross most contemporary American communities? As suggested in the pages of this book, there is much to be learned from reading the American commercial roadside. The overlays of highways, and the buildings that line them, reveal how the automobile, coupled with commerce, has edited the American landscape; while the images in which the buildings were cast reveal how the national psyche has been reduced and encapsulated into twenty-second commercials. The significance of this staggering environmental transformation is still just beginning to come into focus.

We can now, with a hundred years of perspective, see the nineteenth-century Main Street—the portal between factory and consumer—as a valuable window on the industrial revolution. The twentieth-century Miracle Mile, when re-examined in the twenty-first century, is also certain to provide critical insights into the transition from the industrial revolution to a commercial revolution—when Big Macs replaced smokestacks as an icon of American prosperity.

Notes

FROM MAIN STREET TO MIRACLE MILE

1. "Mobility—A Controlling Factor in Design," *Architectural Record* 84 (August 1938): 69.

2. For further discussion of cars versus trains see Warren James Belasco, *Americans on the Road* (Cambridge: MIT Press, 1979), 19–39.

3. Peter Kalm, *Peter Kalm's Travels in North America*, vol. 1, ed. and trans. Adolph B. Bensen (New York: Dover Publications, 1966), 19, 342.

4. Carole Rifkind, *Main Street, The Face of Urban America* (New York: Harper & Row, 1977), 14.

5. For discussion of track towns see John W. Reps, *The Making of Urban America* (Princeton: Princeton University Press, 1965), 397–403.

6. Thomas H. Pitts as quoted in Bayard Still, *Urban America: A History with Documents* (Boston: Little, Brown and Company, 1974), 391–392.

7. Sam B. Warner, Jr., *Streetcar Suburbs: The Process of Growth in Boston, 1870-1900* (Cambridge: Harvard University Press, 1962), 49-52.

8. "Taxpayer" is defined in the *American Heritage Dictionary of the English Language*, New College ed., as "a building intended to cover the expenses of a piece of land until it can be put to a more profitable use." For an example of contemporary usage see "Jack Cinnamon's Market," *Architectural Record* 77 (February 1935): 86.

9. In *Oxford English Dictionary*, s.v. "strip": "A long narrow tract of territory, of land. . . ." In *Dictionary of American Slang*, s.v. "strip": "A newer word, sometimes, but not always, referring to a district rather than a single street." The word came into widespread use by the 1950s to describe developments where commercial or residential buildings were strung out along a highway. In Great Britain, this same phenomenon is referred to as "ribbon development."

10. I. T. Frary, "The Passing of a Famous Avenue," *Architectural Record* 43 (April 1918): 391–392.

11. Winston Churchill, *The Dwelling-Place of Light* (New York: Macmillan Company, 1917), 15–16.

12. Douglas Haskell, "Architecture on Routes U.S. 40 and 66," *Architectural Record* 81 (May 1937): 19.

13. Public Roads Administration, *Highway Practice in the United States of America* (Washington, D.C.: GPO, 1949), 3.

14. American Public Works Association, *History of Public Works in the United States, 1776–1976*, ed. Ellis L. Armstrong (Chicago: American Public Works Association, 1976), 70–73.

15. *Historical Statistics of the United States, Colonial Times to 1970* (Washington, D.C.: U.S. Bureau of the Census, 1975), Series Q 148–162.

16. Lincoln Highway Association, *The Lincoln Highway: The Story of a Crusade That Made Transportation History* (New York: Dodd, Mead & Company, 1935), 77–79.

17. American Public Works Association, *History of Public Works*, 77–82.

18. Robert Bruce, *The National Road* (Washington, D.C.: National Highways Association, 1916), 18, 20.

19. Ibid., 31.

20. *Historical Statistics*.

21. Standard Oil Company of New York, *Historic Tours in SOCONYLAND* (New York: Standard Oil Company of New York, 1925), 56.

22. Frank E. Brimmer, "The 'Nickel-and-Dime' Stores of Nomadic America," *Magazine of Business* 52 (August 1927): 174.

23. John J. McCarthy and Robert Littel, "Three Hundred Thousand Shacks," *Harper's* 167 (July 1933): 184.

24. "The Great American Roadside," *Fortune* 9 (September 1934): 54.

25. Ibid.

26. *Historical Statistics*.

27. Unpublished letter from Arthur A. Shurtleff to *New York Times*, manuscript number 8123.04-108, Boston Public Library.

28. Charles Downing Lay, "New Towns for High-Speed Roads," *Architectural Record* 78 (November 1935): 353.

29. Gilmore D. Clarke, "Transportation—An Expanding Field for Modern Building," *Architectural Record* 90 (October 1941): 44.

30. Brimmer, 174.

31. "Suburban Retail Districts," *Architectural Forum* 93 (August 1950): 107.

32. "Roadtown: The Great American Excursion," *Architectural Forum* 105 (September 1956): 124.

33. "New Type of Suburban Shopping Area Proposed," *American City* 33 (August 1926): 214–216.

34. J. Malcolm Bird, "Tours and Detours," *Scientific American*, November 1921, 6.

35. Harold H. Dunn, as quoted in "New Type," 214.

36. "Mrs. Jones Changes Her Shopping Habits," *Business Week*, 5 October 1929, 29.

37. "Evolution of the Shopping Center," *The Community Builders' Handbook* (Washington, D.C.: Urban Land Institute, 1965), 271.

38. Ibid.

39. Leland F. Champlin, "Michigan: Short-Lived Shopping Center for Unstable Land," *Architectural Record* 84 (July 1938): 44.

40. Geoffrey Baker and Bruno Funaro, *Shopping Centers: Design and Operation* (New York: Reinhold, 1951), 79–85.

41. "Evolution of Shopping Centers," 271.

42. Baker and Funaro, 214–221; "Shoppers' World," *Architectural Forum* 95 (December 1951): 180–186.

43. "A Break-through for Two-Level Shopping Centers," *Architectural Forum* 105 (December 1956): 120.

44. Frank Lloyd Wright, "America Tomorrow," *American Architect* 141 (May 1932): 17.

45. Robert B. Riley, "Understanding the Strip", *Architectural & Engineering News* 10 (January 1968): 32.

46. Diane C. Thomas, "Lonely Road Now," *Atlanta Magazine*, November 1978, 57.

47. Ibid., 59.

ARCHITECTURE FOR SPEED-READING

1. See "Auto Showrooms" chapter.

2. The Dover series of publications of early photographs of American cities is a readily available source, e.g., Robert F. Looney, *Old Philadelphia in Early Photographs, 1839–1914* (New York: Dover Publications, 1976); Mary Black, *Old New York in Early Photographs, 1853–1901* (New York: Dover Publications, 1973).

3. Frank Presbrey, *History and Development of Advertising* (New York: Greenwood Press, 1968), 491–503.

4. See the example of Topeka, Kansas, c. 1900, in Carole Rifkind, *Main Street: The Face of Urban America* (New York: Harper & Row, 1977), 167.

5. John C. Van Dyke, *New New York* (New York: Macmillan Company, 1909), 209, 212–213.

6. For example, Ronald Lee Fleming, "Corporate design: it all looks the same," *Environmental Action*, 3 August 1974, 13.

7. J. B. Jackson, "Other Directed Houses," article first published in *Landscape* magazine, later included in *Landscapes, Selected Writings of J. B. Jackson*, ed. Ervin H. Zube (Amherst: University of Massachusetts Press, 1970), 65.

8. Many accounts of early wayside business owners appear in trade journals such as *Tourist Court Journal* and travel accounts such as Lewis Gannett, *Sweet Land* (Garden City, N.Y.: Sun Dial, 1937), 5.

9. Frederick Lewis Allen, *Only Yesterday: An Informal History of the 1920's* (1931; reprint, New York: Harper & Row, 1964), 73–107; or Alan Gowans, *Images of American Living* (New York: J. B. Lippincott Company, 1964), 423.

10. Robert S. Lynd and Helen Merrell Lynd, *Middletown: A Study in Modern American Culture*, rev. ed. (New York: Harcourt Brace Jovanovich, 1956), 255.

11. Ibid., 103.

12. Herbert Hoover, as quoted in *The Palace or the Poorhouse: The American House as a Cultural Symbol*, by Jan Cohn, (East Lansing: Michigan State University Press, 1979), 237.

13. For example, E. F. Hodgson Co., *Portable Houses* (Boston: E. F. Hodgson Co., 1923), 45.

14. Lynd and Lynd, 100.

15. For example, *How to Build Cabins, Lodges, and Bungalows* (New York: Popular Science Publishing Company, 1934), 209–226.

16. As a postscript, during the late 1950s and early 1960s, domestic imagery resurfaced along the wayside. This "roadside domestic revival" was championed especially by oil companies wishing to silence critics by building gas stations in the image of ranch houses designed to blend in with postwar suburban neighborhoods. Once an expression of shared dreams as well as a desire to fit in, the house motif had become merely a carefully contrived aesthetic palliative. (See "Gas Stations" chapter.)

17. John F. Kasson, *Amusing the Million—Coney Island at the Turn of the Century* (New York: Hill & Wang, 1978), 41.

18. David Gebhard prefers the term "programmatic," as explained in his introduction to Jim Heimann and Rip Georges' *California Crazy–Roadside Vernacular Architecture* (San Francisco: Chronicle Books, 1980), 11–25. For the origin of the term "duck," see Robert Venturi, Denise Scott Brown, and Steven Izenour, *Learning from Las Vegas*, rev. ed. (Cambridge: MIT Press, 1977), 87.

19. Barbara W. Tuchman, *A Distant Mirror* (New York: Ballantine Books, 1979), 158.

20. For early history, see David Gebhard's introduction in *California Crazy*.

21. Reyner Banham, *Los Angeles: The Architecture of Four Ecologies* (New York: Harper & Row, 1971), 125.

22. For example see J. J. C. Andrews, *The Well-Built Elephant and Other Roadside Attractions* (New York: Congdon & Weed, 1984).

23. See, for example, Kathleen Ann Brooker, "Railroad Depots in New Mexico: Southwestern Styles and the Masonry Tradition," (Master's Thesis, University of New Mexico, May 1981).

24. The most useful work for understanding the relationship of Moderne and Modern is David Gebhard, "The Moderne in the U.S., 1920–1941," *Architectural Association Quarterly*, July 1970, 4–20.

25. Jeffrey L. Meikle, *Twentieth Century Limited—Industrial Design in America, 1925–1939* (Philadelphia: Temple University Press, 1979), 33–36.

26. John A. Kouwenhoven, *The Arts in Modern American Civilization* (1948; reprint, Garden City, N.Y.: W. W. Norton & Company, 1967), 26–27.

27. Meikle, 68–69.

28. Ibid., 180–185.

29. For example, in Carl W. Dipman and John E. O'Brien, *Self-Service and Semi-Self-Service Food Stores* (New York: The Progressive Grocer, 1940), 9–10.

30. Scholarly accounts often discuss both fairs' portrayal of modernity. The expositions also contained attractions clothed in popular imagery, like that exploited along the highways of the time, to appeal to a similar mass audience. At Chicago, for example, there was a reproduction of Old Fort Dearborn, 1804,

while in New York there were a number of mimetic exhibits, including the Photomatic Corporation's building in the shape of a giant streamlined snapshot camera.

31. For example, "A Modernization Forecast," *American Restaurant* 22 (January 1938): 25.

32. See, for example, Museum of Modern Art, *Modern Architecture International Exhibition* (New York: Museum of Modern Art, 1932).

33. See "Gas Stations" chapter.

34. For example, see George Anderson and Earl Crawford, "A Furnishing Plan for the Lightfoot Modern Tourist Court," *Tourist Court Journal*, June 1938, 11; also see "Motels" chapter.

35. Le Corbusier, *Towards a New Architecture*, trans. Frederick Etchells (1927; reprint, New York: Praeger, 1972).

36. Probably the richest sources for these advertisements are the wartime issues of *Life*.

37. "New Fields for Architects," *Architectural Record* 70 (August 1931): 116.

38. Daniel Vieyra, *Fill 'er Up: An Architectural History of America's Gas Stations* (New York: Collier, Macmillan, 1979), 59.

39. For example, "Drive-In Restaurant," *American Architect and Building Age* 163 (June 1943): 42.

40. Herbert Smith, "An Architect's Notes on Designing Drive-Ins," *Motor Courts and Drive Ins Construction and Operation* (New York: Ahrens, 1951), 94.

41. See Alan Hess, "California Coffee Shops," *Arts & Architecture* 2 (1983): 42–51.

42. The term "razzle-dazzle" was used to describe this genre of commercial design by Richard J. S. Gutman, Elliott Kaufman, and David Slovic. *American Diner* (New York: Harper & Row, 1979), 60.

43. Hess, 44.

44. Tom Wolfe, *The Kandy-Kolored, Tangerine-Flake Streamline Baby* (New York: Farrar, Straus and Giroux, 1965), 82.

45. Hess, 44.

46. Bevis Hillier, *The Decorative Arts of the Forties and Fifties—Austerity/Binge* (New York: Clarkson N. Potter, 1975), 158–161.

47. For example, Jack Ehli, "Shopping Center Stars," *Signs of the Times*, August 1960, 67.

48. Jane Jacobs, *The Death and Life of Great American Cities* (New York: Random House, Vintage Books, 1961), 7.

49. Rachel Carson, *Silent Spring* (Boston: Houghton Mifflin Company, 1962), 8.

50. Peter Blake, *God's Own Junkyard: The Planned Deterioration of America's Landscape*, rev. ed. (New York: Holt, Rinehart & Winston, 1979; original ed. 1964), 24.

51. Lady Bird Johnson as quoted in *Beauty for America, Proceedings of the White House Conference on Natural Beauty* (Washington, D.C.: GPO, 1965), 22.

52. Ray Kroc, *Grinding It Out: The Making of McDonald's* (Chicago: Henry Regnery Company, 1977), 143.

53. In Arthur J. Krim's "Northwest Cambridge," *Survey of Architectural History in Cambridge* (Cambridge, Mass.: Cambridge Historical Commission, 1977), 116, the author suggests that the cosmetic mansard roof originated in the "rapidly expanding suburbia of metropolitan Texas and Florida" where "it was found that the clear trapezoidal form of the 'French Provincial' mansard roof seemed to provide a domestic scale and secure form to the barren edges of the apartment blocks and tract houses." Further work is still needed, however, to pin down the exact derivation of the motif.

54. For this study, a core sampling was taken of *Sweet's General Building Catalogs* by checking the following years: 1946,

1952, 1955, 1961, 1965, 1970, 1981 to determine changes in materials being marketed for roadside buildings. *Sweet's* has been published since 1906 by McGraw-Hill Publishing Company, New York.

55. Paul Goldberger, "Architecture and Preservation," in *Preservation: Towards an Ethic in the 1980s* (Washington, D.C.: Preservation Press, 1980), 176.

56. For example see Philip Langdon, "Buses Hide Pane Sight," *Buffalo Evening News*, 29 September 1980.

AUTO SHOWROOMS

1. The phrase "auto showrooms" has multiple meanings. Narrowly defined, it is the salesroom where automobiles are displayed. The word has also taken on a broader connotation through popular use as an entire automobile dealership complex, including the sales-and-service building and surrounding car lot.

2. "A Remodeled Livery Stable," *The Horseless Age* 34 (15 July 1914): 92.

3. "The Binghamton Automobile Company's New Garage," *The Horseless Age* 26 (16 March 1904): 314.

4. Ibid.

5. *Historical Statistics of the United States, Colonial Times to 1970* (Washington, D.C.: U.S. Bureau of the Census, 1975), Series Q 148–162.

6. For example, see "Studebaker Will Conduct Model Garage and Salesroom," *The Horseless Age* 30 (25 September 1912): 463.

7. For example, see Ernest L. Ransome and Alexis Saurbrey, *Reinforced Concrete Buildings* (New York: McGraw-Hill, 1912).

8. "The Packard Garage, New York," *Architects' and Builders' Magazine* 40 (December 1907): 110–111.

9. Ibid.

10. "Studebaker Will Conduct," 463.

11. "Rambler Opens New Boston Sales and Service Station," *The Horseless Age* 30 (2 October 1912): 509.

12. "Star Motor Car Co. Sales Building and Garage, Hollywood, California," *Architectural Forum* 46 (March 1927): plate 51.

13. See photo in William F. Wharton, "Architecture and Decoration of Automobile Show Rooms," *Architectural Forum* 46 (March 1927): 311.

14. Ibid., 305–308.

15. "Ford's Broadway Showroom Is Paneled in American Walnut" (advertisement for American Walnut Manufacturers' Association), *Architectural Forum* 46 (March 1927): 76.

16. The preceding account of Alvan T. Fuller and Boston's automobile row was based on field notes, building permits, and files at the Museum of Transportation (Boston) gathered during a survey of Commonwealth Avenue conducted by students in a course in Commercial Archeology at Boston University, under the direction of the author. The material was compiled by Deborah Gilbreath Andrews, then graduate fellow in the Historic Preservation Program, University of Vermont, in an unpublished paper entitled "Merchandizing the Automobile: Early Auto Showrooms along Boston's Commonwealth Avenue."

17. B. W. Rubin, "Exorbitant Rents Result in New Motor Row," *Motor Age* 36 (11 December 1919): 20.

18. Ibid.

19. Ibid., 21.

20. Ibid.

21. "The Automobile Dominates the Plans Being Made for the 'Century of Progress' in 1933 at Chicago," *Automotive Industries* 64 (10 October 1931): 538.

22. *Modern Buildings for Modern Automobile Dealers* (Lansing, Mich.: Olds Motor Works, 1936), 5, 21.

23. A. R. Lee, "Hollywood Likes This Striking Modernized Department," *Gas Station, Garage and Motor Car Dealer* 10 (March 1938): 17.

24. "Design Competition for Dealer Establishments," *Architectural Forum* 83 (October 1945): 117.

25. See "Supermarkets" chapter.

26. Studebaker Corporation, *Postwar Housing and Facilities for Studebaker Dealers* (South Bend, Ind.: Studebaker Corporation, 1944), 2.

27. "Design Competition," 117.

28. *Historical Statistics.*

29. Hubert W. Kelley, Jr., "Mutiny of the Car Dealers," *Harper's* 213 (August 1956): 71.

30. Ibid.

31. See discussion of George Urich in "Gas Stations" chapter and Michael Cullen in "Supermarkets" chapter.

32. "Supermarkets: Dealers in Surplus Cars Go Big Time," *Business Week,* 1 October 1955, 104.

33. Kelley, 70.

34. Ibid.

35. Ibid., 69.

GAS STATIONS

Daniel I. Vieyra, *Fill 'er Up: An Architectural History of America's Gas Stations* (New York: Collier Books, 1979), is a useful guide to the history of gas-station imagery. It is one of two recent works that were very helpful in the preparation of this chapter. The other was John A. Jakle, "The American Gasoline Station, 1920–1970," *Journal of American Culture* 1 (Spring 1978): 520–542, an excellent chronology of gas-station building types.

1. *Historical Statistics of the United States, Colonial Times to 1970* (Washington, D.C.: U.S. Bureau of the Census, 1975), Series Q 148–162.

2. "Money to Be Made: The Oil-Marketing Story," *National Petroleum News* 61 (February 1969): 114.

3. C. A. Crosser, "Curbing the Curb Pump," *American City* 29 (August 1923): 155.

4. *National Petroleum News* 61 (February 1969): 114–115; Harry Bridges, *The Americanization of Shell* (New York: Newcomen Society, 1972), 15.

5. *National Petroleum News* 61 (February 1969): 116.

6. William J. Frappier, "Gasoline Alley: An Aging Ghost of Our Motoring Past," *New England Senior Citizen,* August 1981, 8–9.

7. Lucy Lowe, "Service Stations as an Asset to the City," *American City* 25 (August 1921): 153.

8. For the relationship of the City Beautiful movement and gas-station design, see Vieyra, 27–30.

9. Lowe, 151–153.

10. J. F. Kuntz, "Greek Architecture and Gasoline Service Stations," *American City* 27 (August 1922): 123–124.

11. Lowe, 154.

12. The Pennsylvania Independent Oil Company as quoted in *National Petroleum News,* 29 October 1924, 68.

13. For example, see *California Standard Steel Service Stations* (San Francisco: Michel & Pfeffer Iron Works, 1926).

14. Keith A. Sculle, "C. A. Petersen: Pioneer Gas Station Architect," *Historic Illinois* 2 (June 1979): 11–13.

15. A. H. Packer, "Community Service Stations," *Motor Age,* 6 September 1923, 23.

16. *California Standard Steel Service Stations,* 13.

17. See, for example, "Super Service Station: A Plan for a Corner Lot," *Automobile Digest* 17 (January 1929): 37.

18. For example, John Hocke, "An Up-to-Date Greasing Palace," *American Builder and Building Age* 52 (December 1930): 80–81; also Jakle, 528–529.

19. *National Petroleum News* 61 (February 1969): 116.

20. Ibid., 118–120; Jakle, 529–531; Jeffrey L. Meikle, *Twentieth Century Limited—Industrial Design in America, 1925–1939* (Philadelphia: Temple University Press, 1979), 123–131.

21. Jakle uses the term "oblong box" to categorize this genre of station, 529.

22. "Standardized Service Stations Designed by Walter Dorwin Teague," *Architectural Record* 82 (September 1937): 69–72; Meikle, 125.

23. "Standardized Service Stations," 69–72.

24. See Meikle, 125–131.

25. Interview, Frederick G. Frost, Jr., by author, 26 January 1982.

26. See "Supermarkets" chapter.

27. The term "independent" originally was used in the industry to describe oil companies that were independent of the Standard Oil trust. By the 1930s, the term was being applied to small oil companies that bought petroleum from the major oil companies and sold it under their own "private brands."

28. *National Petroleum News* 61 (February 1969): 118.

29. "Self-Service Stations: New Marketing Pattern?" *Business Week,* 24 July 1948, 68.

30. "Gasoline: Help Yourself Boom," *Newsweek* 30 (29 December 1947): 48.

31. "'Gas-A-Terias': Self-served gasoline saves nickel a gallon for California drivers," *Life* 25 (22 November 1948): 129.

32. "Self-Service Stations," 68.

33. "Gasoline: Help Yourself Boom," 48.

34. "Gasoline: War Against Self-Service," *Newsweek* 33 (25 April 1949): 69.

35. "Self-Service Stations," 68.

36. Don Sweeney, "California's Self Service Stations Still in Limelight," *National Petroleum News* 40 (25 May 1948): 9.

37. John Baeder, *Gas, Food and Lodging* (New York: Abbeville Press, 1982), 42.

38. See "Restaurants" chapter.

39. For example, see advertisement by California Cornice, Steel and Supply Corp., *Gas Station, Garage, and Motor Car Dealer* 32 (February 1949): 16; Richard R. Elwell, "California Is Off Again, As . . . Multipumps Revive the Canopy," *National Petroleum News* 47 (November 1955): 41–42.

40. For example, see "Service Station Design," *National Petroleum News* 42 (29 March 1950): 30; "Designed to Attract Attention," *Architectural Record* 111 (June 1952): 185–187; "Shell Tailors Stations to Fit," *National Petroleum News* 50 (January 1958): 106–107.

41. Richard C. Schroeder, "How and When to Modernize Your Service Station," *National Petroleum News* 50 (October 1958): 86.

42. Mars Bogstahl, "Storm Warnings Up for Stations," *National Petroleum News* 56 (July 1964): 103.

43. "Shell Oil's Newest 'Blend-in,'" *National Petroleum News* 52 (February 1960): 121.

44. See Vieyra, 51–53; "How Ranch Style Is Taking Over Service Station Design," *National Petroleum News* 58 (May 1966): 95–101.

45. "Prototype for Service Stations: Mobil Tests Effect of Design on Sales at 58 Locations," *Architectural Record* 141 (May 1967): 172–175.

46. Wolf Von Eckardt, "Toward a Better Community: Must Gas Stations Be Garish?" *American Home* 70 (June 1967): 40.

47. Joe Link, "Attacks on Service Stations Mount While Oil Remains Silent," *National Petroleum News* 64 (March 1972): 46.

48. For example, see Marvin Reid, "The Sophisticated Self-Serve Comes of Age: Self-Serves and C-Stores," *National Petroleum News* 69 (July 1977): 54–63.

SUPERMARKETS

1. For other early experiments in self-service, see M. M. Zimmerman, *The Super Market: A Revolution in Distribution* (New York: McGraw-Hill, 1955), 19–30.

2. Clarence Saunders, "Self-Servicing Store" patent, U.S. Patent Office, patent number 1,242,872, patented 9 October 1917.

3. "Piggly Wiggly's History Is Long, Colorful," *Piggly Wiggly Turnstile* (from files of *Progressive Grocer*, c. 1960), 12.

4. "The Cousin of the Cafeteria," *Scientific American*, September 1918, 193.

5. Ibid.

6. Walter S. Hayward, Percival White, and John S. Fleek, *Chain Stores* (New York: McGraw-Hill, 1928), 492–494.

7. Zimmerman, 9–15.

8. For a typical layout, see Carl W. Dipman, ed., *Modern Food Stores* (New York: Progressive Grocer, 1935), 29.

9. "The A&P from A to Z," *Business Week*, 30 November 1932, 9.

10. Ibid.

11. Zimmerman, 32–35.

12. "Supermarkets: 50 Years of Progress," *Progressive Grocer* 59 (May 1980): 26.

13. Zimmerman, 40.

14. Zimmerman, 39–43; B. Sumner Gruzen, "Automobile Shopping Centers," *Architectural Record* 76 (July 1934): 43–48.

15. Zimmerman, 17.

16. Ibid., 18.

17. Ibid., 40.

18. Ibid., 24–30.

19. "The Cheapy Thrives," *Business Week*, 8 February 1933, 11–12.

20. "Now Come 'Warehouse' Stores to Threaten the Food Chains," *Business Week*, 20 April 1932, 9.

21. "Supers Reach Peak in Pittsburgh," *Business Week*, 3 July 1937, 26–28.

22. Dipman, *Modern Food Stores*, 7.

23. J. S. Harrison, "Self-Service—A Development of the Machine Age," *Chain Store Age* 15 (May 1939): 39.

24. Dipman, *Modern Food Stores*, 55.

25. For information on development of fixtures and decor, see: ibid., 15, 55; Carl W. Dipman and John E. O'Brien, *Self-Service and Semi-Self-Service Food Stores* (New York: Progressive Grocer, 1940), 15–18; Carl W. Dipman, Robert W. Mueller, and Ralph E. Head, *Self-Service Food Stores* (New York: Progressive Grocer, 1946), 24–42.

26. "25 Years of Progress in Meat Departments," *Chain Store Age: Silver Jubilee Issue* 26 (1950): J29.

27. "Frozen Foods Zoom to New Heights," *Progressive Grocer* 51 (June 1972): 50.

28. Dipman, *Modern Food Stores*, 49–55.

29. Dipman, Mueller, and Head, *Self-Service Food Stores*, 210.

30. "The Supermerchants," *Time* 58 (20 August 1951): 80.

31. Zimmerman, 140–141.

32. "The 1950s," *Progressive Grocer* 51 (June 1972): 29.

33. B. Sumner Gruzen as quoted in Zimmerman, 166.

34. "Commercial Buildings: Prototype Supermarket," *Progressive Architecture*, July 1956, 100–105.

35. "The 1950s," 29.

36. "Super Markets of the Sixties" (study conducted by the Raymond Loewy Corp.), Supermarket Institute, 1960, 21.

37. *Outstanding New Super Markets* (New York: Progressive Grocer, 1969), 29.

38. Ibid., 69.

39. Allan J. Mayer, "Supermarkets in a Crunch," *New York Times Magazine*, 2 February 1976, 52.

40. *Grocery Retailing in the '80s—Part 2* (New York: Progressive Grocer, 1980), 21–25.

MINIATURE GOLF COURSES

1. *The Official Index of the United States Patent Office* (Washington, D.C.: GPO, 1925), 1059.

2. For early history, see "Bobby Joneses of the Vacant-Lot Golf Clubs," *Literary Digest* 106 (23 August 1930): 32–34; Elmer Davis, "Miniature Golf to the Rescue," *Harper's* 162 (December 1930): 5–6; Jesse F. Gelders, "Why Midget Golf Swept Country," *Popular Science* 117 (November 1930): 22–23; Morley B. Thompson, *Miniature Golf, A Treatise on the Subject* (Denver: Central States Publishing Co., 1930), 7. There are many conflicts in accounts of the early history of the game. This would make an excellent topic for further study.

3. Pamphlet in the manager's collection, *Fairyland, Lookout Mountain, Tennessee*, "Fairyland, Where Spring Is 8 Months Long," c. 1927.

4. Thompson, 7.

5. Carter's claim in his advertisement "Thar's Gold in Them Thar Hills, Stranger," *Saturday Evening Post* 202 (31 May 1930): 148.

6. Gelders, 20, 136.

7. Ibid., 137.

8. Ibid.

9. Ibid.

10. Ibid.

11. Ibid., 138.

12. "Hazards of Miniature Golf Courses Listed," *Weekly Underwriter and the Insurance Plan*, 15 November 1930, 1122; also, Joseph P. Quinlan, "Roofing the Tom Thumb Courses Is No Midget Business Opportunity," *Building Age*, September 1930, 71; also, Davis, 6.

13. "Thar's Gold in Them Thar Hills," 148.

14. Gelders, 23.

15. Thompson, p. 8.

16. Ibid., 34.

17. Michael J. Phillips, *How to Play Miniature Golf* (Los Angeles: Keystone, 1930), 53.

18. "Courses in New York City," *Miniature Golf Management* 1 (March 1931): 20. Delanoy and Ledbetter appear to have been associated with Miniature Golf Courses of America.

19. "Large Uses of Steel in Small Ways: Miniature Golf," *Steel* 87 (27 November 1930): 54.

20. "Concrete Supplies Utility and Beauty on Miniature Golf Courses," *Concrete* 37 (October 1930): 46–48.

21. "Lighting: For All-Night Miniature Golf," *Electrical World* 95 (4 October 1930): 644–646.

22. Quinlan, 71.

23. "Tom Thumb Golf," *Nation* 131 (27 August 1930): 216.

24. Davis, 9.

25. Ibid., 7–9.

26. "Bobby Joneses," 32.

27. "Half-Pint Golf," *Outlook and Independent* 155 (27 August 1930): 656.

28. "Rout the Roughnecks," *Miniature Golf Management* 1 (March 1931): 6.

29. "A Brief Survey of Miniature Golf in New England," *Miniature Golf Management* 1 (March 1931): 18.

30. Charles Evans, Jr., "Golf in Your Own Backyard," *Popular Mechanics* 54 (September 1930): 492–497.

31. "Bobby Joneses," 33.

32. "A Theme Song," *Miniature Golf Management* 1 (15 August 1930): 26.

33. "Miniature Golf and Public Policy," *American City* 43 (August 1930): 17.

34. "Civic War Threatened," *Miniature Golf Management* 1 (15 August 1930): 11.

35. "Midget or Colossus?" *Survey* 65 (15 November 1930): 197.

36. For example, *Boston Sunday Post*, 15 March 1931, 21.

37. Davis, 14.

38. "The Status of the Game," *Miniature Golf Management* 1 (May 1931) 6.

39. Interview with Edward Silva, owner, 21 June 1980.

40. Ibid.

41. Ibid.

42. *Miniature Golf Courses* (Chicago: National Golf Foundation, 1949), 2.

43. Eastern Golf Company, Inc., *1980—Our 50th Anniversary Catalog* (North Bronx, N.Y.: Eastern Golf Company, Inc., 1980), 23–26.

44. *Harris Miniature Golf Courses, Inc.* (catalog) (Wildwood, New Jersey, n.d.).

45. Lomma Enterprises, Inc., *Lomma Champion Miniature Golf Courses* (Scranton, Penn.: Lomma Enterprises, Inc., n.d.).

DRIVE-IN THEATERS

1. "The Drive-in Lie-in," *Newsweek* 62 (8 July 1963): 78; Lewis Beale, "Drive-Ins: The Thrill Is Gone," *Washington Post*, 5 June 1983, 1.

2. Richard M. Hollingshead, Jr., "Drive In Theater" patent, U.S. Patent Office, patent number 1,909,537, patented 16 May 1933.

3. Ibid.

4. "Open-Air Movies Are Being Tried," *Architectural Forum* 59 (July 1933): 81.

5. Ibid.

6. Ibid.

7. "Movie Theater Lets Cars Drive Right In," *Popular Science* 123 (August 1933): 19.

8. "Camden's Drive-In Theater," *Literary Digest* 116 (22 July 1933): 19.

9. "Drive-Ins," *Time* 38 (14 July 1941): 66.

10. "Drive-in Theater," *Collier's*, 22 March 1938, 52.

11. "The Drive-In Theaters," *Theatre Catalog*, 1942, G42.

12. "The Legal Position of Design Patents," *Theatre Catalog*, 1949–1950, 165.

13. Mary O'Hara, "The Drive-in Theaters Achieve Their Own Place in the Sun," *Theatre Catalog*, 1942, 146.

14. "Prefabricated All-Steel Screen Towers," *Theatre Catalog*, 1948–1949, 265.

15. O'Hara, 146.

16. American Association of State Highway Officials, Committee on Traffic; Subcommittee on Roadside Control, *Drive In Theater Study 1949*, (Washington, D.C., American Association of State Highway Officials, 1949).

17. "Drive-in Theatres of the 1950 Season," *Theatre Catalog*, 1949–1950, 253.

18. See "Motels" and "Restaurants" chapters.

19. "Drive-in Theatres of the 1950 Season," 196–198.

20. Ibid., 300–302.

21. "Miniature Train Company" (advertisement), *Theatre Catalog*, 1952, 201.

22. Katharine Best and Katharine Hillyer, "Movies under the Stars," *Reader's Digest* 53 (September 1948): 119.

23. Pico usher as quoted in "Drive-in Theater," *Collier's*, 22 March 1938, 52.

24. David Naylor, *American Picture Palaces* (New York: Van Nostrand Reinhold, 1981), 11.

25. Some theater historians have mistakenly called this period the "dark ages"; e.g., see ibid., 172–174.

26. S. Charles Lee, "What the Future May Bring," *Theatre Catalog*, 1941, 12.

27. For example, Rapp & Rapp designed the Niles Outdoor Theater (1944) in Niles, Michigan; S. Charles Lee the Edwards Drive-in (1949) in Los Angeles.

28. "The Gratiot Drive-In," *Theatre Catalog*, 1948–1949, 128.

29. "Another Home in a Screen Tower," *Theatre Catalog*, 1953–1954, 84.

30. Rodney Luther, "Drive-in Theaters: Rags to Riches in Five Years," *Film Quarterly* 5 (Summer 1951): 408.

31. *Encyclopedia of Exhibitions*, New York: National Association of Theatre Owners (1981), s.v. "Drive-in theater statistics."

32. "Drive-in Lie-in," 78.

33. Ibid.

MOTELS

1. Warren James Belasco, *Americans on the Road: From Autocamp to Motel, 1910–1945* (Cambridge: MIT Press, 1979). This excellent social history of the transition from hotel to camp to early motor court was very helpful in the preparation of the first part of this chapter.

2. John J. McCarthy and Robert Littell, "Three Hundred Thousand Shacks," *Harper's* 167 (July 1933): 183.

3. John J. McCarthy, "The Market Business Forgets," *Nation's Business* 21 (August 1933): 40.

4. Frank E. Brimmer, "The 'Nickel-and-Dime' Stores of Nomadic America," *Magazine of Business* 52 (August 1927): 152.

5. Ibid., 151.

6. Ibid., 153.

7. Gilbert S. Chandler, "Starting from Scratch and Building a De Luxe Motor Court," *Tourist Court Journal* 1 (November 1937): 5.

8. See "Architecture for Speed-Reading" chapter for handyman aesthetic.

9. "Originality, Enterprise, Good Taste, and Lots of Effort and Money Make Mission Village," *Tourist Court Journal* 1 (December 1938): 5–6.

10. "A Motor Tourist Camp Designed for Sanitation and Beauty," *American City* 41 (July 1929): 105.

11. Charles (Chic) Sale, 1885–1936, an early-twentieth-century comedian famous for his monologue "The Specialist" consisting of hilarious advice on how to construct an outhouse. See Joe Franklin, *Encyclopedia of Comedians* (Secaucus, N.J.: The Citadel Press, 1979), 289.

12. "The Great American Roadside," *Fortune* 9 (September 1934): 54.

13. McCarthy and Littell, "Three Hundred," 185.

14. "Cabin and Cottage Building Time Is Here," *American Builder* 13 (March 1935): 40.

15. McCarthy and Littell, "Three Hundred," 182.

16. "Roadside Cabins for Tourists," *Architectural Record* 74 (December 1933): 457.

17. "Tourist Cabins," *Architectural Record* 77 (February 1935): 95–96.

18. E. H. Lightfoot, "Constructing a Modern Motor Court," *Tourist Court Journal* 1 (March 1938): 7.

19. John N. Teets, "The Motor Court Moderne; Designed for the Needs of Today and Tomorrow," *Tourist Court Journal* 1 (March 1938): 11–12, 24.

20. "America Takes to the Motor Court," *Business Week*, 15 June 1940, 21–22.

21. Ibid., 22.

22. Anonymous salesman as quoted in Hattie Plemons and Constance Plemons, "Why Many Downtown Hotel Guests Are Switching to Motor Courts," *Hotel Management* 55 (April 1949): 110.

23. McCarthy and Littell, "Three Hundred," 184.

24. Seymour Freedgood, "The Motel Free-for-All," *Fortune* 59 (June 1959): 163.

25. Bernard DeVoto, "Motel Town," *Harper's* 207 (September 1953): 46.

26. Plemons and Plemons, 51.

27. Richard F. Dempewolff, "Drive-In Dream Castles," *Popular Mechanics* 106 (July 1956): 100.

28. Claire Hoffman, "Circle Tour Notes About Courts," *Tourist Court Journal* 10 (September 1947): 6.

29. C. Vernon Kane, *Motor Courts—from Planning to Profits* (New York: Ahrens Publishing Company, 1954), 6.

30. Ernest W. Fair, "When the Highway Leaves You," *Tourist Court Journal* 13 (September 1950): 8.

31. Freedgood, 119.

32. "Best Western: The Independent Alternative," *News* (a publication of the Best Western News Service, Phoenix), n.d.

33. Kemmons Wilson, *The Holiday Inn Story* (New York: Newcomen Society, 1968), 8.

34. Federic A. Birmingham, "Kemmons Wilson: The Inn-Side Story," *Saturday Evening Post* 244 (Winter 1971): 69.

35. "Putting the HJ Seal on Motels," *Business Week*, 23 October 1954, 126–130.

36. "Plan 100 Motor Inns in Chicago District," *Business Week*, 27 May 1931, 16.

37. "Motel and Hotel: The Gap Narrows," *Business Week*, 11 June 1955, 102.

38. Kane, 62.

39. Ibid., 65.

40. C. Vernon Kane as quoted in Richard A. Miller, "The Odds on Motels," *Architectural Forum* 107 (August 1957): 111.

41. Norris Willatt, "The $6 Motel," *Dun's Review* 89 (May 1967): 61.

RESTAURANTS

1. For example, see Guy Gundaker, "Why the Cafeteria Is Successful," *American Restaurant* 2 (January 1920): 22.

2. For example, see Warfield Webb, "The Luncheonette in the Drug Store," *American Restaurant* 2 (May 1920): 30.

3. Ralph Pomeroy, *The Ice Cream Connection* (New York: Paddington Press, Ltd., 1975), 37–39.

4. Ray Giles, "What Does the 'Eating Out' Habit Mean to the Food Advertiser?" *Advertising & Selling*, 4 May 1927, 19.

5. Ibid., 20.

6. Ibid., 44.

7. Raymond S. Tompkins, "Hash-House Visionaries," *The American Mercury* 22 (March 1931): 363.

8. Florence A. McCaskie, "Rustic Colonial House Now a Tea Room," *Tea Room and Gift Shop* 2 (August 1923): 9.

9. "The Bottle Hill Tea Shop," a special publication of *Woman's Home Companion*, 1922, 19.

10. Ibid.

11. "She Teaches People How to Run Wayside Eating Places," *The American Magazine* 91 (April 1924): 69.

12. Ibid.

13. Gordon Gaskill, "That Wild Johnson Boy," *The American Magazine* 131 (March 1941): 34.

14. "The Howard Johnson Restaurants," *Fortune* 21 (September 1940): 82; "Glorified Roadstands Pay," *Business Week*, 17 February 1940, 26–27.

15. Warren J. Belasco, "Toward a Culinary Common Denominator," *Journal of American Culture* 2 (1979): 512.

16. Interview by Michele Plourde with local Middleboro, Massachusetts, historian Mertie Romaine, February 1985.

17. Willard J. Slagle, "Howard D. Johnson," *American Restaurant* 41 (June 1958): 108.

18. "The Great American Roadside," *Fortune* 9 (September 1934): 56.

19. "Ptomaine Joe's Place," *Collier's*, 1 October 1938, 54.

20. "Elevating the Standing of the 'Hot Dog Kennel,'" *American City* 38 (May 1928): 99.

21. Anderson sold his interest to Ingram in 1933.

22. E. W. Ingram, Sr., "All This from a 5-cent Hamburger!" (New York: Newcomen Society, 1964), 10.

23. *Drive-In Operators Handbook*, (Duluth, Minn.: Ojibway Press, 1964), 7.

24. Ibid.

25. Jack Pollexfen, "Don't Get Out," *Collier's*, 19 March 1938, 52.

26. Ibid.

27. *American Builder and Building Age* 65 (June 1943): 42.

28. "Where the Drive-Ins Are," *Drive-In Restaurant* 28 (April 1964): 16.

29. "Lane's Aluminum Industries, Inc." (advertisement), *Drive-In Restaurant* 28 (July 1964): 3.

30. *Drive-In Operators Handbook*, 65.

31. "Tray on Trestle Serves at Drive-In," *Popular Mechanics* 92 (September 1949): 127.

32. John Bigelow, "The Detroit Study of Drive-In Problems," *Drive-In Restaurant* 28 (August 1964): 12.

33. The first mention of the term "fast food" noticed in the course of my research was in "Foods Made Fast Sell Fast," *American Restaurant* 38 (February 1955): 70.

34. Ray Kroc, *Grinding It Out* (Chicago: Henry Regnery Company, 1977), 66.

35. Ibid.

36. "One Million Hamburgers and 160 Tons of French Fries a Year," *American Restaurant* 34 (July 1952): 44.

37. Kroc, 66.

38. "One Million Hamburgers and 160 Tons of French Fries a Year," 44.

39. Ibid.

40. U.S. Department of the Interior, National Park Service, Alan L. Hess and John Beach, "McDonald's Drive-in Restaurant and Sign," *National Register of Historic Places—Nomination Form*, 1983, 3.

41. Kroc, 68.

42. Ibid., 143.

43. Ibid.

44. "'Slice of Pie and a Cup of Coffee—That'll Be Fifteen Cents, Honey,'" *American Heritage* 28 (April 1977): 69.

45. Richard J. S. Gutman, Elliott Kauffman, and David Slovic, *American Diner* (New York: Harper & Row, 1979), 8.

46. Ibid.

47. Gutman, Kauffman, and Slovic, 14.

48. "'Coffee and' in the Doggy Dog-Wagon," *Literary Digest* 112 (20 February 1932): 43.

49. Paul P. Merbach, "Fritz's 20 Years of Progress," *Diner* 6 (March 1948): 10–11.

50. "'Coffee and' in the Doggy Dog-Wagon," 42.

51. "Lunch Wagons De Luxe," *Christian Science Monitor*, 23 March 1938, 14.

52. "'Coffee and' in the Doggy Dog-Wagon," 42.

53. "Lunch Wagons Streamline—Customers Stream In," *Nation's Business* 25 (September 1937): 74.

54. Diana Rice, "The Lunch Wagon Settles Down," *New York Times Magazine*, 19 October 1941, 20.

55. Blake Ehrlich, "The Diner Puts on Airs," *Saturday Evening Post* 220 (19 June 1948): 34.

56. Ibid., 130.

57. "New Trends in Diners," *Diner* 9 (August 1949): 14.

58. Michael Aaron Rockland, "Diner Capital," *New Jersey Monthly*, October 1977, 56.

Selected Bibliography

A NOTE ON SOURCES

Considering the sheer volume of roadside commercial structures, this huge, though comparatively newborn, phylum of American building, while stridently criticized and occasionally romanticized, has been subjected to relatively little serious study. This situation has begun to change. In recent years, roadside commercial architecture has become the topic of an ever-increasing number of articles and books by a scattering of scholars, critics, artists, photographers, journalists, and enthusiasts. The work of Warren J. Belasco, J. B. Jackson, David Gebhard, Robert Venturi, Denise Scott Brown, Steven Izenour, Grady Clay, John F. Kasson, John Stilgoe, John A. Jakle, Daniel I. Vieyra, John Baeder, Alan Hess, Philip Langdon, Jeffrey L. Meikle, J. C. C. Andrews, Paul Goldberger, Bevis Hillier, Bruce A. Lohof, Jim Heimann, Rip Georges, Rudi Stern, Richard J. S. Gutman, Elliot Kaufman, David Slovic, and John Margolies, to name a few, proved helpful in focusing ideas for this book (full citations of their work can be found in the bibliography).

Yet, due to the vastness of the subject matter, no single work offered an overview of the field—one of my main objectives for this book. Lacking any large-scale road map to help steer my research and writing, I began by studying the evolution of individual building types, examining—chronologically—key articles and advertisements appearing in industry trade journals from *Progressive Grocer* and *Theatre Catalog* to the *Tourist Court Journal*. This information was supplemented by an extensive review of a wide range of popular and specialized periodical literature, corporate histories, biographies of business leaders, and numerous other related books and articles written from a variety of disciplinary perspectives including architectural, social, and cultural history and geography and urban planning. A representative sampling of the most helpful works consulted is listed within. Although many of these sources proved valuable in the preparation of a several sections of this book, they are listed only once by the chapter in which they were most useful.

Finally, a word about the greatest repository of evidence on the evolution of twentieth-century roadside commerce—the thousands of structures, signs, and symbols, surviving from different periods, that line the nation's highways. I personally field-checked all key conclusions of my research through more than twenty thousand miles of transcontinental travel along the Main Streets and Miracle Miles of hundreds of communities, looking at patterns, dating structures, interviewing designers, builders, workers, and business owners. Much of this fieldwork and verification is reflected in the visual bibliography—the photographs and captions accompanying the text.

FROM MAIN STREET TO MIRACLE MILE

Abbott, Lawrence F. "The Vices and Virtues of the Automobile." *Outlook* 144 (15 December 1926): 49–50.

Alexander, H. W. "Designing a Suburban Commercial Center." *American City* 47 (July 1932): 67.

American Public Works Association. *History of Public Works in the United States, 1776–1976*. Edited by Ellis L. Armstrong. Chicago: American Public Works Association, 1976.

Baker, Geoffrey, and Funaro, Bruno. *Shopping Centers: Design and Operation*. New York: Reinhold Publishing Corp., 1951.

Bedell, Mary Crebore. *Modern Gypsies*. New York: Brentano's, 1924.

Bird, J. Malcolm. "Tours and Detours." *Scientific American* 125 (November 1921): 6–8.

Borth, Christy. *Mankind on the Move: The Story of Highways*. Washington, D.C.: The Automotive Safety Foundation, 1969.

"A Break-through for Two-Level Shopping Centers." *Architectural Forum* 105 (December 1956): 114–123.

Bruce, Robert. *The National Road: Most Historic Throughfare in the United States*. . . . Washington, D.C.: National Highways Association, 1916.

"By-Pass Highways for Traffic Relief." *American City* 38 (April 1928): 88–90.

Champlin, Leland F. "Michigan: Short-lived Shopping Center for Unstable Land." *Architectural Record* 84 (July 1938): 44.

Clay, Grady. *Close-Up: How to Read the American City*. Chicago: University of Chicago Press, 1973. Phoenix Edition, 1980.

Clay, Grady. "Finding Futures in the Highway Strip." *Landscape Architecture* 64 (October 1973): 458–465.

Cohen, Yehoshua S. *Diffusion of an Innovation in an Urban System: The Spread of Planned Regional Shopping Centers in the United States, 1949–1968*. Chicago: Department of Geography, University of Chicago, 1972.

Collins, George R. "The Linear City." *Architects' Yearbook*, v. 2, 1965, 214–217.

Connolly, Vera. "Tourists Accommodated." *Delineator* 106 (March 1925): 15.

Dale, Crag. "Is Main Street Doomed?" *Popular Mechanics* 55 (May 1931): 756–768.

"A Detour for Roadside America." *Business Week*, 16 February 1974, 44.

"Drafting and Design Problems: Neighborhood Shopping Centers." *Architectural Record* 71 (May 1932): 325–332.

"Evolution of the Shopping Center." *The Community Builders' Handbook*. Washington, D.C.: Urban Land Institute, 1965, 271–272.

Fawcett, Waldon. "Roadside Merchants Organize to Study Mutual Problems." *Sales Management & Advertisers' Weekly* 15 (1 September 1928): 480.

Fink, James J. *The Car Culture*. Cambridge: MIT Press, 1975.

Flagg, James Montgomery. *Boulevards All the Way*. New York: George H. Doran, 1925.

Frazer, Elizabeth. "The Destruction of Rural America." *Saturday Evening Post* 197 (9 May 1925): 39.

"Gasoline Gypsies, 1925." *Survey* 54 (15 May 1925): 229.

Glaab, Charles N. *The American City: A Documentary History*. Homewood, Ill.: The Dorsey Press, 1963.

Gruen, Victor. "Retailing and the Automobile: A Romance Based upon a Case of Mistaken Identity." *Architectural Record* 127 (March 1960): 192–214.

Harvey, W. Clifford. "Atlantic-to-Pacific Turnpike?" *The Christian Science Monitor* weekly magazine section, 24 June 1944, 8–9.

Haskell, Douglas. "Architecture on Routes U.S. 40 and 66." *Architectural Record* 81 (May 1937): 15–21.

Hastings, Charles Warren. "Roadtown, The Linear City." *Architects and Builders Magazine* 10 (August 1910): 445.

"Highway Departments Report on Progress of Interstate Program." *Better Roads* 29 (November 1959): 26–29.

Historical Statistics of the United States, Colonial Times to 1970. Washington, D.C.: U.S. Bureau of the Census, 1975.

Hitchcock, Henry-Russell, Jr. "Traffic and Building Art." *Architectural Record* 68 (June 1930): 455–460.

"How Gridiron Streets Systems Might Be Replanned." *American City* 70 (April 1944): 51–52.

Hungerford, Edward. "America Awheel." *Everybody's Magazine* 36 (June 1917): 678.

"Influence of Bypasses on Land and Business Activity." *Better Roads* 10 (December 1958): 21.

Jackson, John Brinckerhoff. *American Space*. New York: W. W. Norton, 1972.

Jakle, John A., and Mattson, Richard L. "The Evolution of a Commercial Strip." *Journal of Cultural Geography* 1 (1981): 3–25.

Kimball, Winfield A., and Decker, Maurice H. *Touring with Tent and Trailer*. New York: McGraw-Hill Book Company, Inc., Whittlesey House, 1937.

Kowinski, William Severini. "Suburbia: End of the Golden Age." *New York Times Magazine*, 16 March 1980, 16.

Lay, Charles Downing. "New Towns for High-Speed Roads." *Architectural Record* 78 (November 1935): 352–354.

Lewis, Sinclair. *Main Street*. New York: Harcourt Brace & World, 1920.

Lincoln Highway Association. *The Lincoln Highway: The Story of a Crusade That Made Transportation History*. New York: Dodd, Mead & Company, 1935.

"The Lincoln Highway of To-day." *American City* 25 (August 1921): 106–111.

MacKaye, Benton, and Mumford, Lewis. "Townless Highways for the Motorist." *Harper's* 163 (August 1931): 347–356.

McKinley, Blake. *The Urbanization of America*. New Brunswick, N.J.: Rutgers University Press, 1963.

Meinig, D. W., ed. *The Interpretation of Ordinary Landscapes*. New York: Oxford University Press, 1979.

"Mobility—A Controlling Factor in Design." *Architectural Record* 84 (August 1938): 67–70.

"Modern Motor Ways." *Architectural Record* 74 (December 1933): 430–436.

"Mrs. Jones Changes Her Shopping Habits." *Business Week*, 5 October 1929, 28–30.

"New Type of Suburban Shopping Area Proposed." *American City* 35 (August 1926): 214–216.

Nichols, J. C. "Developing Outlying Shopping Centers." *American City* 41 (July 1929): 99–101.

"Northland: A New Yardstick for Shopping Center Planning." *Architectural Forum* 100 (June 1954): 102–119.

"Park and Shop." *American City* 57 (October 1937): 71–72.

"The Passing of a Famous Avenue." *Architectural Record* 43 (April 1918): 391–392.

"Planned Postwar Shopping Centers Come Big: They Are Changing U.S. Buying Habits." *Business Week*, 11 October 1952, 124–126.

"Relieving the Shopper of Parking Worries." *System*, October 1925, 496–497.

Reps, John W. *Cities on Stone*. Fort Worth: Amon Carter Museum, 1976.

———. *The Forgotten Frontier*. Columbia: University of Missouri Press, 1981.

———. *The Making of Urban America*. Princeton: Princeton University Press, 1965.

———. *Town Planning in Frontier America*. Princeton: Princeton University Press, 1969.

Rifkind, Carole. *Main Street: The Face of Urban America*. New York: Harper & Row, Publishers, 1977.

Riley, Robert B. "Understanding the Strip." *Architectural & Engineering News* 10 (January 1968): 32–35.

Roadside Merchant. Chicago: Bamberger Publishing Co., June, July, August, November 1933; February, March, May 1934.

"Roadtown: The Great American Excursion." *Architectural Forum* 105 (September 1956): 124–129.

Rose, Albert C. *Historic American Roads: From Frontier Trails to Superhighways*. New York: Crown Publishers, Inc., 1976.

"Shoppers' World." *Architectural Forum* 95 (December 1951): 180–186.

"Shopping Center for the Post-War 'Shelf.'" *American Builder and Building Age* 65 (June 1943): 45.

Squire, Latham C., and Bassett, Howard M. "A New Type of Thoroughfare: The 'Freeway.'" *American City* 47 (November 1932): 64–66.

"Stage-Coach Days Are Back, with New Luxuries." *Literary Digest* 83 (13 December 1924): 56–57.

Stewart, George R. *U.S. 40: Cross Section of the United States of America*. Boston: Houghton Mifflin Co., 1953.

Stilgoe, John R. *Metropolitan Corridor*. New Haven: Yale University Press, 1983.

Still, Bayard. *Urban America: A History with Documents*. Boston: Little, Brown and Company, 1974.

"Suburban Retail Districts." *Architectural Forum* 94 (August 1950): 105–119.

Thomas, Diane C. "Lonely Road Now." *Atlanta Magazine*, November 1978, 57–59, 123–124.

"Toll Road Projects Menace Small Business in 22 States." *American Restaurant*, June 1953, 42.

Van Leuven, Karl O., Jr. "From Joe's Hot Dog Stand to a Regional Shopping Center." *American City* 88 (April 1953): 98–99.

Warner, Sam B., Jr. *Streetcar Suburbs: The Process of Growth in Boston, 1870–1900*. Cambridge: Harvard University Press, 1962.

Watts, Gilbert S. *Roadside Marketing*. New York: Orange Judd Publishing Co., Inc., 1928.

"Who'll Get Helped or Hurt by Auto Freeways." *U.S. News & World Report*, 21 December 1956, 90–92.

Wright, Frank Lloyd. "America Tomorrow." *American Architect* 141 (May 1932): 16–17, 76.

ARCHITECTURE FOR SPEED-READING

"Acrylic Signs Threaten Neon." *Modern Plastics* 27 (January 1950): 145–146.

Allen, Frederick Lewis. *Only Yesterday: An Informal History of the 1920's*. 1931. Reprint. New York: Harper & Row, Publishers, 1964.

Anderson, Warren H. *Vanishing Roadside America*. Tucson: University of Arizona Press, 1981.

Andrews, J. J. C. *The Well-Built Elephant and Other Roadside Attractions*. New York: Congdon & Weed, 1984.

Automobile Blue Book 1918. Standard Road Guide of America. Vol. II. New York: The Automobile Blue Book Publishing Co., 1918.

Baeder, John. *Gas, Food, and Lodging*. New York: Abbeville Press Publishers, 1982.

Banham, Reyner. *Los Angeles: The Architecture of Four Ecologies*. New York: Harper & Row, Publishers, 1971.

———. *Theory and Design in the First Machine Age*. New York: Praeger Publishers, Inc., 1960.

Barach, Arnold B. *Famous American Trademarks*. Washington, D.C.: Public Affairs Press, 1971.

Baum, Dwight James. "A Plea for Constructive Modernism." *Architectural Forum* 48 (April 1928): 576.

Beauty for America, Proceedings of the White House Conference on Natural Beauty. Washington, D.C.: U.S. GPO, 1965.

The Billboard—A Blot on Nature and a Parasite on Public Improvements. New York: The Moore Press, Inc., 1939.

Black, Mary. *Old New York in Early Photographs, 1853–1901*. New York: Dover Publications, Inc., 1973.

Blake, Peter. *God's Own Junkyard: The Planned Deterioration of America's Landscape*. Rev. ed. New York: Holt, Rinehart & Winston, 1979.

Bliss, Carey S. *Autos Across America—A Bibliography of Transcontinental Automobile Travel: 1903–1940*. Los Angeles: Dawson's Book Shop, 1972.

Boorstin, Daniel J. *The Image or What Happened to the American Dream*. New York: Atheneum, 1962.

"Both Fish and Fowl." *Fortune* 9 (February 1934): 40–43.

Broadbent, Geoffrey; Bunt, Richard; and Jencks, Charles. *Signs, Symbols and Architecture*. Chichester, England: John Wiley & Sons, 1980.

Brooker, Kathleen Ann. "Railroad Depots in New Mexico: Southwestern Styles and the Masonry Tradition." Master's thesis for University of New Mexico, May 1981.

Bush, Donald J. *The Streamlined Decade*. New York: George Braziller, 1975.

Capitman, Barbara Baer. *American Trademark Designs*. New York: Dover Publications, Inc., 1976.

Cheney, Sheldon. *The New World Architecture*. New York: Tudor Publishing Company, 1931.

Cohn, Jan. *The Palace or the Poorhouse: The American House as a Cultural Symbol*. East Lansing: Michigan State University Press, 1979.

Cook, John W., and Klotz, Heinrich. "Ugly Is Beautiful: The Main Street School of Architecture." *Atlantic Monthly* 231 (May 1973): 33–43.

"Does Beauty Sell? Mobil Tries to Find Out." *National Petroleum News* 58 (November 1966): 120.

Dreyfuss, Henry. *Designing for People*. 2nd rev. ed., 1967, with foreword by R. Buckminster Fuller. New York: The Viking Press, Inc., 1974.

"Drive-In Design Attracts Trade." *American Builder* 71 (November 1949): 90–91.

"Drive-In Restaurants and Luncheonettes." *Architectural Record* 100 (September 1946): 99–109.

"Drive-Ins, Building Types Study Number 164." *Architectural Record* 108 (August 1950): 130–152.

Ehli, Jack. "Shopping Center Stars." *Signs of the Times*, August 1960, 67–69.

Fitzgerald, Bob. "Arrows Point the Way to Increased Sales." *Signs of the Times*, November 1955, 36.

Fleming, Ronald Lee. "Corporate Design: It All Looks the Same." *Environmental Action*, 3 August 1974, 13.

———. *Facade Stories*. New York: Hastings House Publishers, 1982.

Gannett, Lewis. *Sweet Land*. Garden City, N.Y.: Sun Dial, 1937.

Gebhard, David. "The Moderne in the U.S., 1920–1941." *Architectural Association Quarterly*, July 1970, 4–20.

Gebhard, David, and Von Breton, Harriette. *L.A. in the Thirties, 1931–1941*. Los Angeles: Peregrine Smith, Inc., 1975.

Gladding, Effie Price. *Across the Continent by the Lincoln Highway*. New York: Brentano's, 1915.

"Glass-Brick Walls Inclose New Buildings." *Engineering News Record* 110 (27 April 1933): 522.

Goldberger, Paul. "Architecture and Preservation." *Preservation: Towards an Ethic in the 1980s*. Washington, D.C.: Preservation Press, 1980.

Gowans, Alan. *Images of American Living*. Philadelphia and New York: J. B. Lippincott & Company, 1964.

Gropius, Walter. *The New Architecture and the Bauhaus*. London: Faber and Faber Limited, 1935. Reprint. Glasgow: The University Press, 1956.

Heimann, Jim, and Georges, Rip. *California Crazy—Roadside Vernacular Architecture*. San Francisco: Chronicle Books, 1980.

Hess, Alan. "California Coffee Shops." *Arts & Architecture* 2 (1983): 42–51.

Hess, Alan. "The Original McDonald's." *Journal of the Los Angeles Institute of Contemporary Art*, April 1983, 28–30.

Hillier, Bevis. *The Decorative Arts of the Forties and Fifties—Austerity/Binge*. New York: Clarkson N. Potter, Inc., Publisher, 1975.

———. *The World of Art Deco*. New York: E. P. Dutton, 1971.

Houck, John W., ed. *Outdoor Advertising: History and Regulation*. Notre Dame: University of Notre Dame Press, 1969.

How to Build Cabins, Lodges, and Bungalows. New York: Popular Science Publishing Company, Inc., 1934.

Jackson, J. B. *The Necessity for Ruins and Other Topics*. Amherst: University of Massachusetts Press, 1980.

Jacobs, Jane. *The Death and Life of Great American Cities*. New York: Random House, Vintage Books, 1961.

Jacobus, John, *Twentieth Century Architecture: The Middle Years, 1940–65*. New York: Praeger, Publishers, Inc., 1966.

Jencks, Charles, and Silver, Nathan. *Adhocism: The Case for Improvisation*. Garden City, N.Y.: Doubleday & Co., 1972.

Kalm, Peter. *The America of 1750: Peter Kalm's Travels in North America* (the English version of 1770). Revised from the original Swedish, and edited by Adolph B. Benson. New York: Dover Publications, Inc., 1966.

Kasson, John F. *Amusing the Million—Coney Island at the Turn of the Century*. New York: Hill & Wang, 1978.

Kouwenhoven, John A. *The Arts in Modern American Civilization*. 1948. Reprint. Garden City, N.Y.: W. W. Norton, 1967.

Le Corbusier. *Towards a New Architecture*. Translated by Frederick Etchells, 1927. Reprint. New York: Praeger Publishers, Inc., 1972.

Lemagny, J. C. Introduction to *Visionary Architects, Boulle; Ledoux; Lequeu*. Houston: University of St. Thomas, 1968.

Liebs, Chester. "Remember Our Not-So-Distant Past?" *Historic Preservation* 30 (January–March, 1978): 30–35.

Looney, Robert F. *Old Philadelphia in Early Photographs 1839–1914*. New York: Dover Publications, Inc., 1976.

Ludlow, William Orr. "Let Us Discourage the Materialistic Modern." *American Architect* 141 (April 1932): 24.

Lynd, Robert S., and Lynd, Helen Merrell. *Middletown: A Study in Modern American Culture*. Rev. ed. New York: Harcourt Brace Jovanovich, 1956.

———. *Middletown in Transition: A Study in Cultural Conflicts*. New York: Harcourt, Brace & World, Inc., 1937.

"The Mansard Madness." *Architectural Review and American Builders' Journal* 55 (August 1869): 67.

Margolies, John. *The End of the Road*. New York: Penguin Books, 1981.

Meikle, Jeffrey L. *Twentieth Century Limited—Industrial Design in America, 1925–1939*. Philadelphia: Temple University Press, 1979.

Miller, Samuel C. *Neon Techniques and Handling*. 3rd ed. Cincinnati: Signs of the Times Publishing Co., 1977.

"Modernize Main Street Competition." *Architectural Record* 78 (July 1935): 1–8.

Museum of Modern Art. *Modern Architecture International Exhibition*. New York: Museum of Modern Art, 1932.

"New Fields for Architects." *Architectural Record* 70 (August 1931): 116–117.

Outdoor Advertising—The Modern Marketing Force. A Manual for Business Men and Others Interested in the Fundamentals of Outdoor Advertising. Chicago: Outdoor Advertising Association of America Inc., 1928.

Plummer, Kathleen Church. "The Streamlined Moderne." *Art in America* 62 (January/February 1974): 46–54.

Presbrey, Frank. *History and Development of Advertising*. New York: Greenwood Press, 1968.

Preziosi, Donald. *The Semiotics of the Built Environment*. Bloomington: Indiana University Press, 1979.

"Ready or not, Mr. Manufacturer, the public expects immediate post-war product changes." *Printers' Ink* 203 (21 May 1943): 16.

Roberts, Kenneth L. "Travels in Billboardia." *Saturday Evening Post* 201 (13 October 1928): 24.

Rosen, Ben. *The Corporate Search for Visual Identity*. New York: Van Nostrand Reinhold Co., 1970.

Rowsome, Frank, Jr. *The Verse by the Side of the Road*. Brattleboro, Vt.: Stephen Greene Press, 1965.

Scarlett, Frank, and Townley, Marjorie. *Arts Decoratifs 1925—A Personal Recollection of the Paris Exhibition*. New York: St. Martin's Press Inc., 1975.

Schlereth, Thomas J. *Artifacts and the American Past*. Nashville: AASLH, 1980.

Scully, Vincent, Jr. *Modern Architecture—The Architecture of Democracy*. Rev. ed. New York: George Braziller, 1974.

Sears, Stephen W. *The American Heritage History of the Automobile in America*. New York: Simon and Schuster, 1977.

———. "Ocean to Ocean in an Automobile Car." *American Heritage* 31 (June/July 1980): 58–64.

"Shopping Facilities in Wartime." *Architectural Record* 92 (October 1942): 63–70.

"Signs and Symbols, Building Types Study Number 238." *Architectural Record* 120 (September 1956): 244–271.

Smith, Herbert. "An Architect's Notes on Designing Drive-Ins." *Motor Courts and Drive Ins Construction and Operation*. New York: Ahrens, 1951, 90–112.

Stern, Rudi. *Let There Be Neon*. New York: Harry N. Abrams, Inc., 1979.

"Stores, Building Types Study Number 88." *Architectural Record* 97 (April 1944): 95–108.

Stott, William. *Documentary Expression and Thirties America*. New York: Oxford University Press, 1973.

Teague, Walter Dorwin. *Design This Day: The Technique of Order in the Machine Age*. New York: Harcourt, Brace & Co., 1940.

Treib, Marc. "Eye-konism (Part One)." *Print* 27 (March/April 1973): 68–72.

———. "Eye-konism: (Part Two) Signs as Building as Signs." *Print* 27 (May/June 1973): 54–57.

———. "Eye-konism: (Part Three) The Word as Image." *Print* 27 (July/August 1973): 49–53.

Tunnard, Christopher, and Pushkarev, Boris. *Man-Made America—Chaos or Control?* 1963. Reprint. New York: Harmony Books, 1981.

Venturi, Robert. *Complexity and Contradiction in Architecture*. New York: Museum of Modern Art, 1966.

Venturi, Robert; Brown, Denise Scott; and Izenour, Steven. *Learning from Las Vegas*. Rev. ed. Cambridge: MIT Press, 1977.

Venturi, Rauch, Architects and Planners. *Sign of Life: Symbols in the American City*. Washington, D.C.: Aperture, Inc., 1976.

"Wayside Stands, Billboards, Curb Pumps, Lunch Wagons, Junk Yards, and Their Ilk." *American City* 44 (April 1931): 104–108.

"What the Past Has Contributed." *Signs of the Times*, May 1966, 50–51.

Whittington, Wayne. *Commercial Los Angeles, 1927–1947*. Glendale, Calif.: Interurban Press, 1981.

"Will the Post War Restaurant Look Like This?" *American Restaurant* 27 (June 1943): 46.

Wolfe, Tom. "From Bauhaus to Our House." Parts 1, 2. *Harper's* 120 (June, July 1981): 33–54, 40–59.

———. *The Kandy-Kolored, Tangerine-Flake Streamline Baby.* New York: Farrar, Straus and Giroux, 1965.

Wurts, Richard, et al. *The New York World's Fair 1939/1940.* New York: Dover Publications, Inc., 1979.

Yorke, Douglas A., Jr. "Mansard Madness." *UpCountry*, September 1978.

Zube, Ervin H., ed. *Landscapes, Selected Writings of J. B. Jackson.* Amherst: University of Massachusetts Press, 1970.

AUTO SHOWROOMS

"An Up to Date Garage—Swan's, at New Rochelle, N.Y." *The Horseless Age* 26 (21 September 1910): 414–415.

Andrews, Deborah Gilbreath. "Merchandising the Automobile: Early Auto Showrooms along Boston's Commonwealth Avenue." Typescript, December 1980. (Student paper, Commercial Archeology course, University of Vermont, Burlington.)

"Are Supermarkets for Autos Next?" *Business Week*, 7 May 1966, 33.

"Auto Dealers Gear for Battle." *Business Week*, 28 March 1953, 27–28.

"Automobile Display, Sales and Service Center: A Rare Example." *Architectural Record* 143 (April 1968): 172.

"The Automobile Dominates the Plans Being Made for the 'Century of Progress' in 1933 at Chicago." *Automotive Industries* 65 (10 October 1931): 538–540.

"Automotive Buildings Reference Number." *Architectural Forum* 46 (March 1927): plates 34–40, 45, 50–56.

"The Binghamton Automobile Company's New Garage." *The Horseless Age* 13 (16 March 1904): 314–315.

Blanchard, Harold F. "Layout of Automotive Buildings." *Architectural Forum* 46 (March 1927): 281–303.

———. "Those Perplexing Questions About Building, and Their Answers." *Automobile Trade Journal* 24 (1 May 1920): 209–229.

Bowditch, Arthur H. "The Noyes-Buick Building, Boston, Mass." *American Architect* 119 (23 February 1921): 195–197.

"Built for Automotive Service." *Motor Age* 36 (10 July 1919): 22–24.

Bury, Martin H. *The Automobile Dealer.* 4th rev. ed. Haverford, Penn.: Philpenn Publishing Company, 1973.

"Combined Sales and Service Establishment." Part I. *Motor Age* 36 (14 August 1919): 22–25.

"Design Competition for Dealer Establishments." *Architectural Forum* 83 (October 1945): 117–124.

"Detroit Woos Its Dealers with. . . a Basic Change in Auto Selling." *Business Week*, 3 March 1956, 104.

Dominguez, Henry L. *The Ford Agency: A Pictorial History.* Osceola, Wis.: Motorbooks International, 1981.

Epstein, Ralph C. *The Automobile Industry: Its Economic and Commercial Development.* Chicago: A. W. Shaw Company, 1928.

Fairbrother, F. A. "The Planning of Automobile Sales and Service Buildings." Parts 1, 2. *Architectural Forum* 33 (August, September 1920): 39–44, 93–100.

Ford Motor Company. *Plans for New and Modernized Sales and Service Buildings for Ford, Mercury and Lincoln Dealers.* Dearborn, Mich., 1945.

"Ford's Broadway Showroom Is Paneled in American Walnut." (Advertisement for American Walnut Manufacturers' Association.) *Architectural Forum* 46 (March 1927): 76.

General Motors Corporation. *Planning Automobile Dealer Properties.* Detroit, Mich.: Service Section, General Motors Corporation, 1948.

———, Oldsmobile Division. *How Oldsmobile Dealers Are Building Profits Today in Facilities Built for Tomorrow.* Lansing, Mich., 1968.

———, Oldsmobile Division. *How to Increase Your Profitability by Design.* Lansing, Mich., 1977.

Hartman Brothers. *75th Anniversary: Hartman Brothers, 1904–1979.* Montrose, Colo.: Hartman Brothers [c. 1979].

"Improving the Show Room Front." *The Horseless Age* 41 (15 January 1918): 37.

Kahn, Albert. "Sales and Service Buildings, Garages and Assembly Plants." *Architectural Forum* 46 (March 1927): 209–214.

Kelley, Hubert W., Jr. "Mutiny of the Car Dealers." *Harper's* 213 (August 1956): 69–75.

Lee, A. R. "Hollywood Likes This Striking, Modernized Department." *Gas Station, Garage and Motor Car Dealer*, March 1938, 17.

Modern Buildings for Modern Automobile Dealers. Lansing, Mich.: Olds Motor Works, 1936.

"New Garages for Savannah." *The Horseless Age* 13 (8 June 1904): 612–613.

"The Packard Garage, New York." *Architects' and Builders' Magazine* 40 (December 1907): 110–111.

Palamountain, Joseph Cornwall. *Politics of Distribution.* Cambridge: Harvard University Press, 1955.

"Rambler Opens New Boston Sales and Service Station." *The Horseless Age* 30 (2 October 1912): 509.

Ransome, Ernest L., and Saurbrey, Alexis. *Reinforced Concrete Buildings.* New York: McGraw-Hill, 1912.

"Razzle Dazzle Selling Makes Hull-Dobbs Biggest Ford Dealer." *Business Week*, 22 May 1954, 46–47.

"A Remodeled Livery Stable." *The Horseless Age* 34 (15 July 1914): 92.

Rowland, Wirt C. "Architecture and the Automobile Industry." *Architectural Forum* 34 (June 1921): 199–206.

Rubin, B. W. "Exorbitant Rents Result in New Motor Row." *Motor Age* 36 (11 November 1919): 20–21.

"Standard Layout for 50-ft. Garage." *Motor Age* 36 (11 September 1919): 33.

Studebaker Corporation. *Postwar Housing and Facilities for Studebaker Dealers.* South Bend, Ind.: Studebaker Corporation, 1944.

"Studebaker Will Conduct Model Garage and Salesroom." *The Horseless Age* 30 (25 September 1912): 463.

"Supermarkets: Dealers in Surplus Cars Go Big Time." *Business Week*, 1 October 1955, 104–106.

Tipper, Harry. "Functions of the Dealer in Car Distribution." *Automotive Industries* 46 (2 February 1922): 240–241.

"Used Car Sales." *Architectural Record* 91 (March 1942): 50.

Watson, Wilbur J. "The Planning of Automobile Service Stations." *American Architect* 121 (4 January 1922): 32–37.

Wharton, William F. "Architecture and Decoration of Automobile Show Rooms." *Architectural Forum* 46 (March 1927): 305–312.

GAS STATIONS

Adrian, A. A. "New Stations Exemplify Advanced Design." *Gas Station and Garage* 11 (October 1938): 8.

"Baker Oil Company Presents Extensive New Calsteel Built Service Facility." *Gas Station and Garage* 34 (May 1950): 10.

Bayer, Linda. "Roadside Architecture." *Historic Huntsville Quarterly of Architecture and Preservation* 9 (Fall/Winter 1982/1983): 5–25.

Bogstahl, Mars. "Storm Warnings Up for Stations." *National Petroleum News* 56 (July 1964): 103–106.

Bridges, Harry. *The Americanization of Shell*. New York: The Newcomen Society in North America, 1972.

"Calcor Built Neighborhood Station Features Complete Service for Every Car." *Gas Station and Garage* 34 (February 1950): 8.

California Cornice, Steel and Supply Corp. (advertisement). *Gas Station, Garage, and Motor Car Dealer* 32 (February 1949): 16.

"Canopies: What's Behind an Old Standby's New Appeal." *National Petroleum News* 50 (November 1958): 99–104.

The Center for Research in Marketing Incorporated. *A Study of Consumer Response to Oil Company Gas Station Signs*. New York, 1957.

"Changes at the Pump." *Time* 86 (9 July 1965): 90.

Claus, Robert James. *Spatial Dynamics of Gasoline Service Stations*. Vancouver: Tantalus Research Ltd, 1969.

Coate, Roland E. "An Auto Service Station." *Architectural Record* 63 (April 1928): 303.

Crosser, C. A. "Curbing the Curb Pump." *American City* 29 (August 1923): 155–156.

"Does Beauty Sell? Mobil Tries to Find Out." *National Petroleum News* 58 (November 1966): 120.

Elwell, Richard R. "California Is Off Again, As . . . Multi-pumps Revive the Canopy." *National Petroleum News* 47 (November 1955): 41–42.

Emond, Mark. "What Marketers Are Doing—or Not Doing—About Closed Stations." *National Petroleum News* 64 (April 1972): 82–85.

"Filling Stations as Embryo Cities." *Literary Digest* 107 (29 November 1930): 44.

Frappier, William J. "Gasoline Alley: An Aging Ghost of Our Motoring Past." *New England Senior Citizen*, August 1981, 8–9.

"Gas-A-Terias': Self-Served Gasoline Saves a Nickel a Gallon for California Drivers." *Life* 25 (22 November 1948): 129.

"Gasoline: Help Yourself Boom." *Newsweek* 30 (29 December 1947): 48.

"Gasoline Stations Become Architectural Assets." *American City* 41 (November 1929): 98–99.

"Gasoline: War Against Self-Service." *Newsweek* 33 (25 April 1949): 69–70.

Giddens, Paul H. *Standard Oil Company*. New York: Appleton-Century-Crofts, Inc., 1955.

Hadley, Aldon. "The Independent Has 'His Place in the Sun' Right Now." *Gas Station, Garage and Motor Car Dealer* 7 (July 1936): 17.

Haynes, J. J. *Standard Oil Company of California*. New York: The Newcomen Society in North America, 1980.

"'High Test' Architecture." *AIA Journal* 21 (21 March 1973): 30–34.

Historic Tours in Soconyland. New York: Standard Oil Company, 1925.

Hocke, John. "An Up-to-Date Greasing Palace." *American Builder and Building Age* 52 (December 1930): 80–81.

"How Ranch Style Is Taking Over Service-Station Design." *National Petroleum News* 58 (May 1966): 95–101.

Jakle, John A. "The American Gasoline Station, 1920–1970." *Journal of American Culture* 1 (Spring 1978): 520–542.

Jones, Charles L. *Service Station Management: Its Principles and Practice*. New York: D. Van Nostrand Company, 1922.

Kuntz, J. F. "Greek Architecture and Gasoline Service Stations." *American City* 27 (August 1922): 123–124.

Lee, A. R. "Our Station Is a Merchandising Display,' Says Richfield Dealer." *Gas Station and Garage* 11 (November 1938): 9.

Link, Joe. "Attacks on Service Stations Mount While Oil Remains Silent." *National Petroleum News* 64 (March 1972): 46–48.

Lohof, Bruce A. "The Service Station in America: The Evolution of a Vernacular Form." *Industrial Archeology* 11 (1974): 1–13.

Londberg-Holm, K. "The Gasoline Filling and Service Station." *Architectural Record* 67 (June 1930): 563–571.

Lowe, Lucy. "Service Stations as an Asset to the City." *American City* 25 (August 1921): 151–153.

"Money to Be Made: The Oil-Marketing Story." *National Petroleum News* 61 (February 1969).

Moore, Stanley T. "Individual Service Station Design." *National Petroleum News* 25 (14 June 1933): 53–57.

"New Life for Old Stations." *National Petroleum News* 56 (September 1964): 101–104.

Packer, A. H. "Community Service Stations." *Motor Age*, 6 September 1923, 23–24.

Partridge, Bellamy. *Fill 'er Up!* Reprint. Los Angeles: Floyd Clymer, 1959.

"Prototype for Service Stations: Mobil Tests Effect of Design on Sales at 58 Locations." *Architectural Record* 141 (May 1967): 172–175.

"Prototype Gas Station Looks Like a Winner—And Is." *Progressive Architecture* 53 (October 1972): 31.

Reid, Marvin. "The Sophisticated Self-Serve Comes of Age: Part I: Self-Serves and C-Stores." *National Petroleum News* 69 (July 1977): 54–63.

Schroeder, Richard C. "How and When to Modernize Your Service Stations." *National Petroleum News* 50 (October 1958): 84–89.

Sculle, Keith A. "C. A. Petersen: Pioneer Gas Station Architect." *Historic Illinois* 2 (June 1979): 11–13.

———. "The Vernacular Gasoline Station: Examples from Illinois and Wisconsin." *Journal of Cultural Geography* 1 (Spring-Summer 1981): 56–74.

"Self-Service Moves in on the Pump." *Business Week*, 1 October 1966, 129–130.

"Self-service Stations: New Marketing Pattern?" *Business Week*, 24 July 1948, 68.

"Service-station beautification is coming in for ever-increasing attention." *National Petroleum News* 58 (March 1966): 81–82.

"Service Station Design." *National Petroleum News* 42 (29 March 1950): 30.

"Service Stations." *Architectural Record* 97 (February 1944): 71–92.

"Service Stations: The Needless Blot." *Fortune* 74 (September 1966): 159–160.

"Shell Oil's Newest 'Blend-In.'" *National Petroleum News* 52 (February 1960): 121.

"Staebler Opens Modern Station in Ann Arbor." *National Petroleum News* 25 (31 May 1933): 34.

"Standardized Service Stations Designed by Walter Dorwin Teague." *Architectural Record* 82 (September 1937): 69–72.

"Striking New Styling in Calcor-Built Hill Top Station Creates Sensation." *Gas Station and Garage* 30 (February 1948): 25.

"Super Service Station: A Plan for a Corner Lot." *Automobile Digest* 17 (January 1929): 37.

Sweeney, Don. "California's Self Service Stations Still in Limelight." *National Petroleum News* 40 (25 May 1948): 9.

———. "New Stations Designed to Stress Eye Appeal in Pushing the Sale of TBA." *National Petroleum News* 40 (14 January 1948): 34.

"Tommorrow's Gas Station." *Popular Science* 149 (November 1946): 100–101.

"Updating the Service Station Image." *Industrial Design in America* 12 (August 1965): 42–49.

"Vacancies on Gasoline Alley." *Business Week*, 15 December 1973, 20–21.

Vieyra, Daniel I. *"Fill 'er Up": An Architectural History of America's Gas Stations.* New York: Collier Macmillan Publishers, 1979.

Von Eckardt, Wolf. "Toward a Better Community: Must Gas Stations Be Garish?" *American Home* 70 (June 1967): 40–41.

SUPERMARKETS

"A&P from A to Z." *Business Week*, 30 November 1932, 9.

"A&P Goes to the Wars." *Fortune* 17 (April 1938): 93–98.

"Big Bear Shopping Center, a Super-Market, Paterson, New Jersey." *Architectural Record* 76 (September 1934): 204–205.

Brand, Edward A. *Modern Supermarket Operation.* New York: Fairchild Publications, 1963.

Chain Store Age. Silver Jubilee issue, 1925–1950. June 1950.

Charvat, Frank J. *The Development of the Supermarket Industry Through 1950.* Ann Arbor, Mich.: University Microfilms, 1954.

"The Cheapy Thrives." *Business Week*, 8 February 1933, 11–12.

"Clarence Saunders' Amazing Innovation Is a Success." *Food Topics* 22 (June 1967): 39–50.

"Commercial Buildings: Prototype Supermarket." *Progressive Architecture* 37 (July 1956): 100–105.

"The Cousin of the Cafeteria." *Scientific American* 119 (7 September 1918): 193.

Cross, Jennifer. *The Supermarket Trap: The Consumer and the Food Industry.* Bloomington: Indiana University Press, 1970.

Daykin, Leonard E. *Outstanding New Supermarkets.* New York: Progressive Grocer, 1969.

Dipman, Carl W., ed. *Modern Food Stores.* New York: Progressive Grocer, 1935.

———. *The Modern Grocery Store.* New York: Progressive Grocer, 1931.

Dipman, Carl W.; Muller, Robert W.; and Head, Ralph E. *Self-Service Food Stores.* New York: Progressive Grocer, 1946.

Dipman, Carl W., and O'Brien, John E. *Self-Service and Semi-Self-Service Food Stores.* New York: Progressive Grocer, 1940.

"Food Fair Supermarkets." *Fortune* 41 (June 1950): 99–101.

"Grocery Checkout by Computer: What It Means to Shoppers." *U.S. News & World Report*, 30 December 1974, 56–57.

"Grocery Retailing in the '80s—Part I—First Stores off the Drawing Board." *Progressive Grocer* 58 (June 1979): 36–54.

"Grocery Retailing in the '80s—Part II." *Progressive Grocer* 59 1980.

Gruzen, B. Sumner. "Automobile Shopping Centers." *Architectural Record* 76 (July 1934): 43–48.

Gruzen, B. Sumner. "Automobile Shopping Centers." *Super Market Merchandising*, September 1938, 44.

Harrison, J. S. "Self-Service—A Development of the Machine Age." *Chain Store Age* 15 (May 1939): 39.

Hayward, Walter S.; White, Percival; and Fleek, John S. *Chain Stores.* New York: McGraw-Hill Book Company, Inc., 1928.

"How Leading Store Engineers Plan New Super Markets." *Progressive Grocer* 37 (May 1958): 54–69.

Jenkins, George W. *The Publix Story.* Downington, Penn.: The Newcomen Society in North America, 1979.

Kline, George E., ed. *Modern Super Markets & Superettes.* New York: Progressive Grocer, 1956.

Martin, Harold H. "Why She Really Goes to Market." *Saturday Evening Post* 236 (28 September 1963): 40–43.

Mayer, Allen J. "Supermarkets in a Crunch." *New York Times Magazine*, 2 February 1976, 10–12, 46–54.

McAusland, Randolph. *Supermarkets: 50 Years of Progress.* Washington, D.C.: Food Marketing Institute, 1980.

Mueller, R. W. "A New and Important Study for America's Food Retailers." *Progressive Grocer* 44 (July 1965): 6.

"Now Come 'Warehouse' Stores to Threaten the Food Chains." *Business Week*, 20 April 1932, 9.

"One-Stop Supermarkets." *Business Week*, 27 July 1946, 70–71.

"Piggly Wiggly's History Is Long, Colorful." *Piggly Wiggly Turnstile* (from files of *Progressive Grocer*), [c. 1960], 12–13.

"Pioneering Combo Superstores." *The Discount Merchandiser* 20 (February 1980): 32–42.

Progressive Grocer. Fiftieth Anniversary Edition. June 1972.

Progressive Grocer's Marketing Guidebook, 1980. New York: Progressive Grocer, 1980.

Restaurant Business. Diamond Jubilee Edition. May 1976.

"A Roadside Supermarket: Shopping Without Standing." *Interiors* 104 (November 1944): 64–65.

"Supermarket's 50th Anniversary." *Time*, 27 October 1980. (Advertising supplement.)

"Supermarkets: 50 Years of Progress." *Progressive Grocer*, May 1980.

"The Supermerchants." *Time* 58 (20 August 1951): 80.

"Supers Reach Peak in Pittsburgh." *Business Week*, 3 July 1937, 26–28.

Sutnar, Ladislav. *Design for Point of Sale.* New York: Pelligrini & Cudahy, 1952.

"Twenty Years of Progress, Convenience Stores." *Progressive Grocer* 59 (Mid-June 1980).

"25 Years of Progress in Meat Departments." *Chain Store Age: Silver Jubilee Issue* 26 (1950): J28–J33.

"What Are They Building Today?" *Progressive Grocer* 31 (October 1952): 71–79.

Zimmerman, Max M. *The Super Market: A Revolution in Distribution.* New York: McGraw-Hill Book Co., Inc., 1955.

MINIATURE GOLF COURSES

Ashe, Harold J. "A New Market." *Domestic Engineering* 132 (6 September 1930): 54–56.

Beard, Marvin. "Original Tom Thumb Golf Course Here Quietly Passing into Oblivion." *Chattanooga New Free Press*, 10 July 1958.

"Bobby Joneses of the Vacant-Lot Golf Clubs." *Literary Digest* 106 (23 August 1930): 32–34.

"A Brief Survey of Miniature Golf in New England." *Miniature Golf Management* 1 (March 1931): 18.

Chlevin, Ben, ed. *Golf Operators Handbook: Miniature Putting Courses, Golf Driving Ranges, Par-3 Golf Courses.* Chicago, Ill.: National Golf Foundation, 1956.

"Civic War Threatened." *Miniature Golf Management* 1 (15 August 1930): 11.

"Concrete Supplies Utility and Beauty on Miniature Golf Courses." *Concrete* 37 (October 1930): 46–48.

"Courses in New York City." *Miniature Golf Management* 1 (March 1931): 20.

Davis, Elmer. "Miniature Golf to the Rescue." *Harper's* 162 (December 1930): 4–14.

Eastern Golf Company, Inc. *1980–Our 50th Anniversary Catalog.* North Bronx, N.Y.: Eastern Golf Company, Inc., 1980.

Evans, Charles, Jr. "Golf in Your Own Backyard." *Popular Mechanics* 54 (September 1930): 492–497.

Gelders, Jesse F. "Why Midget Golf Swept Country." *Popular Science Monthly* 117 (November 1930): 22–23, 136–138.

"Half-Pint Golf." *Outlook and Independent* 155 (27 August 1930) 656.

Harris Miniature Golf Courses, Inc. (catalog) Wildwood, N.J., n.d.

"Hazards of Miniature Golf Courses Listed." *The Weekly Underwriter and the Insurance Plan* 123 (15 November 1930): 1122.

Kahn, E. J., Jr. "Messieurs, Faites Vos Jeux." *New Yorker* 33 (12 October 1957): 144–148.

"Large Uses of Steel in Small Ways: Miniature Golf." *Steel* 87 (27 November 1930): 54.

"Large Volume of Concrete in Miniature Golf Courses." *Concrete* 39 (September 1930): 49–50.

"Lighting: For All-Night Miniature Golf." *Electrical World* 95 (4 October 1930): 644–646.

"Midget or Colossus?" *Survey* 65 (15 November 1930): 197.

"Miniature Golf Again." *American City* 43 (September 1930): 17.

"Miniature Golf and Public Policy." *American City* 43 (August 1930): 17.

Miniature Golf Courses. Chicago: National Golf Foundation, 1949.

"Miniature Golf Helps Many Kinds of Business." *Business Week,* 3 September 1930, 9–10.

National Golf Foundation, Inc. *Miniature Putting Course Manual.* Rev. ed. North Palm Beach, Fla., 1978.

Phillips, Michael J. *How to Play Miniature Golf.* Los Angeles: Keystone Publishing Company, 1930.

Quinlan, Joseph P. "Roofing the Tom Thumb Courses Is No Midget Business Opportunity." *Building Age* 52 (September 1930): 71.

Rice, G. "Small Game Hunters." *Collier's* 86 (20 September 1930): 19.

"Rout the Roughnecks." *Miniature Golf Management* 1 (March 1931): 6.

"Thar's Gold in Them Thar Hills, Stranger." *Saturday Evening Post* 262 (31 May 1930): 148.

"A Theme Song." *Miniature Golf Management* 1 (15 August 1930): 26.

Thomas, George C., Jr. *Golf Architecture in America.* Los Angeles: The Times-Mirror Press, 1927.

Thompson, Morley B. *Miniature Golf, A Treatise on the Subject.* Denver: Central States Publishing Co., 1930.

"Tom Thumb Golf." *Nation* 131 (27 August 1930): 215–216.

"The Tom Thumbs Are Back." *New York Times Magazine,* 21 August 1955, 71.

Trevor, George. "Battle of Lilliput." *Outlook and Independent* 156 (1 October 1930): 194.

DRIVE-IN THEATERS

American Association of State Highway Officials. Committee on Traffic; Subcommittee on Roadside Control. *Drive-In Theater Study 1949.* Washington, D.C.: American Association of State Highway Officials, 1949.

"Another Home in a Screen Tower." *Theatre Catalog.* Philadelphia: Jay Emanuel Publications, 1953–1954, 84.

Best, Katharine, and Hillyer, Katharine, "Movies under the Stars." *Reader's Digest* 53 (September 1948): 117–119.

"Building a Drive-In." *Theatre Catalog.* Philadelphia: Jay Emanuel Publications, Inc., 1956–1957, 94–101.

"Camden's Drive-In Theater." *Literary Digest* 116 (22 July 1933): 19.

Corgan, Jack. "Movies under Texas Skies." *Architectural Concrete* 11 (February 1946): 24–25.

"Depreciation for Tax and Financing." *Theatre Catalog.* Philadelphia: Jay Emanuel Publications, Inc., 1949–1950, 288–289.

"The Drive-In—Implementing an Old American Custom." *Motion Picture Herald* ("Better Theatres" supplement), 8 January 1949, 19–20.

"The Drive-In Lie-In." *Newsweek* 62 (8 July 1963): 78.

"Drive-In Movie Holds Four Hundred Cars." *Popular Mechanics* 60 (September 1933): 326.

"Drive-Ins." *Architectural Record* 108 (August 1950): 130–153.

"Drive-Ins." *Time* 38 (14 July 1941): 66.

"Drive-In Theater." *Business Week,* 5 August 1933, 19.

"Drive-in Theater." *Collier's* 101 (22 March 1938): 52.

"Drive-In Theaters of the 1950 Season."·*Theatre Catalog.* Philadelphia: Jay Emanuel Publications, Inc., 1949–1950, 253–274.

Encyclopedia of Exhibitions. New York: National Association of Theatre Owners. Rev. ed. 1981, s.v. "Drive-in theater statistics."

"The Gratiot Drive-In." *Theatre Catalog.* Philadelphia: Jay Emanuel Publications, 1948–1949, 128.

Hall, Ben M. *The Best Remaining Seats: The Story of the Golden Age of the Movie Palace.* New York: Clarkson N. Potter, Inc., Publisher, 1961.

Lee, S. Charles. "What the Future May Bring." *Theatre Catalog.* Philadelphia: Jay Emanuel Publications, 1941, 12.

Jack H. Levin Associates. *A Study of Influences on Drive-In Theatres in 1952.* New York, 1952.

Levy, Herman M. "The Legal Position of Design Patents." *Theatre Catalog.* Philadelphia: Jay Emanuel Publications, Inc., 1949–1950, 165.

Lewis, Howard T. *The Motion Picture Industry.* New York: D. Van Nostrand Co., Inc., 1933.

Luther, Rodney. "Drive-in Theaters: Rags to Riches in Five Years." *Film Quarterly* 5 (Summer 1951): 401–411.

———. "Who Are the Drive-In Patrons?" *Theatre Catalog.* Philadelphia: Jay Emanuel Publications, Inc., 1949–1950, 196–200.

Moonlight Movies System. *Typical Drive-In Plans.* Rialto, Calif., 1948.

"Movie Theater Lets Cars Drive Right In." *Popular Science* 123 (August 1933): 19.

Naylor, David. *American Picture Palaces—The Architecture of Fantasy.* New York: Van Nostrand Reinhold Company, 1981.

"1949–50 Review of New Drive-In Construction." *Theatre Catalog.* Philadelphia: Jay Emanuel Publications, Inc., 1949–1950, 201–232.

"Open-Air Movies Are Being Tried." *Architectural Forum* 59 (July 1933): 81.

Peterson, George M. "Drive-In Planning and Construction—Post-War Style." *Motion Picture Herald* ("Better Theatres" supplement), 14 February 1948, 19–22.

———. "Drive-In Theatres of Today and Tomorrow." *Theatre Catalog.* Philadelphia: Jay Emanuel Publications, Inc., 1949–1950, 233–236.

———. "Site Selection and Layout Planning." *Theatre Catalog.* Philadelphia: Jay Emanuel Publications, Inc., 1949–1950, 237–241.

Reynolds, Albert H. "Monkey Villages as Promotional Aids." *Theatre Catalog.* Philadelphia: Jay Emanuel Publications, Inc., 1949–1950, 300–302.

Stote, Helen M., ed. *The Motion Picture Theater.* New York: Society of Motion Picture Engineers, Inc., 1948.

Taylor, Frank J. "Big Boom in Outdoor Movies." *Saturday Evening Post* 229 (15 September 1956): 31.

"The Work of S. Charles Lee." *Theatre Catalog.* Philadelphia: Jay Emanuel Publications, Inc., 1949–1950, 1–36.

"Zoning Regulations and Legal Decisions." *Theatre Catalog.* Philadelphia: Jay Emanuel Publications, Inc., 1949–1950, 242–247.

MOTELS

Alexander, Jack. "Host of the Highways." *Saturday Evening Post* 228 (19 July 1958): 16–17.

"America Takes to the Motor Court." *Business Week*, 15 June 1940, 19–22.

Anderson, George, and Crawford, Earl. "A Furnishing Plan for the Lightfoot Modern Tourist Court." *Tourist Court Journal* 1 (June 1938): 11–12.

"The Architect's Role in Hotel-Motel Design." *Architectural Record* 130 (September 1961): 131–132.

Baker, Geoffrey, and Funaro, Bruno. *Motels.* New York: Van Nostrand Reinhold Co., 1955.

Baum, Arthur W. "The New American Roadside." *Saturday Evening Post* 233 (30 July 1960): 32–33, 48–50.

Belasco, Warren James. *Americans on the Road: From Autocamp to Motel, 1910–1945.* Cambridge: MIT Press, 1979.

Berdan, Harry B. "Have We Outgrown the Original Cabin Camp?" *Tourist Court Journal* 1, (September 1938): 13–14.

"Best Western: The Independent Alternative." *News* (a publication of the Best Western News Service, Phoenix), n.d.

Birmingham, Frederic A. "Kemmons Wilson: The Inn-side Story." *Saturday Evening Post* 244 (Winter 1971): 66–71.

Borland, Hal. "From Pup Tents to Motels." *New York Times Magazine*, 16 September 1951, 24–25.

Brimmer, Frank E. "The 'Nickel-and Dime' Stores of Nomadic America." *Magazine of Business* 52 (August 1927): 151–153, 174–175.

Bryant, Robert P. "Why More and More Tourists Are Turning to Motels." *Hotel Management* 52 (August 1947): 33–36.

"Cabin and Cottage Building Time Is Here." *American Builder* 57 (March 1935): 40.

"Can Urban Renewal Renew Your Volume?" *Hospitality* 50 (May 1966): 72–75.

Chandler, Gilbert S. "Starting from Scratch and Building a Deluxe Motor Court." *Tourist Court Journal* 1 (November 1937): 5–6.

Colbert, Haines. "Motor Hotel Resort—Florida Style." *Hotel Management* 64 (November 1953): 48–53.

Cole, Warren M., and Broten, Paul R. "Trends in Guest Room Design." *Cornell H.R.A. Quarterly* 12 (November 1971): 19–21.

Cowgill, Clinton H. "Modern Travel Accommodations." *AIA Journal*, March 1960, 73–92.

Cranley, Elizabeth. "Upward and Inward with Time." *Progressive Architecture* 59 (February 1978): 46–51.

Dempewolff, Richard F. "Drive-In Dream Castles." *Popular Mechanics* 106 (July 1956): 97–103.

DeVoto, Bernard. "Motel Town." *Harper's* 207 (September 1953): 45–48.

Fair, Ernest W. "When the Highway Leaves You." *Tourist Court Journal* 13 (September 1950): 8–9.

Fehler, Edward N. "Beautifying Motor Courts and Lodges by Means of Proper Planning." *Tourist Court Journal* 1 (December 1937): 5–6.

Freedgood, Seymour. "The Motel Free-for-all." *Fortune* 59 (June 1959): 119, 122–123, 163–164, 168, 171.

Goldrath, Bert. "Bypassed." *Hotel Management* 67 (May 1955): 76–78.

"The Great American Roadside." *Fortune* 9 (September 1934): 53–63.

Hanson, A. C. "Building a De Luxe Motor Court." *Tourist Court Journal* 1 (January 1938): 5–8, 28.

Harding, Richard F. "Warnings." *Tourist Court Journal* 10 (November 1946): 26–27.

"HCA Expansion and Motor Hotels." *Hotel Management* 72 (July 1957): 76–77.

"Highway Hotels." *Architectural Record* 98 (July 1945): 66–77.

"Highway Hotels and Restaurants." *Architectural Record* 114 (July 1953): 158–177.

Hillyer, Katharine. "Bed and Butter Letter." *Tourist Court Journal* 10 (February 1947): 12–13.

Hocke, John. "Good Profits Building Tourist Camps." *American Builder and Building Age* 51 (April 1931): 88–89.

Hoffman, Claire. "Circle Tour Notes About Courts." *Tourist Court Journal* 10 (September 1947): 5–7.

"Hotels That Look Like Motels." *Business Week*, 14 March 1953, 62.

"How Concrete Is Used in Building Indian Teepees." *Concrete* 37 (August 1930): 52.

"How Two Ex-G.I.'s Designed and Built Their Own Motor Court." *Hotel Management* 53 (March 1948): 47–51.

"The Inn Crowd." *Newsweek* 81 (19 February 1973): 69–70.

Jakle, John A. "Motel by the Roadside: America's Room for the Night." *Journal of Cultural Geography* 1 (Fall/Winter 1980): 34–49.

Jones, William D. C. "Up in the Air." *Tourist Court Journal* 10 (May 1947): 5–7.

Joseph, James. "Business—Bypass or No." *Hotel Management* 64 (July 1953): 44–45.

———. "TravelLodge." *Hotel Management* 64 (July 1953): 46–47.

Kane, C. Vernon. *Motor Courts—from Planning to Profits.* New York: Ahrens Publishing Company, Inc., 1954.

Koch, Carl. "Design for a Franchise Chain." *Architectural Record* 23 (April 1958): 205–208.

Kulbago, Mary Ellen. "A Thumbnail Guide to Chains." *Hospitality* 57 (December 1973): 18–29.

Leahy's Hotel-Motel Guide and Travel Atlas of the United States, Canada, Mexico and Puerto Rico. 103rd edition. Northbrook, Ill.: American Hotel Register Co., 1978.

Lightfoot, E. H. "Constructing a Modern Motor Court." *Tourist Court Journal* 1 (March 1938): 5–7.

Lightfoot, T. E. "Construction Questions." *Tourist Court Journal* 1 (January 1938): 19.

"Lodgings for Travelers." *Architectural Record* 119 (January 1956): 170–197.

McCarthy, John J. "The Market Business Forgets." *Nation's Business* 21 (August 1933): 38–40.

———. "'Pay Dirt' in Tourist Camps." *Advertising and Selling* 42 (25 May 1933): 26, 44.

McCarthy, John J., and Littell, Robert. "Three Hundred Thousand Shacks." *Harper's* 167 (July 1933): 180–188.

McCullough, C. E. "Simple, Home-Like Arrangement of Court Cottages Is Most Desirable." *Tourist Court Journal* 13 (August 1938): 5–9.

Miller, Richard A. "The Odds on Motels." *Architectural Forum* 107 (August 1957): 110–117.

"Money on the Roadside." *Fortune* 44 (August 1951): 80–84.

"Motel and Hotel: The Gap Narrows." *Business Week*, 11 June 1955, 102–104.

"Motels." *Architectural Record* 113 (May 1948): 95–117.

Motels, Hotels, Restaurants and Bars. 2nd ed. New York: F. W. Dodge Corporation, 1956.

"Motor Court Management." *Hotel Management* 57 (February 1950): 39–61.

Motor Courts and Drive-Ins Construction and Operation. New York: Ahrens Publishing Company, Inc., 1951.

"Motor Hotel Round-up." *Hotel Management* 66 (November 1954): 82–92.

"A Motor Tourist Camp Designed for Sanitation and Beauty." *American City* 41 (July 1929): 105.

O'Moore, Peggy [Jeanne Bowman]. *Tourist Cabins.* New York: Gramercy Publishing Co., 1941.

"Originality, Enterprise, Good Taste, and Lots of Effort and Money Make Mission Village." *Tourist Court Journal* 2 (December 1938): 5–6.

Pawley, Frederic Arden. "Motels." *Architectural Record* 107 (March 1950): 110–131.

Penner, Richard H. "The Commercial Lodging Market." *Cornell H.R.A. Quarterly* 16 (May 1975): 33–34.

"Plan 100 Motor Inns in Chicago District." *Business Week*, 27 May 1931, 16.

Plemons, Hattie, and Plemons, Constance. "Why Many Downtown Hotel Guests Are Switching to Motor Courts." *Hotel Management* 55 (April 1949): 49–51, 110–116.

Podd, George O., and Lesure, John D. *Planning and Operating Motels and Motor Motels.* New York: Ahrens Publishing Company Inc., 1964.

"Putting the HJ Seal on Motels." *Business Week*, 23 October 1954, 126.

Rich, Edson. "A Motor Tourist Camp Designed for Sanitation and Beauty." *The American City* 67 (July 1929): 105.

"Roadside Cabins for Tourists." *Architectural Record* 74 (December 1933): 457–462.

"A Rougher Road for Motel Chains." *Business Week*, 30 March 1974, 94.

"Scheme for a Mid-City Motor Hotel." *Architectural Record* 123 (April 1958): 228–230.

"The Sheraton Franchise Division: A Changing Image for a Changing Market." *Hotel & Resort Industry*, December 1981, 46.

"A Single Standard for Travelers." *Business Week*, 16 November 1963, 114.

Smith, George Cline. "Motor Hotels." *Architectural Record* 128 (July 1960): 145–168.

Solomon, Leo M. "Hotel in Name—Hotel in Plan But Built for Roadside Success." *Hotel Management* 56 (October 1949): 47–51.

Spooner, Harry L. "Traveling Salesmen Build an In-line Type Tourist Court." *Tourist Court Journal* 13 (April 1950): 38–39.

Stedman, Gerald, and Stedman, Margaret. "Miami's Miracle Mile of Motels." *Tourist Court Journal* 15 (July 1952): 10–11.

Taylor, Frank J. "Just What the Motorist Ordered." *Saturday Evening Post* 220 (5 July 1947): 32–33.

Teets, John N. "The Motor Court Moderne; Designed for the Needs of Today and Tomorrow." *Tourist Court Journal* 1 (March 1938): 11–12, 24.

"Tourist Cabins." *Architectural Record* 77 (February 1935): 95–100.

Tourist Court Plan Book. 2nd ed. Temple, Tex.: Tourist Court Journal, 1950.

"Tourists' Cabins That Get the Business." *Popular Mechanics* 64 (July 1935): 151–154.

Trends in the Hotel Industry. New York: Pannell Kerr Forster, 1981.

U.S. Department of Commerce. Bureau of the Census. "Tourists Camps: 1935." *Census of Business: 1935.*

U.S. Lodging Industry. Philadelphia: Laventhol & Horwath, 1981.

U.S. Small Business Administration. *Establishing and Operating a Year-Round Motor Court*, by Harry Barclay Love. Industrial (Small Business) Series No. 50. Washington, D.C.: GPO, 1947.

———. *Motels*, by Howard E. Morgan. Small Business Bibliography No. 66. Washington, D.C.: GPO, 1964.

———. *Starting and Managing a Small Motel*, by Harold Whittington. The Starting-and-Managing Series, Vol. 7. Washington, D.C.: GPO, 1963.

Wade, Dorothy. "Can a Tourist Be 'Laid'?" *Tourist Court Journal* 10 (December 1946): 5–9.

Wilkinson, Walter B. *Profits in Tourist Camps.* Lansing, Mich.: Travel Research, 1940.

Willatt, Norris. "The $6 Motel." *Dun's Review* 89 (May 1967): 61–62.

Wilson, Kemmons. *The Holiday Inn Story.* New York: The Newcomen Society in North America, 1968.

Zachary, Frank. "How Much Has Been Done for and by Motorists in the New York World's Fair?" *Tourist Court Journal* 1 (April 1939): 13–14.

RESTAURANTS

"A&W Shows New Designs." *Drive-In Restaurant* 32 (July 1968): 42.

"Along Came the Drive-Ins." *The Diner* 3 (September 1946): 8–9.

"Always Beckoning Customers . . . the ABC's of Good Design." *American Restaurant* 40 (May 1957): 214–216.

"Architecture for the Autoist." *Country Life* 38 (April 1928): 80.

Atkin, William Wilson, and Adler, Joan. *Interiors Book of Restaurants.* New York: Whitney Library of Design, 1960.

Baeder, John. *Diners.* New York: Harry N. Abrams, Inc., 1978.

———. *Diners of New Jersey.* Wayne: William Paterson College, 1978.

Bailey, K. V. "The Silent Salesmen." *The Diner* 7 (September 1948): 14.

Baraban, Regina. "The Amazing Evolution of Fast Food." *Restaurant Design*, Winter 1981, 30–37.

"Better Drive-In Service with Functional Planning." *American Restaurant* 33 (September 1951): 59.

"Big Business with Small Menu." *American Restaurant* 38 (July 1955): 86.

Bigelow, John. "The Detroit Study of Drive-In Problems." *Drive-In Restaurant*, August 1964, 12.

Boas, Max, and Chain, Steve. *Big Mac: The Unauthorized Story of McDonald's.* New York: New American Library, 1976.

"The Burger Queen." *Drive-In Restaurant* 27 (September 1963): 16.

Burroughs, A. D. "First Impressions Are Lasting Impressions. . . ." *Drive-In Restaurant and Highway Cafe Magazine* 20 (March 1956): 8.

"The Butterfly." *Drive-In Restaurant and Highway Cafe Magazine* 19 (July 1955): 15.

Buzzell, Paul W. "Lindholm's a Vermont Institution." *The Diner* 5 (February 1948): 10–11.

"Catching the Eye of the Consumer." *Fast Service* 36 (January 1977): 35.

"Cedric's: 19th Century Decor and 20th Century Service." *Fast Service* 36 (May 1977): 48.

Chain Store Age: Variety Store Managers' Edition, Section Two, Fountain—Restaurant, 1925–1950. June 1950, 17–54.

Childs, Leslie. "'Hot Dog Kennels' as Nuisances to Adjoining Property Owners." *American City* 63 (February 1928): 137.

"Church's Fried Chicken: A Corporate Profile." *Fast Service* 38 (January 1979): 43.

Clark, Blake. "Who Is Howard Johnson?" *Reader's Digest* 55 (July 1949): 127–130.

Claudy, C. H. "Organizing the Wayside Tea House." *Country Life in America* 29 (June 1916): 54.

Clifford, J. C. "The Investor Views the Chain Restaurant." *The Magazine of Wall Street*, 17 October 1931, 848–872.

"Clip On a New (Brick) Face." *Drive-In Restaurant* 27 (February 1963): 36.

"'Coffee and' in the Doggy Dog-Wagon." *Literary Digest* 112 (February 1932): 42–43.

Collins, B. L. "Competition Cleans-Up!" *American Restaurant* 38 (October 1955): 106–107.

"Coming . . . A New Restaurant Trend." *American Restaurant* 31 (April 1949): 125–126.

"Consumer Research: A Tool to Use or Abuse." *Fast Service* 36 (February 1977): 19.

"Cooking Up Profits, Southern Style." *Business Week*, 24 June 1967, 176.

Crossman, Ralph. "World's Largest Drive-In." *The Diner* 8 (February 1949): 10.

Crump, Spencer. "Cinema Capitol Creates Ideas You Can Use." *American Restaurant* 31 (July 1949): 37–39.

"Customers Love Fast Service from Hostess and Two-Way Radio." *Drive-In Restaurant and Highway Cafe Magazine* 20 (September 1956): 14.

"Design Ideas by Bastian-Blessing." *Drive-In Restaurant and Highway Cafe Magazine* 20 (February 1956): 21.

"Designed to Stop Both Eye and Car." *Drive-In Restaurant* 25 (July 1961): 8.

"Designing Interiors to Stimulate Sales." *Soft Serve & Drive-In Field* 13 (July–August 1968): 38.

Dickson, Paul. *The Great American Ice Cream Book.* New York: Atheneum, 1972.

Divine, Charles. "The Thousand and One Night Owls." *The New York Times Magazine*, 24 December 1922, 8.

Doyle, Jerry. "Success—'Savage Style.'" *Drive-In Restaurant* 10 (February 1946): 7.

"Drive-In Design Attracts Trade." *American Builder* 71 (November 1949): 90–91.

"Drive-In Magazine's Architectural Editor Looks into the Future." *Drive-In Magazine* 21 (December 1957): 11.

Drive-In Operators Handbook. Duluth, Minn.: Ojibway Press Inc., 1964.

"Drive-In Ordinance Roundup." *Drive-In Restaurant* 29 (October 1965): 32.

"Drive-In Profit Season Lengthened by Heaters." *American Restaurant* 38 (September 1955): 51.

"Drive-In Restaurant." *American Building and Building Age* 65 (June 1943): 42.

"Drive-In Restaurants and Luncheonettes." *Architectural Record* 100 (September 1946): 99–106.

"The 'Drive-Thru.'" *Drive-In Restaurant and Highway Cafe Magazine* 21 (January 1957): 11.

"The Eccentric." *Drive-In Restaurant* 27 (November 1963): 31.

Ehle, Henry S. "Do New Super-Roads Doom Restaurants?" *American Restaurant* 42 (June 1959): 51–58.

Ehrlich, Blake. "The Diner Puts on Airs." *Saturday Evening Post* 220 (19 June 1948): 34–35.

"Elevating the Standing of the 'Hot Dog Kennel.'" *American City* 38 (May 1928): 99.

Emerson, Robert L. *Fast Food: The Endless Shakeout.* New York: Lebhar-Friedman, Inc., 1979.

Esposito, Michael J. "Wendy's International." *Fast Service* 38 (April 1979): 14.

"Everyone Likes Donuts." *Drive-In Magazine* 24 (April 1960): 20.

"Eye-Catching Roofs Catch More." *American Restaurant* 40 (June 1957): 110–112.

"Family Friendly: More Evolution Than Revolution." *Fast Service* 36 (April 1977): 26.

"Fast Food." Washington, D.C.: Center for the Visual Environment, 1975.

"Fast Food as a Barometer of City Growth." *Fast Service* 36 (January 1977): 20E.

"The Fast Food Challenge." *Progressive Grocer*, November 1977, 1–15.

"Fast Food Goes Urban Chic." *Fast Service* 35 (November 1976): 36.

Fengler, May. *Restaurant Architecture and Design.* New York: Universe Books, 1969.

"50 Ideas for Drive-Ins." *American Restaurant* 42 (July 1959): 52–53.

"Formula Profits." *Time* 44 (25 August 1947): 80.

"41 in Florida." *Drive-In Restaurant and Highway Cafe Magazine* 19 (June 1955): 19.

"Franchises Listed for Single Items or Full Restaurant Operations." *American Restaurant* 41 (June 1958): 57.

Fraser, Nancy. "Hamburger University." *Life* 61 (21 October 1966): 100.

"Frozen Custard: Money in It." *Changing Times* 10 (May 1956): 41–42.

Furniss, Ruth MacFarland. "The Ways of the Tea House." *Tea Room Management* 1 (August 1922): 5.

Garfunkel, Louis X. *Sandwich Shops, Drive-Ins and Diners: How to Start and Operate Them.* New York: Greenberg Publisher, 1955.

Gaskill, Gordon. "That Wild Johnson Boy." *The American Magazine* 131 (March 1941): 34.

Gaston, H. P. *Roadside Marketing in Michigan*. Special Bulletin 185. East Lansing, Michigan: Michigan State College Agricultural Experiment Station, 1929.

"Glorified Road Stands Pay." *Business Week*, 17 February 1940, 26–27.

Gundaker, Guy. "Why the Cafeteria Is Successful." *American Restaurant* 2 (January 1920): 22.

Gutman, Richard J. S.; Kauffman Elliot; and Slovic, David. *American Diner*. New York: Harper & Row, 1979.

"Half a Million." *Drive-in Restaurant and Highway Cafe Magazine* 20 (April 1956): 10.

Harrison, Ed. "What's Cooking on the Strip?" *Drive-In Carry-Out*, December 1970, 16.

Hempt, Grace Elizabeth. "Old Grist Mill Is Now a Tea Room." *Tea Room and Gift Shop* 2 (March 1923): 7.

Hicks, Clifford B. "Computerburgers Hit the Assembly Line." *Popular Mechanics* 90 (September 1966): 80–83.

"Highway Business Survey Completed." *Drive-In Restaurant and Highway Cafe Magazine* 21 (February 1957): 10.

"Highway Restaurant for a 100-Octane World." *Architectural Record* 98 (October 1945): 102–104.

"Highway Restaurants." *Architectural Record* 126 (October 1954): 163–169.

"Highways Are Happy Ways." *American Restaurant* 37 (May 1954): 124–125.

Hirshorn, Paul, and Izenour, Steven. *White Towers*. Cambridge: MIT Press, 1979.

Hocke, John A. "An Up-to-Date Greasing Palace." *American Builder and Building Age* 52 (December 1930): 80–81.

"Home Atmosphere Makes Many Friends." *Tea Room and Gift Shop* 2 (May 1923): 9.

Hoopes, Lydia Clawson. "From Root Beer Stand to Millions." *American Restaurant* 31 (May 1948): 39.

"Hot Dogs De Luxe." *Woman's Home Companion*, March 1930, 4.

"How Bob Christian Licked the By-Pass." *Drive-In Restaurant*, October 1963, 16.

"How Drive-Ins Compare with Other Restaurants." *Drive-In Restaurant* 32 (April 1968): 40.

"How the Frosted Scotchman Solved the Teenager Problem." *Soft Serve & Drive-In Field* 72 (March–April 1967): 22.

"Howard Johnson Redesigns." *Architectural Forum* 102 (March 1955): 162–165.

"The Howard Johnson Restaurants." *Fortune* 2 (September 1940): 82–87.

"How's Business with Diners?" *American Restaurant* 31 (February 1949): 120–125.

Huxtable, Ada Louise. "Architecture for a Fast Food Culture." *New York Times Magazine*, 12 February 1978, 23–25.

"'I'd Never Return to the Old Operation.'" *The Diner* 9 (December 1949): 16.

"In Atlanta, All Roads Lead to the Varsity." *Business Week*, 8 October 1966, 132–133.

Ingram, E. W., Sr. *All This from a 5-cent Hamburger! The Story of the White Castle System*. New York: The Newcomen Society in North America, 1964.

Ireland, William Francis. "Where the Cafeteria Was Born." *American Restaurant* 2 (May 1920): 15.

Jackson, Howard E. "Operation 'Eye Appeal.'" *The Diner* 7 (August 1948): 10.

Karsten, T. Robert. "Self-Service: Psychology in Cafeteria Operation." *American Restaurant* 1 (November 1919): 29.

Keally, Francis. "Planning Roadside Inns for Today's New Patronage." *Hotel Management* 48 (October 1945): 31.

"Kitchen Layout and Equipment Design Give Fast Service at Hardee's." *Drive-In Restaurant* 26 (August 1962): 10.

Knutson, L. W. "Ideas from 20 Years in Drive-Ins." *Drive-In Restaurant* 30 (April 1966): 37.

Kottak, Conrad P. "Ritual at McDonald's." *Natural History* 87 (January 1978): 74–83.

Kroc, Ray. *Grinding It Out: The Making of McDonald's*. Chicago: Henry Regnery Company, 1977.

Kurtz, Stephen A. *Wasteland: Building the American Dream*. New York: Praeger Publishers, Inc. 1973.

"Laventhol and Horwath Study Second Tier Food Chains." *Fast Service* 37 (April 1977): 16J.

"Lunch Wagons De Luxe." *The Christian Science Monitor*, 23 March 1938, 14.

"Lunch Wagons Streamline—Customers Stream In." *Nation's Business* 25 (September 1937): 74.

Lundberg, Donald E. *The Hotel and Restaurant Business*. Boston: CBI Publishing Co., Inc., 1975.

"Main Street 1910." *Fast Service* 39 (October 1980): 34.

Marshall, Thomas Farley. "Tourist Taverns Make Bid for Motorists' Food Trade." *American Restaurant* 16 (June 1933): 30.

Martin, Rebecca. "Once Around Florida." *The Diner* 7 (October 1948): 12.

McAllister, Antoinette. "Cities OK Fast-Food Chains—But Hold the Golden Arches." *American Society of Planning Officials* 42 (October 1976): 20–21.

McCaskie, Florence A. "Rustic Colonial House Now a Tea Room." *Tea Room and Gift Shop* 2 (August 1923): 9.

McNeel, John P. "From Ice Cream to a Motor Lodge Chain." *Hotel Management* 71 (March 1957): 70–73.

McPherson, A. Pearl. "Historical Feasts Featured in Restaurant Advertising." *American Restaurant* 5 (January 1922): 34.

"Mexican Foods—Family Style." *Drive-In & Carry-Out*, April 1969, 46.

Mitgang, Herbert. "For the Love of Pizza." *Collier's* 131 (7 March 1953): 66–69.

Morgenstern, Joseph. "Roadside Gourmet: Pop Goes the Food." *Newsweek* 80 (25 September 1972): 76–78.

Morton, David. "They Did It All for You." *Progressive Architecture* 59 (June 1978): 64–67.

"The Most Innovative McDonald's of the Future." *Progressive Architecture* 60 (March 1979): 22.

"Motormat 'Magic.'" *American Restaurant* 31 (September 1949): 48.

Mozzocco, Edward A. "The Diner That Wouldn't Give Up." *American Restaurant* 32 (January 1950): 34.

Munroe, Charles C. "When You Buy an Electric Sign—." *American Restaurant* 7 (December 1924): 42.

"A New Breed of McDonald's: Glendale Station: A McDonald's on the Right Track." *Fast Service* 36 (September 1977): 21.

"The New Outlet—Roadside Refreshment Stands." *Printer's Ink* 135 (22 April 1926): 127.

"New Trends in Diners." *The Diner* 9 (August 1949): 14.

"Off the Highways." *Business Week*, 19 June 1943, 60.

O'Leary, Jay. "The Fast Food Entrepreneur: Four Stories of Success." *Fast Service* 38 (April 1979): 23.

O'Meara, John B. "Drive-In Service Do's and Don'ts." *American Restaurant* 39 (July 1956): 70.

"On the Road Again." *Business Week*, 25 August 1945, 52.

"104-Point Check List for Planning a Restaurant." *American Restaurant* 39 (February 1956): 92–93.

"One Hundred Truckers Stop Here Daily." *American Restaurant* 39 (July 1956): 67.

"One Million Hamburgers and 160 Tons of French Fries a Year." *American Restaurant*, July 1952, 44–45.

"Palaces of the Hot Doges." *Architectural Forum* 63 (August 1935): 30.

"A Palate Revolution." *Forbes* 107 (15 February 1971): 35.

Patterson, C. A. "A Modernization Forecast." *American Restaurant* 21 (January 1938): 25.

"Period Architecture for Tea Rooms." *Tea Room and Gift Shop* 2 (June 1923): 5.

Peterson, Elmer T. "Hamburgers Incorporated." *Nation's Business* 15 (May 1927): 71–74.

"Pick Your Spot Scientifically." *The Diner* 8 (February 1949): 15.

Pomeroy, Ralph. *The Ice Cream Connection*. New York: Paddington Press, Ltd., 1975.

"Ptomaine Joe's Place." *Collier's* 102 (1 October 1938): 54.

"Restaurant Design as a Marketing Tool." *Fast Service* 36 (May 1977): 20.

Restaurant Hospitality: 60th Anniversary Issue. December 1979.

"A Restaurant with Built-In Sales Appeal." *American Restaurant* 40 (May 1957): 216–218.

"A Restaurant with Mechanical Brains." *American Restaurant* 7 (May 1924): 54.

Rice, Diana. "The Lunch Wagon Settles Down." *New York Times Magazine*, 19 October 1941, 20.

"Roadside Beauty and You." *Drive-In Restaurant* 29 (November 1965): 24.

"The Roadside Stand Grows Up—Ultra Modern, Magnificent." *Drive-In Restaurant and Highway Cafe Magazine*, November 1955, 21.

Rockland, Michael Aaron. "The Rest of America May Belong to the Fast-Food Chains, but New Jersey Is Proud to Be Its Diner Capital." *New Jersey Monthly*, October 1977, 53–59.

"A Root-Beer Franchiser Regains Its Fizz." *Business Week*, 20 October 1973, 54–56.

"A Roving Restaurant." *American Restaurant* 5 (April 1922): 44.

"Sales Increase 300% with Custom-Built 'Skookum-matic' Serving System." *Drive-In Restaurant and Highway Cafe Magazine* 20 (June 1956): 5.

Sargeant, Winthrop. "Roadside Restaurant." *Life* 31 (13 August 1951): 75–76.

Schwartz, Barney. "Two Cars for One." *The Diner* 7 (June 1948): 9.

Seliger, Nancy. "Fast Food Architecture: Keeping Pace with the Changing Culture." *Fast Service* 39 (May 1980): 22.

"Sell Passers-by with Smarter Fronts." *American Restaurant* 36 (September 1953): 62–63.

"Serving 300 Million Customers a Year...Howard Johnson's in 33 States." *American Restaurant* 41 (June 1958): 58–59.

"75 Years of Foodservice History." *Restaurant Business* 75 (May 1976): 43–44.

"She Teaches People How to Run Wayside Eating Places." *The American Magazine* 97 (April 1924): 69.

Siekman, H. C. "Modernization Puts Business Spotlight on the Restaurant Profit Picture." *American Restaurant* 22 (January 1940): 26.

———. "Restaurant Industry Plans Modernization Drive." *American Restaurant* 20 (January 1938): 27.

Skidmore, H. B. "Open Day and Night: Silver Line Diner, Jersey City." *Woman's Journal* 13 (1928): 22.

Slagle, Willard J. "Howard D. Johnson." *American Restaurant*, June 1958, 108.

"'Slice of Pie and a Cup of Coffee—That'll Be Fifteen Cents, Honey.'" *American Heritage* 28 (April 1977): 68–71.

Society for Commercial Archeology. "All Night, All-Night Diner Tour." Boston: Society for Commercial Archeology, April 1980.

Society for Commercial Archeology News Journal, September 1978.

Soule, Gardner B. "The Old Dog Wagon Puts on the Dog." *Popular Science* 162 (March 1953): 138–141.

Stern, Jane, and Stern, Michael. "Road Food." *New York Magazine* 11 (16 May 1977): 38–45.

"Streamlined Restaurants Will Not Sell Tomorrow's Customers.'" *Drive-In Restaurant and Highway Cafe Magazine* 19 (June 1955): 9.

Taylor, Frank J. "This 'Burger Business." *Collier's* 17 (25 January 1941): 22.

Tea Room Booklet. Woman's Home Companion, 1922.

Tompkins, Raymond S. "Hash-House Visionaries." *The American Mercury* 22 (March 1931): 361.

"Tray on Trestle Serves at Drive-In." *Popular Mechanics* 72 (September 1949): 127.

Trott, Harlan. "Take from a Wayside Drive-In." *The Christian Science Monitor*, 29 June 1940, 8–9.

"Turnpike Business Is Different." *Business Week*, 6 September 1952, 42.

"28 Flavors Head West." *Life* 25 (6 September 1948): 71.

Van Leewaarden, J. H. "Drop a Coin and Get Your Pie." *American Restaurant* 2 (July 1920): 20.

Watts, Gilbert S. *Roadside Marketing*. New York: Orange Judd Publishing Co., Inc., 1928.

"When the Lunch Wagon Made Its Bow." *New York Times Magazine*, 7 February 1926, 20.

"Where Do We Eat?" *Ladies' Home Journal* 49 (August 1932): 46.

"Where the Drive-Ins Are." *Drive-In Restaurant* 28 (April 1964): 16.

White, E. F. "The Possibilities of the Chocolate Shop or Tea Room." *American Restaurant* 2 (February 1920): 28.

"Will the Post War Restaurant Look Like This?" *American Restaurant* 25 (June 1943): 46.

"Your Curb Is Your Atmosphere." *Drive-In Magazine* 24 (March 1960): 32.

Sources of Illustrations

The source of each illustration reproduced in this book is indicated in parentheses following its caption as well as below.

Photographs by Chester H. Liebs (credited "Author") are located on pages 5, 14 (right), 16 (top; bottom left), 22 (left), 23 (both), 24 (both), 25 (both), 27 (left), 30 (left), 34 (left), 35 (all), 38, 41, 43, 49 (right), 51, 53, 56 (top; bottom left), 59, 62 (all), 63, 64, 66, 67 (both), 68, 69 (both), 72, 74, 78 (bottom), 80, 81, 82, 85 (right), 88 (right), 91, 92, 98 (right), 103, 107 (bottom), 114 (both), 115, 130 (right), 134 (right), 135, 136, 146–147 (all), 149 (both), 150 (bottom), 151, 158, 163 (bottom), 164 (right), 165 (both), 167, 170 (bottom right), 182 (both), 187, 190 (bottom), 191, 204, 214 (bottom right), 215, 216, 223 (both), 224, 227.

Illustrations owned by Chester H. Liebs (credited "Author's collection") are located on pages 2, 4 (bottom), 9, 198, 220, and 221 (top).

The author is grateful to the individuals, institutions, and publications named below who generously provided illustrations on the pages indicated and granted permission to reproduce them.

Albany Institute of History and Art, Collection of McKinney Library: 8

Albuquerque Museum Photoarchives: 50, 139

American Architects' and Builders' Magazine: 11 (top) [August 1910]

American Association of State Highway and Transportation Officials, *Drive-In Theater Study—1949*, Washington, D.C., © 1949, used by permission: 157 (both)

American Hotel and Motel Association, New York, N.Y.: 189 [by permission of Imperial 400 National Inc.]; 190 (top) [by permission of Days Inns of America]

American Petroleum Institute, Washington, D.C.: 97 (left), 99 (bottom)

Arizona Historical Society, Arizona Heritage Center, Tucson: 10 (left), 15, 19 (left), 76, 87 (right), 170 (top)

John Baeder's collection, Nashville, Tenn.: 200 (top left), 218

John Baeder watercolor: 222 (top)

Brewer-Perkins, Inc., North Adams, Mass.: 83

Broadway Chevrolet, Louisville, Ky.: 88 (left)

California Department of Transportation, Sacramento: 33

William H. Chapin, Lookout Mountain, Tenn.: 138

Coca-Cola Company Archives, Atlanta, Ga.: 42 (right)

Colorado Historical Society, Denver: vi, 19 (right)

Community Theatres, Southfield, Mich.: 152, 162, 163 (top)

The Edison Institute, Henry Ford Museum, Dearborn, Mich.: 13 [neg. (189) 1496]; 42 (left) [neg. 0-2411]; 87 (left) [neg. 63525-D]; 100 [neg. (833) 66979-C]

John and Eugenie Fauver, Perrysburg, Ohio, by permission of T. Brock Saxe: 70 (top left; top right), 71 (top left)

Charles W. Fish, San Diego, Calif., by permission of Stanley C. Meston: 214 (bottom left)

Fisher Music Corporation, New York, N.Y.: 45 (left)

Florida State University Photographic Archives, Tallahassee: 18, 26

Food Marketing Institute, Washington, D.C.: 131

Free Library of Philadelphia, Theatre Collection: 155 (left)

Frederick G. Frost, Jr., Dorset, Vt.: 101

Peter Fuller, Boston: 84 (both), 85 (left)

Georgia Historical Society, Savannah: 192, 209, 210 (both)

Gruen Associates, Los Angeles: 32 (bottom left), 134 (left)

Hartman Brothers, Montrose, Colo.: 77

Kathlyn Hatch, Burlington, Vt.: 56 (bottom right), 178 (bottom)

Dr. Alan D. Hathaway, Davenport, Iowa: 16 (bottom right)

Historic American Engineering Record, Washington, D.C.: 195 (right)

Holiday Inns, Inc., Memphis, Tenn.: 186

Howard Johnson Company, Braintree, Mass.: 34 (right), 70 (bottom left; bottom right), 71 (bottom left; bottom right), 199, 200 (top right; bottom), 201 (all)

Mary M. Humstone, Denver: 112 (left)

Huntington Library, San Marino, Calif.: 11 (bottom), 14 (left), 46 (left), 54, 94, 97 (right), 123 (right), 155 (right), 156, 212

Imperial 400 National Inc.: *see* American Hotel and Motel Association

Albert Kahn Associates, Inc., Detroit: 79, 129

Kansas City Public Library, Montgomery Collection, Missouri Valley Room, Kansas City, Mo.: 32 (top)

Ladies' Home Journal, reprinted with permission, Family Media, Inc., New York, N.Y., © 1932: 45 (right)

Landis Aerial Surveys, Phoenix: 27 (right)

Steve Levin, San Francisco: 166

Library of Congress, Washington, D.C.: 20 (right), 44, 46 (top right), 49 (left), 171, 175, 205

Life: 17 [7 October 1907]; 195 (left) [19 September 1907]

Lomma Enterprises, Inc., Scranton, Pa.: 150 (top)

Richard Longstreth, Washington, D.C.: 30 (right), 52 (bottom), 55, 99 (top), 101 (left), 102, 106 (right), 107 (top), 132, 159, 161 (right), 164 (left), 178 (top), 222 (bottom)

McDonald's Corporation, Oak Brook, Ill.: 214 (top)

Mobil Oil Corporation, Fairfax, Va.: 21, 113

Motor Age Magazine: 78 (top) [14 August 1919]

National Archives, Washington, D.C.: 52 (top), 109, 161 (left), 188

National Golf Foundation, North Palm Beach, Fla.: 148

National Petroleum News: 10 (right) [8 October 1924]

Nebraska State Historical Society, Solomon D. Butcher Collection, Lincoln: 40 (right)

New-York Historical Society, New York, N.Y.: 194

Popular Mechanics, © The Hearst Corporation, all rights reserved: 48 (top) [December 1918]; 48 (bottom) [April 1921]; 172 [July 1935]

Progressive Grocer, Stamford, Conn.: 116, 118, 120 (bottom), 121, 123 (left), 125, 126, 128 (both), 130 (left)

Roadside Merchant: 22 (right) [July 1933]

Lars H. Rolfsen, Tampa, Fla.: 170 (bottom left)

Santa Fe Industries, Inc., Los Angeles: 4 (top)

Gloria E. Scott, Bowling Green, Ohio: 71 (top right)

Daniel V. Scully, Peterborough, N.H.: 226

Sears, Roebuck and Company, Chicago: 36 (all)

Society for the Preservation of New England Antiquities, Boston: 12, 119

John E. Stef, Jr., Portsmouth, N.H.: 98 (left)

Texaco Corporation Archives, White Plains, N.Y.: 105, 112 (right)

Morley B. Thompson, *How to Play Miniature Golf* (Denver: Central States Publishing Company, 1930); 142

Miriam Trementozzi, Albany, N.Y.: 174

University of Louisville Photographic Archives, Louisville, Ky.: 32 (bottom right); 122 (both); 140

University of Texas at Austin, Norman Bel Geddes Collection, Theater Arts Library, Harry Ransom Humanities Research Center, by permission of Edith Lutyens Bel Geddes: 106 (left)

University of Vermont Library Special Collections, Burlington: 20 (left), 46–47, 110, 176–177

University of Wyoming, American Heritage Center, Laramie: 40 (left), 96

U.S. Patent Office, Washington, D.C.: 120 (top), 154

Weichert-Isselhardt Collection, Bennington, Vt., photograph by Robert L. Weichert: 168, 173

White Castle, Columbus, Ohio: 206–207 (all)

Eve C. Yorke, Brooklyn, N.Y.: 221 (bottom)

Index

Page numbers in italic type refer to illustrations and captions. Cities and towns are listed under their state.